1 ENOCH AS CHRISTIAN SCRIPTURE

1 ENOCH AS CHRISTIAN SCRIPTURE

A Study in the Reception and Appropriation of 1 Enoch in Jude and the Ethiopian Orthodox *Tewahǝdo* Canon

Bruk Ayele Asale

Foreword by Loren T. Stuckenbruck

◆PICKWICK *Publications* • Eugene, Oregon

1 ENOCH AS CHRISTIAN SCRIPTURE
A Study in the Reception and Appropriation of 1 Enoch in Jude and the Ethiopian Orthodox *Tewahǝdo* Canon

Copyright © 2020 Bruk Ayele Asale. All rights reserved. Except for brief quotations in critical publications or reviews, no part of this book may be reproduced in any manner without prior written permission from the publisher. Write: Permissions, Wipf and Stock Publishers, 199 W. 8th Ave., Suite 3, Eugene, OR 97401.

Pickwick Publications
An Imprint of Wipf and Stock Publishers
199 W. 8th Ave., Suite 3
Eugene, OR 97401

www.wipfandstock.com

PAPERBACK ISBN: 978-1-5326-9115-7
HARDCOVER ISBN: 978-1-5326-9116-4
EBOOK ISBN: 978-1-5326-9117-1

Cataloguing-in-Publication data:

Names: Asale, Bruk Ayele, author. | Stuckenbruck, Loren T., foreword.

Title: 1 Enoch as Christian scripture : a study in the reception and appropriation of 1 Enoch in Jude and the Ethiopian Orthodox Tewahǝdo Canon / Bruk Ayele Asale ; foreword by Loren T. Stuckenbruck.

Description: Eugene, OR: Pickwick Publications, 2020. | Includes bibliographical references and index.

Identifiers: ISBN 978-1-5326-9115-7 (paperback). | ISBN 978-1-5326-9116-4 (hardcover). | ISBN 978-1-5326-9117-1 (ebook).

Subjects: LCSH: Ethiopic book of Enoch—Criticism, interpretation, etc. | Christianity—Ethiopia. | Bible—Canon. | Bible. Jude—Criticism, interpretation, etc.

Classification: BS1830 E7 A52 2020 (print). | BS1830 (ebook).

Manufactured in the U.S.A.   06/01/20

This monograph is dedicated to the many Ethiopian Christians who have striven and become part of ecumenical movement in Ethiopia.

And

Among these Christians, Rev. Gudina Tumsa stood out in being instrumental for the practical initiation of inclusive Ecumenical Council of Churches in Ethiopia. He was murdered for the faith he believed in!

Rev. Gudina Tumsa believed not only in the possibility and inevitability of ecumenism, he rather believed more in the God of the Bible Who has the power to miraculously bring churches into unity.

He said:

It seems to be necessary to remind ourselves of the mighty power of the Bible's God, because there are Christians who argue that there cannot be a unity among the churches. Biblical faith is based on the impossible, on miracles . . . Miracles are contrary to the laws of nature. Ours is still the God of miracles, and one of the miracles he may perform today is to bring about unity among His churches. Let us then talk about His Church rather than our churches (Gudina Tumsa 2003:19).

It is, therefore, to this committed martyr, the Rev. Gudina Tumsa, this monograph is dedicated with complements.

CONTENTS

Foreword by Loren T. Stuckenbruck | ix
Acknowledgments | xi
Abbreviations | xii

1 Introduction | 1

2 1 Enoch: An Overview of the Transmission History of the Text and Contemporary Academic Dialogue | 6

ADDENDUM I: A CRITIQUE OF EPHRAIM ISAAC'S PROPOSITION | 19

3 1 Enoch in Jude and Other Early Christian Texts | 23

ADDENDUM II: SCRIPTURAL VS. CANONICAL | 57

4 1 Enoch in Other Early Jewish and Christian Texts | 62

5 1 Enoch in the EOTC: Reception and Transmission of Scriptures | 78

6 1 Enoch in the EOTC: Literary and Cultural Appropriation | 87

ADDENDUM III: THE INFLUENCE OF ENOCH AMONG ETHIOPIAN EVANGELICAL CHRISTIANS | 113

7 Concluding Remarks | 118

Bibliography | 121
Subject Index | 133
Author Index | 143
Scripture Index | 147

FOREWORD

IN 1821 RICHARD LAURENCE, then Regius Professor of Hebrew and canon of Christ Church at Oxford, published the first translation of a complete Geʻez version of "The Book of Enoch the Prophet" into a modern European language.¹ Although this translation of one of several Enoch manuscripts brought to Europe from Ethiopia by James Bruce in 1773² had been long anticipated, the book was not appreciated as an emblem of living religious tradition. It was, instead, regarded as a lost book from antiquity that could shed historical light on ideas found in the New Testament. Eventually, in 1912 R. H. Charles even claimed that 1 Enoch (as it is now called), wielded more influence on the New Testament than any other non-biblical writing, though for him it nonetheless served more as a foil for Christian origins.³ The view that the Geʻez version of 1 Enoch preserves tradition from the Second Temple period was confirmed by the discovery of corresponding fragments among the Dead Sea Scrolls, many of which were published by J. T. Milik in 1976.⁴ Dated from the third to the first centuries BCE, materials relating to many parts of 1 Enoch (except for the Parables in chapters 37 to 71, a Dream Vision in 83 to 84, and an Exhortation in 108) contributed to a resurgence of scholarly interest as well as renewed speculative attention

---

1. The original full title of this first edition was መጽሐፈ፡ ሄኖክ፡ ነቢይ፡፡ *The Book of Enoch the Prophet: An Apocryphal Production, supposed to have been lost for ages, but discovered at the close of the last century in Abyssinia; now first translated from an Ethiopic ms. in the Bodleian Library* (Oxford: Oxford University Press).

2. On this, see Erho and Stuckenbruck, "A Manuscript History of *Ethiopic Enoch*," 87–133; and Boccaccini, "James Bruce's 'Fourth' Manuscript," 237–63.

3. Cf. Charles, *The Book of Enoch*, xcv.

4. Milik, *The Books of Enoch*.

among several religious groups fascinated by claims that it transmits "secret" revelation.[5]

However, its unbroken transmission for at least one and a half millennia in Ethiopia reminds that 1 Enoch's religious and cultural significance is firmly rooted in the Horn of Africa. It is not simply a collection of Second Temple traditions that happens to have been preserved in the Ethiopian Orthodox tradition. The manifold witnesses to the text in well over one hundred manuscripts, beginning with the late fourteenth century, and its wide-ranging mention, citation, appeal to, and commentary in literature from that time until today demonstrates a vitality in both oral and written culture that has profoundly shaped the Christian landscape of Ethiopia. This vitality is rapidly becoming the focus of research among "western" scholars in the Americas, Europe, and the Middle East, while it is undergoing a revival of formal interest among Ethiopian Orthodox, Catholic, and Protestant scholars in Ethiopia, where the rich manuscript tradition of 1 Enoch has its home. In Ethiopia, the importance of this attention cannot be underestimated; the book, with *de facto* recognition of it in the Ethiopian Orthodox *Tewahǝdo* Church as scripture, has sometimes functioned as a marker of religious identity that distinguishes one Christian tradition from others.

The present study by Dr. Bruk Ayele Asale treats readers to the first monograph-length analysis of the traditional importance of "the Book of Enoch" from an Ethiopian Protestant perspective. Extraordinarily sensitive to both theological and historical issues, Dr. Bruk promotes the need for mutual listening and constructive dialogue along religious and cultural boundaries. As Dr. Bruk shows, the exploration of 1 Enoch offers an opportunity for Christians in Ethiopia (and elsewhere) of all persuasions, not only to come to terms with more indigenous tradition but also to catapult it onto the global stage where it can reinvigorate longstanding expressions of faith.

Loren T. Stuckenbruck
Chair, New Testament Studies
Ludwig Maximilian University of Munich

---

5. For a representative, though still incomplete bibliography until 2014, see Charlesworth, *O Livro de Enoque Etíope* ou *1 Enoque*, 249–526.

ACKNOWLEDGMENTS

MOST IMPORTANTLY, I WOULD like to give incomparable thanks to the Triune God, who is worthy of honour and glory, for His calling me to His Kingdom and ministry, for His providential care during this study, and for His abundant guidance in writing this monograph. He has made everything possible through His matchless help and support. All glory be to God.

I am especially grateful to my mentor and special guide, Prof. Loren T. Stuckenbruck, without whose support and advice this book would have not been a reality. Thank you, Loren. You are so kind and special. My heartfelt gratitude also goes to my friend and colleague, Meron T. Gebreananaye, who edited this work with several special contributions. Your sincere encouragement enabled me to make this work a reality in a very impossible time of my career. Your contribution was priceless.

I am also indebted to Prof. Fr. Paul Decock, for his both academically rigorous and fatherly supportive approach from the very beginning to the end in going through all the drafts of this book, encouraging and challenging me to attempt to be fair and open to the many views on the topic, and providing me with a number of documents. It is both honor and privilege to be your student.

Finally, above all, I wish to express my profound and heartfelt love and gratitude to my wife, Charis (χαρίς), who has taken all the responsibilities and burdens of our home and supported me, sharing all my administrative and academic pains patiently at every moment in my work and ministry responsibilities; and without her help my success would have been impossible. I would like to express my sincere gratitude to Behulum and Tamagne, God's incredible gifts, our lovely two sons, who became my source of inspiration, joy, shifting the mood of agony to a world of freedom and happiness.

ABBREVIATIONS

I. Journals, Series, Reference Works, and Texts

ABD	*Anchor Bible Dictionary*
AC	*Andəmta* Commentary
BST	The Bible Speaks Today
CBQ	*Catholic Biblical Quarterly*
HTR	*Harvard Theological Review*
JETS	*Journal of the Evangelical Theological Society*
JSJ	*Journal for the Study of Judaism*
JSJS	Journal for the Study of Judaism Supplements
JSNT	*Journal for the Study of the New Testament*
JSNTSup	Journal for the Study of the New Testament Supplements
JTS	*Journal of Theological Study*
LXX	Septuagint
MT	Masoretic text
NICNT	*The New International Commentary on the New Testament*
NIDNTT	*The New International Dictionary of New Testament Theology*
NT	New Testament
NTS	*New Testament Studies*
OT	Old Testament
VT	*Vetus Testamentum*

II. General

AD	*Anno Domini* (i.e. referring to years after Jesus Christ was born)
BC	before Christ
BCE	before the Common Era
BSE	Bible Society of Ethiopia
B.S.P.E.	Berhanena Selam Printing Enterprise
c. (ca.)	*circa* (i.e. approximately)
CE	Common Era
cf.	*confer* (i.e. compare)
diss.	dissertation
E.C.	Ethiopian Calendar
ed(s).	editor(s); edition
e.g.	for example
EECMY	The Ethiopian Evangelical Church Mekane Yesus
EKHC	The Ethiopian *Kale Hiwot* Church
EMML	The Ethiopian Manuscripts Microfilm Library
EOC	Ethiopian Orthodox Church
EOTC	Ethiopian Orthodox *Tewahədo* Church
et al	*et alia* (i.e., and others)
etc.	*et cetera* (i.e., and other similar things)
i.e.	that is
IES	The Institute of Ethiopian Studies
n(n).	note(s)
n.d.	no date
no.	number
PhD	Doctor of Philosophy
SOAS	The School of Oriental and African Studies
STL	Second Temple Period Literature
trans.	translator; translated
UBS	United Bible Societies
v.(vv.)	verse(s)
vol(s).	volume(s)

ABBREVIATIONS

III. Biblical Books (Protocanonical)

Gen	Genesis	Exod	Exodus
Num	Numbers	Deut	Deuteronomy
Judg	Judges	1–2 Sam	1–2 Samuel
1–2 Kgs	1–2 Kings	Est	Esther
Job	Job	Ps(s)	Psalm(s)
Prov	Proverbs	Isa	Isaiah
Jer	Jeremiah	Ezek	Ezekiel
Dan	Daniel	Joel	Joel
Amos	Amos	Mic	Micah
Nah	Nahum	Hab	Habakkuk
Zeph	Zephaniah	Hag	Haggai
Zech	Zechariah	Mal	Malachi
Matt	Matthew	Mark	Mark
Luke	Luke	John	John
Acts	Acts	Rom	Romans
1–2 Cor	1–2 Corinthians	Gal	Galatians
Eph	Ephesians	Phil	Philippians
Col	Colossians	1–2 Thess	1–2 Thessalonians
1–2 Tim	1–2 Timothy	Tit	Titus
Heb	Hebrews	Jes	James
1–2 Pet	1–2 Peter	Rev	Revelation

IV. Biblical Books (Deuterocanonical)

1 En	1 (Ethiopic) Enoch	Jub	Jubilees
Tob	Tobit	Jdt	Judith
Esg	Esther (Greek)	Wis	Wisdom of Solomon
Sir	Sirach (Ecclesiasticus)	Bar	Baruch
1–2 Macc	1–2 Maccabees	1–2 Es	1–2 Esdras

V. Extrabiblical Books

2–3 *En*	*2–3 Enoch*
Sib. Or.	*Sibylline Oracles*
2 Bar	*2 Baruch*
T. Reu.	*Testament of Reuben*
T. Levi	*Testament of Levi*
T. Jud.	*Testament of Judah*
T. Dan	*Testament of Dan*
T. Naph.	*Testament of Naphtali*
T. Ass	*Testament of Asher*
Asc. Isa.	*Ascension of Isaiah*
Pss. Sol.	*Psalms of Solomon*
Barn	*Epistle of Barnabas*

VI. The Dead Sea Scrolls

CD	Damascus Document
1QapGen	Genesis Apocryphon
1QH	Thanksgiving Hymns
1QM	War Scroll
1QS	Manual of Disciples
4QFlor	Florilegium
4QDeut	Deuteronomy at Qumran
4QpIs^a	Pesher or Qumran Commentary on Isaiah

1

INTRODUCTION

Background to the Study

THIS STUDY FOCUSES ON the reception and appropriation of 1 Enoch amongst Christians both in the earliest church and its continued use in the Ethiopian Orthodox *Tewahǝdo* Canon [EOTC]. The contemporary academic study of 1 Enoch has by and large focused on identifying the textual transmission history and the authorial context with little reference to the interpretive and theological impact of this text on subsequent traditions, including Christians. It of course goes without saying that historical and textual studies have offered very important insights into elucidating the historical and social context in which the text(s) were written, the literary structure and character as well as the history of its transmission. Even so, as the pseudepigraphal status of 1 Enoch in relation to both the Old and New Testament canons has meant that the influence of this text outside of the Second Temple Literature and its possible influence on the background of New Testament texts is yet to be adequately studied.

In placing 1 Enoch in relation to a thriving Christian tradition, the Ethiopian Orthodox *Tewahǝdo* Church, and its related influence on contemporary religious and social practices, as well as its use in a New Testament book, this study hopes to suggest the possibility of viewing 1 Enoch as scripture with theological significance.

My interest in this research stems from both academic and deeply practical concerns. On the academic front, considering the significant interest which 1 Enoch has attracted both in contemporary academic discussion understanding its influence and appropriation in Christian traditions seems to offer potential insight into the meaning(s) of the text to the contemporary interpreter. It is particularly important to understand the significance of this text considering that the full text of 1 Enoch has been preserved only by the EOTC in Ge'ez.¹ This both indicates the significance of this text in the Ethiopian church as well as suggesting the importance of the historical and social contexts that has shaped its transmission history.

Practically, my interest in understanding of the reception and appropriation of 1 Enoch in the EOTC stems for the significance of this church and its traditions on the contemporary religious and social context in Ethiopia. This context is particularly important and in need of elaboration for Christian discourse amongst the different denominational traditions in Ethiopia. I therefore posit understanding the appropriation of 1 Enoch in Jude, which is part of the canon of all Christian traditions, will serve to better understand the canonical status of this text in the EOTC.

Approach and Structure

Reception history proposes a model which allows us to bring historical interpretations into the contemporary dialogue between reader and text resulting in a three-way interaction.² This approach allows us to study the influence of different interpretations on subsequent generations of interpreters. A reception-historical approach makes use of the philosophical hermeneutics of Hans-Georg Gadamer and the literary hermeneutics of Hans Robert Jauss. Gadamer's critique of the historicist quest served to reintroduce the significance of tradition in the act of interpretation.³ He determined that each reader is a historically located, finite being and thus part of a process in which past and present are in constant dialogue. Accordingly, "two regulative norms determine the validity of any interpretation: the subject matter of the text and those interpretations which are

---

1. Even if it is essentially true that the full text of 1 Enoch is preserved only in Ge'ez text, it should be noted that there are important differences between the Aramaic fragments and the Ge'ez materials; for example, the Astronomical Book in the Aramaic fragments is significantly longer than the present 1 En 78–82 found in the Ge'ez version.

2. Parris, *Reading the Bible with Giants*.

3. Volmer, *The Hermeneutics Reader*, 261.

recognized by tradition (consciously and/or part of our pre-understanding) as authoritative."[4]

Gadamer defines tradition as the sum of what "we understand [about] ourselves in a self-evident way in the family, society, and state in which we live."[5] Accordingly, each individual is located within formative traditions and cannot remove to a vantage point outside of history for the purposes of objective reflection.[6] The presuppositions or fore-understandings that interpreters possess describe the familiarity or bond with the subject matter which, according to Gadamer, is the most basic precondition of the hermeneutic event.[7]

Therefore, within Gadamer's hermeneutics, conscious acceptance of what he terms as "legitimate prejudices" or presuppositions serves to give proper credence to the historically mediated nature of all understanding.[8] This affirmation, however, does not necessarily imply unyielding captivity to traditions, because traditions are themselves fluid, and horizons are always broadening in interaction with the inherent strangeness of the "historically intended and distant object."[9] Gadamer proposes that the hermeneutic event occurs in the "*in-between*" space between the unfamiliarity of the text and the interpreters prejudices or presuppositions which facilitate understanding.[10] He describes this event as the fusion of horizons of expectations. This fusion assumes that "understanding happens through a gradual and perpetual interplay between the subject matter and the interpreter's initial position—a fusion of one's own horizon and the horizon of the text or other."[11] The horizon of the text—the given subject matter—and the horizon of the interpreter—which constitutes the sum of the traditions and prejudgments which she brings to the text—thus interact in a dynamic dialogue.[12]

---

4. Parris, "Reception Theory," 104.

5. Gadamer, *Truth and Method*, 278.

6. Porter and Robinson, *Hermeneutics*, 88. Gadamer's conception of tradition is formulated against the Enlightenment antithesis between tradition/authority and reason.

7. Gadamer, *Truth and Method*, 294–95.

8. Porter and Robinson, *Hermeneutics*, 91.

9. Westphal, *Whose Community?*, 71.

10. Gadamer, *Truth and Method*, 295.

11. Porter and Robinson, *Hermeneutics*, 86.

12. Porter and Robinson, *Hermeneutics*, 82.

According to Gadamer this interaction allows not only for the reproduction but also the production of meaning extending beyond the author.[13] The *"otherness"* of the text—or its potential to continually evolve in light of the new questions brought to it by successive interpreters—results in the dynamic and unfinished character of texts. This character allows texts to reveal new meaning in reaction to the new horizons of expectations brought to the process of interpretation by successive readers.[14] This, however, does not imply relativism or aesthetic subjectivism as every text has a fixed boundary or *"givenness"* which limits the potential range of meanings that can be derived from it at any given time.[15]

Gadamer's idea of the fusion of horizons—or the co-creation of meaning between text and reader—means that the historical distance between the interpreter and the text is no longer a problem that requires correction. On the contrary, this distance serves as the productive ground for interpretation whereby the interpreter can experience the meanings and understandings of the subject matter in previous interpretations enhancing her ability to understand the potential of meaning that is to be discovered in the text.

The literary theorist Hans Robert Jauss built upon Gadamer's critique to argue that literary history, which was founded on the ideal of objective historiography, enforces a "closed past" that ignores both the "otherness of the past" and the "lived praxis" of the reader's experience.[16] Jauss proposes instead a theoretical model that combines "Marxism's historical mediation and Formalism's advances in the realm of aesthetic perception with his concept of the horizon of expectation of the reader" to analyze the dialogical relationship between the text and successive readers.[17] Jauss's model offers a corrective to both Marxism and Formalism by recognizing the reader as a formative agent. Thus, the dialogue between work and audience is not only reproductive but also productive of meaning.[18] Jauss allows for a reciprocal relationship between text and reader whereby a literary work is understood both in terms of its influence on its readers and in relation to,

---

13. Gadamer, *Truth and Method*, 296.
14. Porter and Robinson, *Hermeneutics*, 91.
15. Porter and Robinson, *Hermeneutics*, 91.
16. Thiselton, "Reception Theory," 290.
17. Thiselton, "Reception Theory," 137.
18. Jauss, *Toward an Aesthetic of Reception*, 28–32.

how encountering successive generations of interpreters with new horizons of expectation leads to new production.[19]

In this study, I will employ the theoretical insight offered by both the philosophical hermeneutics of Gadamer and the literary theory of Jauss to understand the process by which 1 Enoch is received in Jude and in the Canon and interpretive traditions of the EOTC. To this end I will begin by briefly looking at the transmission history of the text of 1 Enoch and the status of relevant studies in contemporary academic contexts (chapter 2). I will then go on to look at the reception of 1 Enoch in Jude (chapter 3), the status of 1 Enoch in the early Jewish and Christian traditions (chapter 4), and in the canon of the EOTC (chapter 5), and its significance in the interpretive traditions and theology of the EOTC (chapter 6). I will finally offer some concluding reflections on the contemporary significance of 1 Enoch for Ethiopian Christianity (chapter 7). Connected to the main topic of the book, there are three relevant addenda following some chapters related to the issues each addendum deals with.

---

19. Jauss, *Toward an Aesthetic of Reception*, 19.

2

1 ENOCH

An Overview of the Transmission History of the Text and Contemporary Academic Dialogue

Introduction

THE TEXT OF 1 Enoch, in its entirety, survived only in Geʻez through its use by the Ethiopian Orthodox *Tewahǝdo* Church (EOTC). The text is also discovered in fragmentary form in Greek and Aramaic. Its survival can thus be classified in three stages and in three languages. Here I will attempt to offer a brief overview of the manuscripts witnesses to 1 Enoch, with a focus on the transmission history of the text in the Geʻez and its ultimate survival in this language. I will then move on to offer a brief overview of the contemporary academic discussion of 1 Enoch and its status as scripture amongst different interpretive communities.

Transmission History of 1 Enoch

The Qumran Aramaic Texts

Since the discovery of the Dead Sea Scrolls, the proposition that the Book of Enoch originated among a Jewish community of the Second Temple

Period, having been originally written in Aramaic, has achieved consensus in contemporary scholarship.[1] The discovery of the Aramaic fragments of 1 Enoch at Qumran served to establish the previously debatable early dating and Jewish origin of the book. The fragments discovered include portions from all parts of the book—the *Book of Watchers*, the *Book of Dreams*, the *Epistle of Enoch*, and the *Astronomical Book*—except the *Parables of Enoch*. Nonetheless, significant damage to the manuscripts means that the fragments contain only limited portions of the text.

Following the discovery made at Qumran, Józéf T. Milik tried to reconstruct the fragments, based on the Greek and Ethiopic texts available. He went on to conclude that "for the first book of Enoch, the *Book of Watchers*, we can calculate that exactly 50 percent of the text is covered by the Aramaic fragments; for the third, the *Astronomical Book*, 30 percent; for the fourth, the *Book of Dreams*, 26 percent; for the fifth, the *Epistle of Enoch*, 18 percent."[2]

This conclusion has, however, been challenged and strongly criticized as misleading by subsequent studies. Edward Ullendorff and Michael Knibb, in their critical review of Milik's book, contend that "the true proportion of genuinely recognizable Aramaic material is thus of the order of about 5% of the total [of the Ethiopic book of Enoch]."[3] According to the analysis offered by Knibb, there are about 200 verses, out of a total of more than 1000, in Aramaic that correspond to the Ethiopic verses.[4] He goes on to conclude, "we are very far from possessing the equivalent in Aramaic of 196 verses of the Ethiopic version," because of the damaged state of the Qumran fragments.

Irrespective of the size of the fragments, the discovery of the Aramaic text at Qumran has had significant influence on the study of 1 Enoch. In addition to serving as an important textual witness,[5] the Aramaic texts of 1 Enoch, discovered in one of the greatest archaeological finds of the modern

---

1. Nickelsburg, *1 Enoch 1: A Commentary*, 19.
2. Milik, *The Books of Enoch*, 5.
3. Ullendorff and Knibb, Review of J. T. Milik, 601.
4. Knibb, *The Ethiopic Book of Enoch*, 12.
5. It is not surprising that all prominent scholars involved in major translation and text-criticism of 1 Enoch have used these Aramaic texts as evidence for their text whenever available. So, Milik, *The Books of Enoch*; Black, *The Book of Enoch*; Isaac, "Ethiopic Apocalypse," 5–89; Nickelsburg, *1 Enoch 1: A Commentary*; and Knibb, *Ethiopic Book of Enoch*.

era,[6] witness to the Jewish origin of this text and its significance within the context of the community which preserved it.

The Greek Texts

In addition to the large number of Aramaic fragments of 1 Enoch, some tiny Greek papyrus fragments were also found in Cave 7 at Qumran. While these serve to shed light on the difficult question of the period in which 1 Enoch was translated into Greek, the fragmentary nature of the witnesses leaves us with a range of questions related to translation including date, provenance, and transmission history.

Based on his study, comparative study of the Greek translation and Aramaic texts of the *Book of Watchers* and the *Epistle*, James Barr suggests that the Greek translation of 1 Enoch "belonged to the same general stage and stratum of translation as the Septuagint translation of Daniel," as both the books reflect similar apocalyptic form and content.[7] Pushing the discussion further, Knibb argues that the formation of a fivefold integrated Pentateuchal structure was introduced at this stage of translation and transmission. He notes:

> in any case, whatever the origin of Greek translation, and whether any part of it was known at Qumran, it is plausible to think that it was at the Greek stage in the transmission of the text that the *Parables* and the *Astronomical Book* were inserted between the *Book of Watchers* at the beginning and the *Book of Dreams* and the *Epistle* at the end to [produce the book familiar from?] the Ethiopic version with its fivefold structure.[8]

However, Matthew Black conjectures that such redaction may have been completed in the beginning of the second century AD, probably by a Jewish-Christian "redactor-translator" for Christian interest.[9] This argument seems plausible as no portion of the *Book of Parables*, the largest component of the five books of *1 Enoch*, appears in the Dead Sea Scrolls corpus.

---

6. For a complete edition and translation of the entire Dead Sea Scrolls, see Martínez and Tigchelaar, *The Dead Sea Scrolls* (2 volumes). For the edition and translation of specific text of Aramaic fragments of 1 Enoch, see Martínez and Tigchelaar, *The Dead Sea Scrolls*, vol. 1, 398–445.

7. Barr, "Aramaic-Greek Notes," 191.

8. Knibb, *Essays on the Book of Enoch*, 20.

9. Black, *The Book of Enoch*, 11.

However, the date of this part of the Enochic corpus—given its various implications on other major topics—has been strongly disputed academically until recently.[10] Following Michael E. Stone, in the second volume of his comprehensive work on 1 Enoch,[11] Nickelsburg and VanderKam convincingly conclude that "the Parables [should be dated] between the latter part of Herod's reign and the early decades of the first C.E., with some preference for the earlier part of this time span."[12]

About a quarter of the entire enochic corpus has been discovered in the surviving manuscripts of the Greek translation of 1 Enoch,[13] and the copies are dated from the fourth to ninth centuries AD. Isaac[14] and Nickelsburg[15] list the principal Greek manuscripts, where partial texts from all books of 1 Enoch, except the *Book of Parables*, are contained. These include: (1) a fifth or sixth century AD manuscript, discovered in 1886/87 in a grave, which contains a complete text of 1 En 1:1—32:6a (from the *Book of Watchers*);[16] (2) preserved in the Chronographia of George Syncellus are 1 En 6:1—9:4; 8:4—10:14; 15:8—16:1 (from the *Book of Watchers*); (3) some fragments which come from the fourth century CE and contain 1 En 77:7—78:1; 78:8;

---

10. The proposed dates of the *Book of Parables* spans from as early as 94-79 BC by Charles (*The Book of Enoch*, 72-73) to as late as AD 270 by Milik (*The Book of Enoch*, 91-96). Some other studies which give attention to this particular problem, following Milik's proposal for a late date, include Greenfield and Stone, "The Enochic Pentateuch," 51-65; Knibb, "The Date of the Parables," 345-59; Mearns, "Dating the Similitudes," 360-69; Black, "The Composition, Character," 19-30; Nickelsburg, *Jewish Literature*, 254-56; Bampfylde, "The Similitudes of Enoch," 9-31; Sacchi "Qumran and the Dating," 377-95. See also the articles presented on this specific topic at the Third Enochic Seminar (2005) in Camaldoli, Italy, and published in Gabriele Boccaccini, *Enoch and the Messiah*. These include Piovanelli "A Testimony for the Kings," 363-79; Suter "Enoch in the Sheol," 415-43; Stone, "Enoch's Date in Limbo," 444-49; Charlesworth, "Can We Discern the Composition Date," 450-68; Hannah, "The Book of Noah," 469-77; Arcari, "A Symbolic Transfiguration," 478-86; Eshel "An Allusion in the Parables of Enoch," 487-91; and Olson "An Overlooked Patristic Allusion," 492-96.

11. Stone, "Enoch's Date in Limbo," 449.

12. Nickelsburg and VanderKam, *1 Enoch 2: A Commentary*, 62.

13. Nickelsburg (*1 Enoch 1: A Commentary*, 12, 20) approximates between 28 percent (p. 12) and 25 percent (p. 20) of the surviving *1 Enoch*'s Greek translation.

14. Isaac, "1 (Ethiopic Apocalypse of) Enoch," 6.

15. Nickelsburg, *1 Enoch 1: A Commentary*, 14.

16. As Nickelsburg (*1 Enoch 1: A Commentary*, 12) demonstrates, this codex, known as Codex Panopolitanus, contains portions from the *Gospel of Peter* and the *Apocalypse of Peter* together with the Enochic text, which, according to him is likely because of their shared interest in journeys to the realm of the dead.

1 Enoch as Christian Scripture

85:10—86:2; 87:1–3 (from the *Book of Luminaries* and the *Book of Animal Apocalypse*);[17] (4) manuscripts discovered in the Vatican Library containing 1 En 89:42–49 (from the *Book of Animal Apocalypse*); and (5) another papyrus codex containing 1 En 97:6—107:3 (from the *Epistle of Enoch*).

The preservation of all the Greek manuscripts of 1 Enoch discovered is associated with Christian communities or individuals.[18] As the manuscripts come from the beginning of the fourth century CE, evidently the book enjoyed some status among Christians which was not matched by its position amongst Jews of the period. In summary, despite the fragmentary nature of extant witnesses, the significance of the Greek text, mainly for textual criticism, is notable.

The Geʿez Texts

The transmission and translation history of the Enochic text in Ethiopia—even at time when the significance of this work seems to have been declining in the larger Christian world—is part and parcel of the broader process of translation of scripture.[19] The church has traditionally ascribed the preliminary translation of scripture to the first Bishop of the EOTC, Abba Frumentius, *Abuna Selama Kesate Berhan* (Father of Peace, Revealer of Light), in the fourth century. The church also holds that the main work of translation in this early period was carried out in the fifth and sixth centuries by the so-called "Nine Saints," missionaries who came from Asia Minor.[20] Consequently, it is possible that 1 Enoch was translated into Ethiopic, at the latest, in the fifth and sixth centuries.[21]

---

17. This partition is not included in Isaac's list.

18. For instance, Codex Panopolitanus (or the Gizeh fragment, as designated by Matthew Black (*Apocalypsis Henochi Graece*, 8)) was discovered in a Christian grave, bound with other Christian writings, including portions of the apocryphal *Gospel of Peter* and the *Apocalypse of Peter*. These Greek fragments of 1 Enoch, with some quotations and allusions from early Christian writings and Church Fathers, has been published by Matthew Black (*Apocalypsis Henochi Graece*).

19. There is strong scholarly consensus that the translation of *Enoch* into Geʿez is part of the translation and transmission process of the entire biblical corpus between the fourth and sixth centuries AD. Cf. Reed, *Fallen Angels and the History*, 8; Knibb, "Christian Adoption and Transmission," 403; Nickelsburg, *1 Enoch 1: A Commentary*, 17; Ullendorff, *The Ethiopians*, 55–56.

20. For a comprehensive discussion on the translation of Scriptures into Ethiopic, see Knibb, *Translating the Bible*, 1–54.

21. Knibb, *Essays on the Book of Enoch*, 177.

However, while this early dating of the translation is theoretically plausible, the oldest manuscripts of 1 Enoch, so far attested, mainly come from the fourteenth century onwards, as is true for most Ethiopic manuscripts.[22] In spite of the absence of earlier manuscript witnesses it ought to be noted that significant portions of quotations in other works from the same period, suggest that translations of Enoch from earlier periods were in use.[23] Examples of such books that preserved large portions of 1 Enoch include መጽሐፈ ምዕላድ *Metshafe Mi'lad* (the *Book of Nativity*), መጽሐፈ ብርሃን *Matshafe Berhan* (the *Book of Light*), and መጽሐፈ ምስጢር ሰማይ ወምድር *Metshafe Mistira Semay Womeder* (the *Book of the Mysteries of Heaven and Earth*).[24]

For instance, መጽሐፈ ምዕላድ *Metshafe Mi'lad*, in addition to some other portions, quotes the entire text of 1 En 46:1—51:5 and 62:1–16. As Knibb noted, these are the same passages, which "have attracted the interest of modern scholars concerned with messianism."[25] In addition to such texts, which reflect Christological themes, መጽሐፈ ምዕላድ *Metshafe Mi'lad* raises and defends "the authority of Enoch who is presented as the first prophet, the first who announced the coming of Christ."[26]

More importantly, these references from significant works and periods in the history of the EOTC, indicate important reasons as to persistent influence and authority of 1 Enoch, in the Ethiopian Church, which in turn could be a possible explanation for its survival. The use of the Book

---

22. While Knibb ("The Translation of 1 Enoch 70.1," 340–54) concludes that the oldest manuscripts so far come from the fifteenth century or a little earlier, Olson ("Enoch and the Son of Man," 30–32) argues that the oldest Geʽez Enochic manuscripts date from the twelfth century AD, a claim which Knibb ("The Translation of 1 Enoch 70.1," 347) strongly rejects as "certainly wrong." However, recent studies indicate that the earliest manuscript is EMML 8400 from around the year 1400 (Loren Stuckenbruck, personal communication, 2015).

23. For a list of quotations from the *Book of Enoch* in printed texts and some discussions on some, see Milik *The Books of Enoch*, 85–88. Following Milik, Klaus Berger ("Review of Michael Knibb," 100–109) also worked through the list of quotations and concluded that the quotations came from works whose compositions were earlier than the oldest Ethiopic manuscripts of *1 Enoch*.

24. For brief descriptions about these books, see Ullendorff, *The Ethiopians*, 141. For a detailed discussion on some quotations and their text-critical values, see Knibb, *Essays on the Book of Enoch*, 176–87.

25. Knibb, *Essays on the Book of Enoch*, 180.

26. Knibb, *Essays on the Book of Enoch*, 183.

1 ENOCH AS CHRISTIAN SCRIPTURE

of Enoch "in this period also of interest because of the light shed on the doctrinal and ecclesiastical controversies of the time."[27]

One of the ways ancient biblical texts have survived is their public usage through various means, such as the use of texts in amulets. While the tradition of using amulets among religious people of the ancient period is common for purposes such as protection, medicine, and good fortune, this tradition has continued to date among many Ethiopians. T. de Bruyn defines amulet "as an item that [is/was] believed to convey in and of itself, as well as in association with incantation and other actions, supernatural power for protective, beneficial, or antagonistic effect, and that is worn on one's body or fixed, displayed, or deposited at some place."[28] In addition, among many people, amulets are often associated with and inherent to magical power, even if this point itself is debatable.[29]

From the earliest period of Christianity in Ethiopia—as in other religious traditions and Christian traditions across the world[30]—the use of amulets was a commonplace practice and one that persists to this day. In this regard, it is notable that 1 Enoch is one of the prominent texts used for this purpose.

M. de Jonge, strongly argues that pseudepigrapha of the Old Testament "were transmitted because copyists regarded them as important and were of the opinion that they could function meaningfully in the communities

---

27. Knibb, *Essays on the Book of Enoch*, 187. The theological debates of the fifteenth century are mainly Christological and ecclesiastical. According to Jacopo Gnisci ("Continuity and Tradition," 31–32), there were two prominent figures—a priest and a king—in the fifteenth century controversies in Ethiopian history, whose writings are still extant. Gnisci explains that whereas the priest, Gyorgis of Sagla, who was prominent in the first half of the century, mainly focuses on Christological controversies, where 1 Enoch has been influential, the King, Zer'a Yacob, active in the second half of the century, was occupied in ecclesiological issues and Mariology.

28. de Bruyn, "Papyri, Parchments, Ostraca, and Tablets," 147.

29. For a long list of references on the on-going debate on this issue, see de Bruyn, "Papyri, Parchments, Ostraca, and Tablets," 147, no.8.

30. For instance, de Bruyn ("Papyri, Parchments, Ostraca, and Tablets," 166–83) makes a catalogue of a long list of amulet manuscripts from the fourth to eighth centuries AD, which were used by Christians, written in Greek, and found in Egypt. In addition, de Bruyn ("Papyri, Parchments, Ostraca, and Tablets," 159) notes that "from Isidore of Pelusium, John Chrysostom, Augustine, and other patristic sources that Christians wore 'gospels' around their necks, hung them at their bedside, or used them in other ways for apparently protective purposes." He offers full references for each of the citations from the writings of the Church Fathers (de Bruyn, "Papyri, Parchments, Ostraca, and Tablets," 159, n.60).

for which they copied them. *Transmission clearly presupposes the enduring relevance of what is transmitted*" (italics mine).[31]

Other Texts

In addition to the three versions discussed here—the Aramaic, the Greek, and the Ethiopic—there are three other languages or versions in which some portions of 1 Enoch have been preserved. (1) In Latin, 1 Enoch has been preserved in several quotations and references by Church Fathers. While these extracts could potentially suggest a Latin translation of the book,[32] Nickelsburg rejects this possibility arguing that "the evidence is slim and far from compelling."[33] (2) Two Coptic fragments, containing a few verses of 1 En 93, were also discovered in 1939. (3) A Syriac excerpt from the *Book of the Watchers,* 1 En 6:1–6, serves as further textual evidence for the wider use of the Book of Enoch. These witnesses all serve to demonstrate that "Enochic texts and traditions circulated across a surprisingly broad geographical range."[34]

1 Enoch as Scripture: Contemporary Academic Discussions

Among Jewish Second Temple Literature, 1 Enoch is arguably the most researched "pseudepigraphical" work in the last century, especially after the discovery of the Dead Sea Scrolls containing Aramaic fragments of the book. Most of the scholars in the field have focused predominantly on the text and translation of the book, developing and revising their works in conjunction with the continuing discovery of new manuscripts. R. H. Charles, at the turn of the twentieth century, came up with the authoritative text in 1906[35] and translation in 1912[36] of the book, which scholars relied upon for several decades.

---

31. de Jonge, *Pseudepigrapha of the Old Testament*, 1–2.
32. Knibb (*The Ethiopic Book of Enoch*, 21) has some inclination to that end.
33. Nickelsburg, *1 Enoch 1: A Commentary*, 14.
34. Reed, *Fallen Angels and the History*, 9.
35. Charles, *The Ethiopic Version*.
36. Charles, *The Book of Enoch*.

1 Enoch as Christian Scripture

Following his groundbreaking work, three other scholars—J. T. Milik (1976),[37] M. A. Knibb (1978) and E. Isaac (1983:5–89)—are particularly notable for their work on the text and translation of 1 Enoch, in its entirety or in parts.[38] It is likely that they each conducted this work unaware of the work being done by the others. While Milik's edition mainly focuses on the Aramaic fragments, both Isaac and Knibb base their text and translation on the Ethiopic version. Volume one of Knibb's work contains one of the Ethiopic texts with critical apparatus of the Ethiopic and Greek variants. The second volume contains an introduction, an English translation, and notes on the text in which all the major Aramaic evidence is presented and discussed. Nevertheless, neither Milik nor Knibb consider the historical background of this work in the Ethiopian context, including the reasons as to how and why it was preserved in this church only. This question is one of the central foci of this current study.

Ephraim Isaac, notable for being the only Ethiopian scholar, contributed a significant article on 1 (Ethiopic Apocalypse of) Enoch[39] in Charlesworth's monumental work, *The Old Testament Pseudepigrapha*. Isaac's lengthy article mainly consists of a translation of the entire book based on one of the Ethiopic manuscripts and a thorough comparison with some other important manuscripts. Isaac notes in this study that his efforts to sketch the main themes of the book of Enoch from an Ethiopian perspective seeks to offer insight into the enduring impact of 1 Enoch on Ethiopian Christianity over the centuries. Most important is Isaac's introduction where he acknowledges the historical, theological, and cultural influence of the book, and especially its formative impact on the Ethiopian Church. With some exaggeration, Isaac contends that "it is hardly possible to understand *any aspect* of the religious tradition and thought of Ethiopia, the country in which it [1 Enoch] survived, without an understanding of it."[40] He also goes on to suggest an interesting if uncorroborated possibility: "What distinguishes Ethiopian Christian theology from that of either

---

37. More recently scholars such as Greenfield and Stone ("The Enochic Pentateuch,"), Nickelsburg ("Review of The Books of Enoch), Charlesworth ("The SNTS Pseudepigrapha Seminars"), VanderKam ("Some Major Issues"), and Dimant ("The Biography of Enoch") have strongly criticized several of Milik's conclusions and assumptions.

38. Besides these English translations, the German translation by Siegbert Uhlig ("Chronography"), which is potentially the best existing modern translation from Ge'ez deserves mention.

39. As designated by Isaac.

40. Isaac, "1 (Ethiopic Apocalypse of) Enoch," 10; italics mine.

1 Enoch

Western or Eastern Christendom may well be the emphases on Enochic thoughts."[41] This may potentially highlight the primary shortcoming of his work, despite the uniqueness of his contribution to the field. In my research here, I will attempt to engage the possibility he raises through a nuanced investigation of the influence of 1 Enoch on the socio-religious make-up of Ethiopia and the extent to which it could be said to have contribute to the unique nature of the Church.

More recently, a commentary by George W. E. Nickelsburg titled *1 Enoch 1: A Commentary on the Book of 1 Enoch, Chapters 1–36; 81–108*, is a notable addition, both in terms of the depth and breadth of its approach. Nickelsburg treats issues of history, text, text criticism, hermeneutics, exegesis, and form-critical study with deftness and precision. This first volume of the study includes a comprehensive introduction, an English translation with critical apparatus, thorough critical commentary mainly focusing on The Book of the Watchers (chapters 1–36), The Dream Vision (chapters 83–90), The Epistle of Enoch (chapters 91–105), and the two appendices— The Birth of Noah (chapters 106–7) and Another Book by Enoch (chapter 108). This monumental work had recently been completed with the publication of a second volume that deals with The Book of Similitudes (chapters 37–82), co-authored by James C. VanderKam, another renowned scholar in the field.[42] Based on their commentary, Nickelsburg and VanderKam published a new translation of the entire book in which they made some changes to the text based on recently discovered Enochic manuscripts.[43]

In addition to the extensive commentary on the books mentioned above, the introduction of the first volume offers an in-depth analysis of the unique place of 1 Enoch in the shaping of Ethiopian Christianity.[44] Here I aim to build upon the important foundation laid by Nickelsburg to investigate the influences of 1 Enoch on the larger culture as well as on the church. This study will therefore also explore the book's literary and socio-cultural influence on the Ethiopian Church and on the community at large.

---

41. Isaac, "1 (Ethiopic Apocalypse of) Enoch," 10.
42. Nickelsburg and VanderKam, *1 Enoch 2: A Commentary*.
43. Nickelsburg and VanderKam, *1 Enoch: A New Translation*.
44. Nickelsburg ("The Book of Enoch") later took portions from his book to develop an article on the specific area of *1 Enoch*'s influence on the Ethiopian Church. This article serves as a major foundation to initiate broader research on the topic.

1 ENOCH AS CHRISTIAN SCRIPTURE

Noteworthy in relation to our specific topic—the status of 1 Enoch in Christian traditions—is an article by VanderKam.[45] Here, VanderKam demonstrates the historical and theological significance of Enochic literature in general, and 1 Enoch and the Story of the Watchers, in particular. He supports his arguments through a detailed chronological survey of the status of Enochic literature in early Christianity produced by seven major Christian writers, from Jude to Origen. He also notes the extent to which the Enochic Angel Story and the person of Enoch permeates early Christian writing and theological interpretation. On these bases, he concludes that Enochic literature influenced most centres of early Christianity from early New Testament times until the early fourth century CE. Because of the depth of the discussion and the breadth of the evidence it presents, VanderKam's article is likely to remain a major reference for all future studies of the influence and authority of 1 Enoch in the earliest Christian literature. However, this remarkable work refrains from making even a single note on the influence of this literature on Ethiopian Christians, in spite of the fact that only in Ethiopia the entire book of 1 Enoch has been retained.

In addition to all these publications that evidence the contemporary study of 1 Enoch, the Enoch Seminar, established in 2001 offered a special forum for collaborative research in Enochic and other Jewish literature from the Second Temple Period.[46] With all the outstanding contributions that have resulted from this seminar and its publications, however, the role and influence of this literature in Ethiopia is yet to be addressed.

Loren T. Stuckenbruck, in addition to his many significant works on 1 Enoch,[47] is exceptional for engaging the influence and unique place of

---

45. VanderKam, "1 Enoch, Enochic Motifs," 33–101.

46. The bi-annual seminar papers that were delivered by distinguished scholars have resulted in the production of several books, each devoted to a major subject, edited by Gabriele Boccaccini (*Enoch and Qumran Origins*; *Enoch and the Messiah*; *The Origins of Enochic Judaism*), who is the founding director of the seminar. Of the seven seminars held from 2001 until 2013, the proceedings of the first six seminars have been published as books. The more recent ones await publication as books and the papers presented at each seminar are posted on the *4 Enoch* website. Besides the forum created for publications by the seminar, it has posted an immense quantity of material on a website under the name *4 Enoch: The Online Encyclopedia of Second Temple Judaism*, that is edited by Boccaccini and others and that represents an important resource. This online encyclopedia is arguably the most comprehensive scholarly resource on contemporary discussions of the Enochic corpus.

47. For some relevant works of Loren Stuckenbruck in this connection, see Stuckenbruck, "The 'Angels' and 'Giants' of Genesis 6:1–4," 354–73; Stuckenbruck, "Apocrypha and Pseudepigrapha," 143–62; Stuckenbruck, "The Book of Enoch," 7–40; Stuckenbruck,

this text in Ethiopia. He has particularly engaged with these questions in two meaningful ways. Firstly, he has made field study in Ethiopia to visit various locales to identify, document, and preserve Enochic manuscripts. Secondly, he established an informal Ethiopian "Enoch Seminar" in which Ethiopian Enochic scholars and interested individuals may participate, creating a vibrant space for discussions that promise great fruit.

The Canon Debate

The concept of canonicity has been and remains a subject of heated scholarly debate. Roger Beckwith's work, *The Old Testament Canon of the New Testament Church and Its Background in Early Judaism*, is recognized as a definitive study of canon, particularly in Protestant scholarship.[48] Here, and in a later article,[49] Beckwith, in opposition to Albert Sundberg,[50] argues that the OT canon had already been closed before the advent of Christianity. The discussion of both scholars engages with the various elements of what has been known as the canon debate. However, aside from a brief description of the canonical history of the early Ethiopian Church by Beckwith,[51] these studies fail to consider the significance or influence of the canon of the EOTC. Similarly, the collection of studies edited by Lee Martin McDonald and James A. Sanders,[52] which serve to establish the *status quaestionis* in relation to most major Christian traditions with due regard to historical, theological, and methodological concerns, does not discuss the canon of the EOTC in any way. It is hoped that this present study will make a start towards addressing this lacuna.

The Book of Giants from Qumran; Stuckenbruck, "The Early Traditions Related to 1 Enoch," 41–63; Stuckenbruck, "Revision of the Aramaic-Greek," 13–49; Stuckenbruck, "Review of *The Books of Enoch*," 411–19.

48. Beckwith, *The Old Testament Canon*.

49. Beckwith, "A Modern Theory of the Old Testament," 385–95.

50. Sundberg, *The Old Testament of the Early Church*; Sundberg, "Canon of the NT"; Sundberg, "Re-Examining the Formation."

51. Beckwith, *The Old Testament Canon*.

52. McDonald and Sanders, *The Canon Debate*.

1 Enoch as Christian Scripture

The Scriptures/"Canon" and Its Influence in the History of EOTC

As demonstrated above in our brief review of major examples of the secondary literature on the canon debate studies that take into account the EOTC and the historical status of 1 Enoch within the context of this canon are not readily available. The primary academic contribution, in this regard, remains Roger Cowley's short article from 1974.[53] It is, however, important to note the works produced by scholars of the EOTC that demonstrate the ecclesiastical, historical, and theological perspective of canon from within the context of this tradition. Notable amongst these is the authoritative summary of the life and beliefs of the church—*The Ethiopian Orthodox Tewahǝdo Church Faith, Order of Worship and Ecumenical Relations*.[54] The central focus of canon discussion in the Ethiopian context, as indicated is of course the issue of the number of books included in the Ethiopic canon and the different combinations of Jewish and Christian texts that make up this number. While this issue will be dealt with in greater detail in chapter 4, it is significant to note here that there are currently several lists, all enjoying some level of acceptance and authority within the church. It also bears mentioning that no modern translation of the Bible by the EOTC claims to present the entire canonical collection.

---

53. Cowley, "The Biblical Canon," 318–23. In this study Cowley lists the primary difficulties that he encountered: (1) the concept of canonicity is regarded more loosely by the EOTC than it is by most other churches; (2) the number of canonical books is reckoned to be 81, but this total is reached in various ways; (3) the naming of a book in a list does not necessarily uniquely identify it; (4) some of the books assigned canonical authority have never been printed in Ge'ez, or they have been printed only outside Ethiopia, or they are difficult to obtain; (5) the authorities of the Ethiopian Orthodox Church have never said of an edition of the Ge'ez or Amharic Bible that it was complete.

54. EOTC, *The Ethiopian Orthodox Tewahǝdo Church*. In addition to this resource the following offer interesting insight into discussions about canon within the Ethiopian context: Wondmagegnehu and Motovu, *The Ethiopian Orthodox Church*; and, Sergew, *The Church of Ethiopia*.

ADDENDUM I
A Critique of Ephraim Isaac's Proposition

To my knowledge, Ephraim Isaac[1] is the first scholar to clearly assert the extent of the influence and legacy of 1 Enoch on the Ethiopian church and its worldview.[2] In the more than three decades since Isaac addressed this important gap in the study of Enoch, his observations have barely been augmented by further study. The only major exception, in this regard, has been the work done by Nickelsburg as part of his monumental commentary on 1 Enoch, as well as a later article.[3] Here, I wish to engage with Isaac's groundbreaking work towards better understanding the influence of 1 Enoch on Ethiopian Christianity and the development of its worldview—because of its significance and because it has inspired this current study.

Two important propositions raised by Isaac in this study focus on the breadth and extent to which 1 Enoch has influenced Ethiopian religious tradition, both internally and relative to other Christian traditions. While these propositions articulate challenging and bold claims, the brevity with which they are explained suggests a number of questions that need answering.

Isaac articulates the first proposition as follows: "it is hardly possible to understand *any aspect* of religious tradition and thought of Ethiopia, the

---

1. Isaac, "1 (Ethiopic Apocalypse of) Enoch," 5–89.

2. After summarizing some few examples which note the influence of Enoch in Ethiopia, Nickelsburg notes that: "[a]mong the editions of 1 Enoch published since 1821, only the 1983 translation by Ephraim Isaac has addressed the issue of the Ethiopian use of 1 Enoch—but then only briefly" (Nickelsburg, "The Book of Enoch," 612).

3. Nickelsburg, *1 Enoch 1: A Commentary*, 104–8; Nickelsburg, "The Book of Enoch," 611–19.

1 Enoch as Christian Scripture

country in which it survived, without an understanding of it [i.e. 1 Enoch]."[4] He reaches this conclusion following a discussion that compares the status of 1 Enoch in the ETOC vis-à-vis its influence on Western ideology, which according to Isaac was negligible to "the development of the intellectual history of modern Western culture."[5] He goes on to assert that "all aspects" of Ethiopian religious thought and related traditions uniquely reflect Enochic influence. While, anecdotally at least, this may seem like a plausible claim the breadth and extent of influence which Isaac suggests is not borne out by the limited examples of literary appropriation in the EOTC he uses as evidence.[6] While the literature does support the use of quotes, motifs, and themes from Enoch it does not serve to establish it as the singular text shaping the worldview of Ethiopian Christianity. Such a claim would have likely been better supported had he included its influences in other arenas such as theological formulations and cultural practices.

Another shortcoming of his discussion is the extent to which it minimizes the influence of 1 Enoch on the Western world. It seems hasty, if not outright wrong, to reach such a conclusion without thoroughly assessing and properly considering the legacy of Enoch in the Judeo-Christian scriptures. In this instance, therefore, the claim—while it may form the basis for further in-depth study—fails to convince because it is too general and too absolute.

The second and related proposition argues that: "What distinguishes Ethiopian Christian theology from that of either Western or Eastern Christendom may well be the Ethiopian emphases on Enochic thought."[7] He supports this by arguing that a central tenet of Christian theology, the doctrine of sin is uniquely formulated in Ethiopia because of Enochic influence: "[s]in does not originate from Adam's transgression alone; Satan, the demons, and evil spirits (the fallen angels) are equally responsible for its origin; they continue to lead man astray, causing moral ruin on the earth."[8] While the influence of an Enochic framework of sin is recognized in Ethiopic theological literature, it is nonetheless misleading to conclude that EOTC theology

---

4. Isaac, "1 (Ethiopic Apocalypse) of Enoch," 10; italics mine.
5. Isaac, "1 (Ethiopic Apocalypse) of Enoch," 10.
6. Isaac ("1 (Ethiopic Apocalypse) of Enoch," 10) briefly mentions how the Book of Mysteries of Heaven and Earth has been misunderstood to 1 Enoch in the seventeenth century Europe and how other books like *Kebre Negest* and others are influenced by it.
7. Isaac, "1 (Ethiopic Apocalypse) of Enoch," 10.
8. Isaac, "1 (Ethiopic Apocalypse) of Enoch," 10.

does not recognize the percept of original sin. Indeed, a cursory look at the commentary tradition of the church as well as the Christology and Mariology of the church—frequently, formulated in terms of a Second Adam; Second Eve paradigm, whereby the sin of the original couple is redeemed by the obedience worked out through Christ and Mary.[9] Moreover, even were we to concede some degree of nuance in the Ethiopian understanding of sin as a result of Enochic influence this is still not the most apparent factor which distinguishes the EOTC from other churches. Indeed, considering his other writings,[10] it is surprising that Isaac here seems to be overlooking the major distinguishing factors of the EOTC, which are mainly Jewish practices, including the *tabot* (the Ark of the Covenant), male circumcision, observance of two Sabbaths, dietary laws, fasting of two days, church buildings (replica of the Temple), and ritual cleanliness.[11] Concluding that the influence of 1 Enoch, is the primary element which makes Ethiopian Christianity different from other Christian traditions fails to convince.

Besides the abovementioned Jewish practices in the EOTC, which would be the reasons for some to consider the church as a Judeo-Christian church, other elements such as its Christology; traditions such as the Finding of the True Cross; some hierarchical positions of the church, which includes the *debteras*; the Yaredic hymnology and music; and the Ge'ez literature and its liturgy can be listed as factors distinctive to the church. Even if some of these may have been influenced by 1 Enoch, directly or indirectly, they have their own tradition and development without being linked exclusively to 1 Enoch.

Upon critical assessment, therefore, it is possible to identify strong reservations about Isaac's decidedly exclusive and limited argument about the influence of 1 Enoch on the EOTC. As I have attempted to show the limitations of the arguments he presents are made even more pronounced

---

9. Wondmagegnehu and Motovu, *The Ethiopian Orthodox Church*, 94–95. The writers note that the church, while acknowledging the external influence of evil spirits the EOTC affirms the fallen-ness of humanity in its doctrines.

10. From his PhD dissertation, Isaac has closely studied the origins and character of Hebraic elements in Ethiopian Christianity. Isaac, "A Study of Mashafa Berhan"; Isaac, "An Obscure Component in Ethiopian Church History," 225–58; Isaac, *The Ethiopian Orthodox Täwahïdo Church*.

11. Ullendorff notes an alternative view on the sources and traditions of uniquely Ethiopian Christian practices suggesting that these facets are pre-Christian and hence evidence for the influence of indigenous elements in the process of the appropriation of Christianity (Ullendorff, *The Ethiopians*, 114–15).

because of the misleading nature and the inadequacies of the examples and evidence he employs to support his arguments.

3

1 ENOCH IN JUDE AND OTHER EARLY CHRISTIAN TEXTS

Introduction

THE FOLLOWING DISCUSSION WILL demonstrate the extent to which Jewish literature in general and particularly 1 Enoch exerted influence on Jude. This influence is evident not only in the citations and allusions, themes and motifs, and the use of vocabulary permeating the book, but can also be seen in the literary style that demonstrates Jude's conscious uses in clear contrast with the biblical literature. Both the form and the content reveal Jude's affinity towards and knowledge of the Second Temple Period literature, his awareness of its continuity with the biblical literature, and the authoritative status he grants the source material upon which he is dependent. Hence, a discussion on some literary issues is appropriate.

The book of Jude is acknowledged to be one of the most neglected books in the New Testament. Richard Bauckham[1] and Cory D. Anderson[2] affirm the appropriateness of the description "The Most Neglected Book in the New Testament"[3] given to Jude.[4] The reasons proffered as

---

1. Bauckham, *Jude and the Relatives*, 134.

2. Anderson, "Jude's Use of the Pseudepigraphal," 47.

3. This is the title of an article by D.J. Rowston who argues that the main reasons behind this neglect are Jude's use of 1 Enoch and the uncertain historical background to the letter (Rowston, "The Most Neglected Book," 554–63).

4. Some examples of the academic studies of Jude that have been conducted bear

1 Enoch as Christian Scripture

to why this book has been neglected range from its brevity, its citation of non-canonical Jewish writings, "its burning denunciation of error,"[5] and the apparent absence of main Christian teachings as well as the widely acknowledged dependence of Jude on 2 Peter.[6] Despite these reasons, which have generally inhibited academic interest in Jude, this book is significant, and arguably unique, for the extent of its allusions to ancient Judaism and the status it accords to 1 Enoch and other Second Temple Period literature. This characteristic is reflected in the extent of citations, references and allusions which does not reflect its much-touted brevity.

In this chapter, I will look at the use of Second Temple Literature, generally, and 1 Enoch, particularly, to better understand the reception and appropriation of this work in Christian traditions. Towards this end, I will begin with a brief look at the literary and interpretative strategies employed in Jude. This will be followed by a discussion of the use of Jewish literature, including a look at use of the OT, followed by the use of "extra-canonical" literature including 1 Enoch. Selected texts, both from Jude and 1 Enoch, will be exegeted and compared so as to illuminate the authority accorded "extra-canonical" works in the book of Jude.

Preliminary Issues: Literary and Interpretative Strategies

Though it is generally understood that Jude is generically a letter,[7] it has been rightly noted that the body of the book is "a performed midrash on the theme of judgment."[8] E. Earle Ellis notes that as an interpretative activity

mentioning: Bauckham, *Jude, 2 Peter*; Bauckham, *Jude and the Relatives*; Charles, "The Angels, Sonship," 171–78; Charles, "Jude's Use of Pseudepigraphical," 130–45; Charles, "Literary Artifice," 106–24; Charles, "'Those' and 'These,'" 109–24; Dunnett, "The Hermeneutics of Jude," 287–92; Fossum, "Kurios Jesus as the Angel," 226–43; Osburn, "Discourse Analysis and Jewish Apocalyptic," 287–319; Osburn, "1 Enoch 80:2-8," 296–303; Osburn, "The Christological Use of 1 Enoch," 334–41; Osburn, "The Text of Jude 5," 107–15.

5. Blum, "Jude," 384.

6. Bauckham describes this point as follows: "The tradition of scholarly contempt [i.e. considering Jude merely as nothing but an excerpt from 2 Peter] has also led to scholarly neglect of Jude hence to ignorance of Jude" (Bauckham, *Jude and the Relatives*, 134).

7. The Epistle of Jude has almost all the features of an ancient letter form: the sender, the receivers, greetings, purpose and occasion, the main body, and doxology. For a discussion on epistolary framework of the letter see Osburn, "Discourse Analysis and Jewish Apocalyptic," 288–94.

8. Ellis, *The Making of the New Testament*, 120; Ellis uses the term "performed

the midrash procedure (1) is oriented to the Scriptures, (2) adapting it to the present (3) for the instruction or edification of the current reader. Along these lines he notes that Jude has reworked the midrash by giving it the form of a letter.[9] Bauckham explicates the structure of Jude in terms of a sermon delivered in an epistolary framework—which he notes is a form that might have already been in use both in Judaism and Christianity before Jude's time.[10] The expository characteristics of Jude described in terms of midrash or sermon are readily observed from an analysis of the strategies and devices used by Jude. The careful composition indicates the extent to which, in Jude, "exegetical method is indivisible from his message."[11]

Structure and Literary Analysis of Jude

The literary structure and analysis, adopted here, is indebted to Ellis[12] and the subsequent refinement offered by Bauckham.[13]

1–2	**Address and Greeting**	
3–4	**Occasion and Theme**	
3		A. The Appeal to Contend for the Faith
4		B. The Background to the Appeal: The False Teachers, their character and Judgement (forming Introductory Statement Theme for B')

---

midrash" to denote interpretive renderings of various kinds of "text + exposition" patterns as described here: Ellis, "Biblical Interpretation in the New Testament," 703.

9. Ellis, *The Making of the New Testament*, 20–25. He notes the performed piece constitutes c. 72 percent of the letter.

10. Bauckham, *Jude, 2 Peter*, 3.

11. Charles, "'Those' and 'These,'" 119.

12. Ellis, *Prophecy and Hermeneutics*, 221–26.

13. Bauckham extensively discusses and elaborates the structure and its significance to offer a clear understanding of every aspect of the letter in his various works. This study adopts his latest analysis in Bauckham, "Jude, Epistle of," 1098. His major refinement of Ellis's analysis is that he regards the whole vv. 8–10 as a commentary on vv. 5–7, with the 'citation' in verse 9 introduced as a secondary 'text' to aid the interpretation of vv. 5–7. For a recent discussion on Jude's structural analyses from different perspectives see: Clark, "Discourse Structure in Jude," 125–37; Smith, "Unlocking the Structure of Jude," 138–42. While both propose different structures for Jude, they agree with Bauckham and Ellis that the structure of the letter is part of the author's technique of conveying his message.

5–23 Body of the Letter

5–19   B'. The Background: A Midrash on Four Prophecies of the Doom of the Ungodly

5–7   "Text" 1: The Old Testament Types

8–10   + interpretation

(9)   including secondary "text": Michael and the Devil

11   "Text" 2: Three More Old Testament Types

12–13   + interpretation

(12–13) including secondary allusions

14–15   "Text" 3: A Very Ancient Prophecy

16   + interpretation

17–18   "Text" 4: A Very Modern Prophecy

19   + interpretation

20–23 A'. The Appeal

24–25 Concluding Doxology

This analysis elucidates the epistolary framework of the letter, which contains a "midrash" or a section of formal exegesis (vv. 5–19). The initial statement of the theme of the letter (vv. 3–4) contains two parts (A and B), which correspond, in reverse order, to the two parts of the body of the letter (B' and A').[14]

Bauckham further contends that the midrashic style used in vv. 5–19 is "a very carefully composed piece of scriptural commentary which argues for the statement made in v. 4."[15] In these verses, scriptural examples and quotations become "texts" which are then interpreted to apply to the situation facing Jude's readers. This midrashic pattern of "text" followed by interpretation is repeated four times. The first two "texts," are actually allusions to biblical stories which are then interpreted to apply to Jude's opponents. The latter two are taken from authoritative sources which are equally applied to the readers' situation.[16]

---

14. For further explanation on how the whole fits together, see Bauckham, *Jude and the Relatives*, 179–86.

15. Bauckham, "Jude, Epistle of," 1098.

16. Bauckham, *Jude and the Relatives*, 234.

1 Enoch in Jude and Other Early Christian Texts

Among these texts, texts 1 and 2 reference three groups of characters—Israel in the wilderness (Num 14), the watchers or fallen angels (1 En 6-19), and the people of Sodom and Gomorrah (Gen 19)—and three individuals—Cain (Gen 4:8), Balaam (Num 22:1—31:16) and Korah (Num 16)—all appropriated from Jewish scripture.[17] These are all well-known scriptural examples of judgment, and not verbal prophecies. They are here used as historical types of the false teachers, known to Jude's addressees, who are similarly doomed to judgment.[18] The second pair of texts, 3 and 4, on the other hand, *are* verbal prophecies of the false teachers, quoted from 1 En 1:9 and oral tradition of the teaching of the apostles respectively.[19]

A number of stylistic features mark a distinction between "texts" and interpretation. First, there is a shift in tense from "texts" to interpretation. The tense of the verbs in the "texts" is past or future, referring to types in the past or prophesying the future, whereas the interpretations use present tenses, referring to the fulfilment of the types and prophecies, in the present time.[20] Secondly, transition from "text" to interpretation is also marked by phrases with οὗτοι used in a formulaic way to introduce each section of interpretation.[21] They serve to identify the false teachers as the people to whom the prophecies address. In this way, the transition from the prophecy to its application to the opponents was achieved. Thirdly, the "texts" are introduced by the formulae like ὅτι (5, 11) and λέγω (14, 17) distinguishing them from the interpretation.[22] Bauckham notes that in addition to the four

---

17. It is noted that this is an acceptable way of citing the text of a midrash, (cf. 1 Cor 10:1-5; Heb 7:1-3) (Bauckham, *Jude and the Relatives*, 182).

18. But for some verbal allusions to the actual texts of the Scriptures see Bauckham, *Jude and the Relatives*, 182-83. In another work, Bauckham (*Jude, 2 Peter*, 79-84) suggests that the references to Cain, Balaam and Korah are not merely to the OT texts as such but to some other Second Temple Period traditions about these figures which had grown up around the OT texts.

19. Bauckham, "Jude, Epistle of," 1098. As indicated in the analysis, that is "text" 3: (A Very Ancient Prophecy) and "text" 4: (A Very Modern Prophecy), they show that the opponents and their judgment have been prophesied about from the very earliest times up to the most recent times.

20. Ellis, *Prophecy and Hermeneutic*, 225. For some exceptions, see Bauckham, "Jude, Epistle of," 1089.

21. This resembles similar formulae used in the Qumran commentaries (4QFlor 1:2, 3, 11, 12, 17; 4QpIs^a 3:7, 9, 10, 12; 4QpIsa^b 2:6-7, 10) and occasionally in the NT (Gal 4:24; 2 Tim 3:8).

22. Ellis (*Prophecy and Hermeneutic*, 224) notes that these formulae are used elsewhere in the NT to introduce quotations, e.g., 2 Cor 10:17; Gal 3:11; Mark 12:26.

1 Enoch as Christian Scripture

primary "texts" there is a secondary "text" (v. 9), which helps the interpretation of "text" 1.[23]

Typology, Catchwords, and Triplets

Within the framework of his literary structure, Jude make use of an interweaving of typology, catchwords and triplets. One of the characteristic methods employed by NT writers in their use of OT (or other Jewish traditions) is typology. Typology presupposes continuity between the two testaments in terms of promise (prophecy) and fulfilment[24] or correspondence between type and antitype. For Jude, the OT types apply prophetically to his opponents with historical correspondence between the ungodly of the past and those of the present.

The first instance of Jude's typological triplet cites "three classic examples of sin which incurred divine judgment":[25] the unbelieving Israel (v. 5), the rebellious angels (v. 6) and Sodom and Gomorrah (v. 7) all of which exhibit "unnatural rebellion"[26] The second triplet, Cain, Balaam, and Korah (v. 11), are brought together as "objects of a woe-cry, [that is], a prophetic denunciation, issued by the writer."[27]

Besides these typological triplets, the relatively brief book of Jude is inundated by the abundance of descriptions listed in groups of three. Charles observes twenty sets of triplets which dominate the only twenty-five verses,[28] beginning from the writer's self-designation in v. 1 through to

---

23. Bauckham, "Jude, Epistle of," 1099; Ellis, *Prophecy and Hermeneutic*, 224. However for Ellis v. 9 is a citation with equal weight as the others because it fits all the features which the other citations would have.

24. For a detailed discussion on "typology" as promise and fulfilment, see: von Rad, "Typological Interpretation," 28–46; France, *Jesus and the Old Testament*, 1971.

25. Bauckham, *Jude and the Relatives*, 186.

26. Green, *The Second Epistle General*, 166–67.

27. Charles, "'Those' and 'These,'" 116.

28. Charles, "'Those' and 'These,'" 124 n.24. Charles further relates Jude's usage of triplets with his Jewishness that he tries to find three-fold witnesses to validate his testimony as a tradition in the OT (Deut 17:6; 19:15) and later on affirmed by the NT (John 5:31-33; 8:17-18; Matt: 18:16; 2 Cor 13:1; 1 Tim 5:19; Heb 10:28).

the final doxology in v. 25.²⁹ The many sets of triads indicate the urgency, depth, vividness and strength of the author's argument.³⁰

Jude is also marked by strong and consistent use of catchwords designed to connect various elements in the structure of the letter.³¹ Both the extensive and consistent usage of catchwords shows that the literary device is not accidental on the writer's part, but is rather, "the hall-mark of the midrashic procedure."³² Most of the catchwords, which occur more than four times in their different forms, as listed by C. Landon, are: (1) ἀσεβής / ἀσέβεια vv. 4, 15 (3x), 18; (2) σύ vv. 3 (3x), 5 (2x) 12, 17, 18, 20 (2x) 24; (3) οὗτος vv. 4, 8, 10, 11, 12, 14, 16, 19; (4) κύριος vv. 4, 5, 9, 14, 17, 21, 25; (5) ἁγίοις vv. 3, 14, 20 (2x), 24 (ἄμωμος); (6) σάρξ, ἐπιθυμίας vv. 7, 16, 18, 23; (7) ἀγάπη / ἀγαπητός vv. 1, 2, 3, 12, 17, 20, 21; (8) ἔλεος / ἐλεέω vv. 2, 21, 22, 23; (9) κρίμα, κρίσις vv. 4, 6, 9, 15; (10) πᾶς vv. 3, 15 (4x), 25 (2x).³³ This confirms the general tendency of the writer to structure and enforce his

---

29. As noted by Charles ("Literary Artifice," 131 n.5) these are discovered in: the self-designation of the writer in: v.1 (Ἰούδας, δοῦλος, ἀδελφός)("Literary Artifice," 132, n.5) and the attributes ascribed to the readers (ἠγαπημένοις, τετηρημένοις, κλητός); elements in the greeting in v.2 (ἔλεος, εἰρήνη, ἀγάπη); the participles modifying the main verb in v.4 (προγεγραμμένοι, μετατιθέντες, ἀρνούμενοι); paradigms of judgement (unbelieving Israel, the rebellious angels, Sodom and Gomorrah); actions of the οὗτοι in v. 8 (μιαίνουσιν, ἀθετοῦσιν, βλασφημοῦσιν); the actions of Michael in v.9 (διελέγετο, ἐπενεγκεῖν, εἶπεν); examples of woe v.11 (Cain, Balaam, Korah); escalation of rebellious action (ἐπορεύθησαν, ἐξεχύθησαν, ἀπώλοντο); traits of those at the love-feasts in v.12 (σπιλάδες συνευωχούμενοι ἀφόβως); characteristics of the waves v.13 (ἄγρια, ἐπαφρίζοντα, αἰσχύνας); actions of the Lord vv. 14–15 (ἦλθεν, ποιῆσαι κρίσιν, ἐλέγξαι); characteristics of the οὗτοι v.16 (γογγυσταὶ μεμψίμοιροι κατὰ τὰς ἐπιθυμίας ἑαυτῶν πορευόμενοι); further characteristics v.19 (ἀποδιορίζοντες, ψυχικοί, πνεῦμα μὴ ἔχοντες); Trinitarian language vv. 20–21 (Holy Spirit, God, Jesus Christ); participles relating to the writer's imperative in the same verses (ἐποικοδομοῦντες, προσευχόμενοι, προσδεχόμενοι); final imperatives in vv. 22–23 (ἐλεᾶτε (2x), σῴζετε); divine designations in v. 25 (θεός, σωτήρ, κύριος) and threefold view of time (πρὸ παντὸς τοῦ αἰῶνος καὶ νῦν καὶ εἰς πάντας).

30. In the same line, Steven J. Kraftchick argues that "the triple formulations underscore the urgency of the letter, attempting to make the readers see and feel the magnitude of the danger in their midst. Their use lends depth and vividness to the author's argument, causing his positive statements about God and the community to stand in direct contrast with the negative portrait of the antagonists" (Kraftchick, *Jude & 2 Peter*, 19).

31. As Ellis observes, the catchwords join "text" to "text" (e.g., κρίσις 6, 9, 15), "text" to interpretation (e.g., λαλέω 15, 16), "text" to introduction (e.g., κύριος 4, 15), "text" to final application (e.g., σῴζω 5, 23), or they may join all four elements (τηρέω 1, 6, 13, 21; κύριος 4, 5, 14, 17, 21) (Ellis, *Prophecy and Hermeneutic*, 225).

32. Ellis, *Prophecy and Hermeneutic*, 225.

33. Landon, *A Text-Critical Study*, 52–53.

message by repeating certain key words—a practice "paralleled at Qumran and elsewhere (e.g., 1 Pet 2:4–10)."[34]

Jude also employs other minor literary devices and motifs which may not be readily be detected but are common to the Second Temple Jewish tradition as a continuation and development of the OT.[35] Thus Jude, in his literary strategy and hermeneutics, proves himself to highly depend on and follow early Jewish traditions, both in form and content.

Jude's Use of Jewish Literature: I—OT

Jude's keen awareness of both the OT and STL is evident from his extensive usage of both traditions in an interwoven and systematic way, as revealed in his structure and expository interpretation. To offer a better understanding of this appropriation we will briefly look at the reception of the OT in Jude before moving on to more fully investigate the use and status of 1 Enoch.

Jude's extensive use and dependence on the OT, is evident in at least five notable ways: (1) types and examples of OT figures and traditions, (2) motifs common to the OT, (3) theophanic expression in a judgment context, (4) the notion of names being written in heavenly books, and (5) typological exegesis. Let us briefly look at examples of these uses of the Old Testament.

Some of the OT figures and groups used as types and examples at different levels in Jude include; unbelieving Israel, the fallen angels, Sodom and Gomorrah, Michael the archangel, Moses, Adam, Cain, Balaam, Korah, and Enoch.[36] The sheer extent of these references—which is unparalleled in most of the other books in the New Testament—particularly relative to the brevity of the book of Jude—supports the conclusion that the author is very well versed in Old Testament literature.

Second, one of the ways Jude uses the OT is his dependence on OT motifs. He uses two sets of triplets in order to make an antithesis of the

---

34. Bauckham, "Jude, Epistle of," 1099.

35. For instance, we can see a major antithesis of the ungodly, basically represented as οὗτοι (vv. 8, 10, 11, 12, 14, 16, 19), and the faithful, who are unidentified as ὑμεῖς (vv. 5, 17, 18, 19) (Charles, "'Those' and 'These,'" 120). As Charles notes, juxtaposition is a notable feature of both canonical and non-canonical Jewish wisdom literature. Other dependence on Jewish tradition in general and Enochic motifs in particular, such as theophanic appearances and judgment themes will be seen below.

36. For a detailed discussion on Jude's use of the OT, see Charles, "'Those' and 'These,'" 124.

ungodly and the faithful. Whereas the ungodly are typified by the examples from the OT, the faithful are portrayed by terms common in the OT, such as ἅγιος (holy) (v.14), μισοῦντες καὶ τὸν ἀπὸ τῆς σαρκὸς ἐσπιλωμένον χιτῶνα v. 23 ("hating even the garment stained from corrupted flesh"), and ἀμώμους v. 24 ("blameless"). Such juxtaposition "is a notable feature of OT wisdom literature."[37]

A third example of Jude's dependence on the OT is his use of theophanic language within a judgment context. While Jude 14–15 is explicitly derived from 1 Enoch (see below), its relation to the Sinai Theophany and the blessing of Moses in Deut 33:1–29 is clear. "Behold (for) he comes ...,"[38] "with the myriads of his holy ones ..."[39] "to execute judgment upon all ..."[40] "and he will destroy all the wicked ..."[41] "and he will reprove all flesh ...,"[42] all are reminiscent of common patterns of theophany-statements in the OT which are taken up by the apocalyptic literature, including 1 Enoch.[43]

Fourth, another aspect of Jude's appropriation of the OT, as well as the apocalyptic literature, is the notion of names being written in heavenly books (v. 4), with the motif of divine foreknowledge.[44]

The fifth example of Jude's appropriation of the OT, the use of typological exegesis, is arguably the most significant illustration of his dependence on the OT because typology[45] is an important factor in addressing the question of the NT use of the OT. Jude's use of OT types reflects his awareness of continuity between the two testaments. While these examples demonstrate the extent to which Jude is dependent on the OT, it is also

---

37. Charles, "'Those' and 'These,'" 111. This is particularly common in the book of Proverbs, where the righteous and the foolish stand as diametrically opposed.

38. Deut 33:2; Judg 5:4; Ps 18:9; Isa 19:1; 26:21; 31:4, 27; 40:10; Amos 1:2; Mic 1:3; Hab 3:3; Zeph 1:7; Zech 9:14; 14:1, 3; Mal 3:1–3.

39. Deut 33:2; Ps 68:17; Isa 40:10; 66:15; Dan 7:10.

40. Deut 10:18; Pss 76:9; 96:13; Isa 33:5; Jer 25:31; Dan 7:10, 13, 16; Joel 3:2; Zeph 3:8; Hab 1:12; Mal 2:17; 3:5.

41. Pss 46:8–9; 76:3–6; Isa 19:3; 27:1; 66:15–16; Jer 25:31; Zeph 3:8–18; Hag 2:22; Zech 14:2–3, 12.

42. Isa 66:15–24; Jer 25:31; Zeph 1:8, 9, 12; Mal 3:3–5.

43. Charles, "'Those' and 'These,'" 111.

44. Ex 32:32–33; Pss 40:4; 56:8; 69:29; 139:16; Isa 4:3; Jer 22:30; Dan 7:10; 12:1; Mal 3:16; 1 En 81:1–2; 89:62; 90:14, 17, 20, 22; 104:7; 108:3, 7; T. Ass 7:5; 2 Bar 24:1; Rev 3:5; 5:1, 7, 8; 10:8–11; 20:12.

45. For a detailed discussion on the problem arising from the lack of a common definition of typology, four different views and three major characteristic features, see: Glenny, "Typology: A Summary," 627–38.

important to note that this use is informed by his awareness and appropriation of later Jewish thoughts. "Jude combines typological treatment of the OT with conventions and imagery contemporary to sectarian Judaism which would have been readily understood by his readership."[46]

Jude's Use of Jewish Literature: II—1 Enoch

Besides the explicit quotation in vv. 14-15, a range of different images, expressions, allusions, motifs, and theological themes from 1 Enoch can be discovered in Jude. The writer employs Enochic themes both in form and content, much in the same manner he uses the OT. The undistinguished use of 1 Enoch, alongside and following the same pattern of the use of the OT seems to be a clear indication of the authority of 1 Enoch for the writer of Jude. Below I will look more closely at the direct quotation from 1 Enoch discovered in vv. 14-15, followed by a look at the other Enochic themes and allusions in Jude.

It has long been recognized that Jude 14-15 is a quotation of 1 En 1:9.[47] Bauckham rightly notes that this is the only section of Jude's midrash which employs a formal quotation from a written source.[48] The use of a standard formula in which τούτοις, "these," identifies the false teachers as those to whom the prophecy applies is notable here.[49] Jude makes certain modifications, in accordance with the practice of his period, so that the text may best reflect his exegesis.[50] This can be seen in a comparison of Jude with the Greek and Ethiopic versions of 1 Enoch.[51]

---

46. Charles, "'Those' and 'These,'" 115.

47. This has been noted from the time of the earliest Christian interpreters, Clement of Alexandria and Tertullian.

48. Bauckham, *Jude, 2 Peter*, 93.

49. Cf. 4QpIsa^b 2:7; 4QFlor 1:16; Act 2:16; 4:11.

50. Osburn, "The Christological Use of 1 Enoch," 340-41.

51. Here the Greek of 1 Enoch is from Black's (*Apocalypsis Henochi Graece*) edition and the Ethiopic is represented by Knibb's (*The Ethiopic Book of Enoch*) translation. For a comparison that includes Qumran Aramaic and a Latin version, see Bauckham, *Jude, 2 Peter*, 95.

1 Enoch in Jude and Other Early Christian Texts

Comparison of Jude 14–15 and 1 Enoch 1:9

1 Enoch 1:9 (Ethiopic)⁵²	1 Enoch 1:9 (Black)	Jude 14–15 (UBS)
ወናሁ መጽአ በትእልፊት ቅዱሳን ከመ ይግበር ፍትሐ ላዕሌሆሙ ወያጠፍኦሙ ለረሲዓን ወይትዋቀሥ ኵሎ ዘሥጋ በእንተ ኵሉ ሐጢኣ ወረሲዐ ላዕሉ ኃጥኣን ረሲዓን።	ὅτι ἔρχεται σὺν ταῖς μυριάσιν αὐτοῦ καὶ τοῖς ἁγίοις αὐτοῦ, μυριάσιν αὐτοῦ κατὰ πάντων, καὶ ἀπολέσει πάντας τοὺς ἀσεβεῖς καὶ ἐλέγξει πᾶσαν σάρκα περὶ πάντων ἔργων τῆς ἀσεβείας αὐτῶν ὧν ἠσέβησαν καὶ σκληρῶν ὧν ἐλάλησεν λόγων καὶ περὶ παωτων ων κατελαλησαν κατ' αὐτοῦ ἁμαρτωλοὶ ἀσεβεῖς.	Ἰδοὺ ἦλθεν κύριος ἐν ἁγίαις μυριάσιν αὐτοῦ ποιῆσαι κρίσιν κατὰ πάντων καὶ ἐλέγξαι πᾶσαν ψυχὴν περὶ πάντων τῶν ἔργων ἀσεβείας αὐτῶν ὧν ἠσέβησαν καὶ περὶ πάντων τῶν σκληρῶν ὧν ἐλάλησαν κατ' αὐτοῦ ἁμαρτωλοὶ ἀσεβεῖς.

A brief look at the texts above demonstrates interesting instances of convergence and divergence that need to be considered:

1) Ἰδοὺ: against the Greek, Jude here agrees with the Ethiopic (ወናሁ) which could suggest that Jude follows the Aramaic text.⁵³

2) ἦλθεν: Jude uses an aorist where both the Ethiopic and the Greek are in the present tense. It is probable that Jude's aorist in this case represents a Semitic "prophetic perfect," and may indicate a literal translation of the Aramaic, whereas the Greek and the Ethiopic are more idiomatic renderings.⁵⁴

3) κύριος: as a subject is an addition made by Jude. The subject of the sentence in 1 Enoch is God.⁵⁵ Various suggestions are given for Jude's

---

52. Translation: "And behold! He comes with ten thousands holy ones, to execute judgment upon them and to destroy the impious and to contend with all flesh concerning everything which the sinners and the impious have done and wrought against him."

53. Black, "The Maranatha Invocation," 195; VanderKam, "The Theophany of Enoch," 129–50; Knibb suggests that both the Ethiopic and the Greek derive from an original 'אָ֫ה (Knibb, *Ethiopic Book of Enoch*, 2:59).

54. VanderKam, "The Theophany of Enoch," 148; Osburn, "The Christological Use of 1 Enoch," 337.

55. Even though the last explicit mention of God in 1 En 1 is in v.4, it is clear from the context that he continues to be the subject until v. 9.

introduction of κύριος: (a) it has Christological significance that allows the verse to be applied to Jesus as the "eschatological Redeemer."[56] (b) It could also be employed by analogy with other theophany texts[57] which were applied to the Parousia in primitive Christianity.[58]

4) ἐν ἁγίαις μυριάσιν αὐτοῦ: Once again Jude agrees with the Ethiopic against the Greek.[59] Whether the expansion of the Greek text is the result of a secondary gloss or scribal error in the Greek version[60] the Semitism reflected in Jude's use of ἐν instead of the use σύν illustrates that he is here not following the Greek.[61]

5) καὶ ἐλέγξαι πᾶσαν . . . : As can be seen in the comparison, Jude's text at this point is abbreviated.[62] Both the Ethiopic and the Greek texts (verbs) indicate three purposes for the anticipated coming of God: (1) to judge, (2) to destroy, (3) to convict. Jude omits the idea of destruction by merging it with conviction. The omission of "destroy," which comes rather oddly before "convict" in 1 Enoch, is likely intended to emphasize the judicial conviction of the false teachers before their destruction.[63]

6) πᾶσαν σάρκα: The original object of the conviction, "all flesh," is omitted from Jude. Here also, the omission may be explained in line with

---

56. Osburn, "The Christological Use of 1 Enoch," 341; Black, "The Maranatha Invocation," 195.

57. Isa 40:10; 66:15; Zech 14:5; cf. 1 En 91:7.

58. Bauckham, "A Note on a Problem," 136 n.5.

59. Bauckham attempts to explain the longer reading of the Greek, σύν ταῖς μυριάσιν αὐτοῦ καὶ τοῖς ἁγίοις αὐτοῦ . . ., as a Christian interpretation of the text. He suggests, the rendering of the Greek must be either "a Christian interpretative gloss on a Greek text which originally rendered the Aramaic more accurately, or possibly an indication that [the Greek] represents an originally Christian translation of *1 Enoch*," which combined two Christian interpretations of Zech 14:5 (Bauckham, "A Note on a Problem," 138).

60. Osburn, "The Christological Use of 1 Enoch," 337.

61. Bauckham, "A Note on a Problem," 94. Osburn notes that the agreement of the Ethiopic with the Aramaic fragment in 1 En 1:9 would support Ullendorff's (*Ethiopia and the Bible*) thesis that parts of the Ethiopic texts were derived directly from the Aramaic (Osburn, "The Christological Use of 1 Enoch," 338).

62. Note the alteration of ἀπολέσει by ἐλέγξω later on left out, which reduces Jude's verbs by one.

63. Bauckham, *Jude, 2 Peter*, 94, 96.

the intended effect of the text exclusively to the ἀσεβεῖς, whom Jude identifies as the false teachers.[64]

7) περὶ πάντων τῶν σκληρῶν ὧν ἐλάλησαν κατ' αὐτοῦ: here the Greek is longer than both Jude and the Ethiopic. Knibb explains that the longer text of the Greek may be dittography.[65] It is also possible that Jude abbreviated the text once again, "as the Ethiopic has certainly done here."[66] It is further suggested that the longer Greek text maybe "reflecting a conflation of two readings" from the Aramaic originals.[67]

Despite these minor divergences, the close word for word similarities between the Greek text of 1 Enoch and Jude need to be noted: (1) μυριάσιν αὐτοῦ, (2) μυριάσιν αὐτοῦ κατά πάντων (3) πάντας τοὺς ἀσεβεῖς (4) περὶ πάντων (τῶν Jude) ἔργων (τῆς 1 En) ἀσεβείας αὐτῶν ὧν ἠσέβησαν (5) καὶ περὶ πάντων (6) κατ' αὐτοῦ ἁμαρτωλοὶ ἀσεβεῖς.

The analysis above serves to demonstrate that Jude's quote of 1 En 1:9 is remarkably accurate. The level of accuracy, and the minor differences noted are explained variously. Two credible explanations, which are possible if unlikely, are: (1) Jude was quoting the Greek version from memory hence the minor discrepancies,[68] or (2) that the close parallel between the Greek text and Jude is merely accidental, assuming in both cases a literal rendering of the Aramaic with Jude's few alterations for his own purposes.[69] Another and more convincing alternative, however, is that "Jude *knew* the Greek version but made his own translation from the Aramaic."[70]

Jude 14–15 in Context

According to the literary structure of Jude 14–15 make-up "text" 3: one of his four scriptural texts, each followed by an interpretation. The literary devices utilized in this context indicate that this quotation was accorded special attention by the author.

---

64. Bauckham, *Jude, 2 Peter*, 94.
65. Knibb, *Ethiopic Book of Enoch*, 2:60.
66. Bauckham, *Jude, 2 Peter*, 96.
67. Bauckham, *Jude, 2 Peter*, 96.
68. Kelly, *A Commentary on the Epistles*, 276.
69. Milik quoted in Bauckham, *Jude, 2 Peter*, 96.
70. Bauckham, *Jude, 2 Peter*, 96.

1 Enoch as Christian Scripture

1) Προεφήτευσεν, the aorist active of προφητεύω, "prophesied," used in this context can possibly be understood in different ways.

   (a) Donald Guthrie suggests that Jude uses this term as a formula to introduce 1 Enoch, but hesitates to conclude that this supports the idea it was considered as Scripture, mainly because Jude is the only one in the NT to quote in such a way.[71]

   (b) George L. Lawlor argues that Jude is not quoting 1 Enoch, but offering a prophecy of his own, given to Jude by inspiration. This is hardly credible as the text unambiguously states that "Enoch, in the seventh generation from Adam, prophesied, saying . . ."[72]

   (c) Blum denies the claim of the prophecy because it "does not give any startling new information but is simply a general description of the return of the Lord in Judgment."[73] While this may, in essence, be true it nonetheless fails to convince because every prophetic message need not necessarily have brand new information.

   (d) Reicke, on the other hand, suggests that Jude genuinely regards the quotation from Enoch as an ancient prophecy referring to the destruction of the same false teachers he is contending with.[74]

   (e) Likewise, Bauckham maintains that "prophesied" indicates that Jude regarded the prophecies of 1 Enoch as inspired by God without regarding the book as canonical Scripture.[75]

   (f) Finally, Duane F. Watson equates the prophecy of Enoch with any other OT prophecy, as used in Jude. He argues that for Jude, this serves as a prophecy by Enoch, prophesied long ago against the false teachers.[76]

---

71. Guthrie, *New Testament Theology*, 978–79. Ladd (*A Theology of the New Testament*, 636) likewise argues that Jude not including γραφη—the most common formula used by the NT—in his formula demonstrates that he did not consider 1 Enoch as Scripture. This argument, however, seems to discount that NT writers are by no means limited to formula's containing γραφη.

72. Lawlor, *The Epistle of Jude*, 102.

73. Blum, "Jude," 393.

74. Reicke, *The Epistles of James*, 210. Reicke further notes that Jude applies the prophecy of Enoch to his opponents in the same way as the Qumranites used Habakkuk to identify the enemies referenced by the prophet with their contemporary seducers of the elect.

75. Bauckham, *Jude, 2 Peter*, 96–97.

76. Watson, *The Letter of Jude*, 478, 474.

1 Enoch in Jude and Other Early Christian Texts

2) ἕβδομος ἀπὸ Ἀδάμ, "in the seventh generation from Adam": is a conventional description of Enoch in 1 Enoch (60:8; 93:3; cf. Jub. 7:39).[77] Traditionally the number seven signifies perfection and is likely applied here to enforce the importance of the prophecy which comes from a perfect Enoch.[78]

3) λέγων, the participial form of λέγω "saying": This is another clear indication for the scriptural status of the quotation. One of the major reasons for the objections raised against the quotation's authoritative status is the absence of a traditional quotation formula indicating the use of Scripture, i.e. γραφη.[79] This argument, however, fails to completely convince in as much as that scriptural quotations and allusions are introduced in the NT in diverse manners. For instance, D. A. Carson lists more than a dozen various formulae only in the Gospel of John.[80]

One example of this in the New Testament can be discovered in Matthew's use of the OT where there are at least twelve citations introduced without including the word γραφη, but in all these cases he uses either λέγω or προφητεύω, or both, which is exactly what Jude does, to introduce his quotation in this instance.[81]

Finally, what I seek to highlight here is that in using both λέγω and προφητεύω, in depicting the special prophetic status of Enoch, in appropriating this text strategically in his midrash, and in inserting a Christological amendment of the quotation, Jude seems to most likely be assuming or asserting the status of 1 Enoch as Scripture.

---

77. That these texts allude to other parts of 1 Enoch, especially 60:8, suggests that Jude knows more than merely the Book of Watchers, which would mean that the Book of Parables was preserved alongside the Book of Watchers in the tradition received by Jude. The allusions discussed below, also strengthen this suggestion.

78. Bauckham (*Jude, 2 Peter*, 96) writes that number seven "indicates Enoch's very special character in the genealogy of the patriarchs, as the man who walked with God and was taken up to heaven (Gen 5:24)—the root of all legends and literature about Enoch in the Second Temple Period Judaism. The description here is probably intended to stress, not so much Enoch's antiquity as his special status which gives authority to his prophecy."

79. So: Moo, *The Epistle to the Romans*, 273; Ladd, *A Theology of the New Testament*, 655.

80. Carson, "John and the Johannine Epistles," 247.

81. Matt 1:22; 2:15, 17; 3:3; 4:14; 8:17; 12:17; 13:14, 35; 15:7; 21:4; 22:43. See also Heb 2:6, 12; 12:26, where only λέγων is used as an introductory formula of the citation.

1 Enoch as Christian Scripture

Other Enochic Themes, Motifs, and Allusions in Jude

Besides the quotation in vv. 14-15 and a citation in v. 6, the extensive amount of material from 1 Enoch in Jude serves to underscore the significance of 1 Enoch for Jude. The following discussion looks at textual allusions and echoes of 1 Enoch at different levels as well as some major themes and motifs from 1 Enoch reflected in Jude.

Allusions, Echoes, and Catchwords of 1 Enoch in Jude

That Jude is influenced by 1 Enoch to a remarkable extent is evident in the allusions, echoes and catchwords as well as direct citations as discovered in 14-15.[82]

1) v. 4, οἱ πάλαι προγεγραμμένοι, "who long ago were designated," is related to God's foreknowledge of the destiny of each person—a concept which also captivated the imagination of the author of 1 Enoch (89:62-71; 19; 108:7) as well as that of other Jewish apocalyptic writers.[83] Bauckham specifically relates this concept of the heavenly books as being reminiscent of Enoch's heavenly tour and his prophecies: "Jude could have taken up this idea of heavenly tablets of destiny from 1 Enoch.... Jude applied to the false teachers the prophecies of Judgment on the wicked which he found in 1 Enoch, where they allegedly derived from Enoch's reading of heavenly tablets."[84]

2) v. 4, ἀσεβής, (ungodly) and its cognates, serve as a catchword, appearing 6 times in this brief letter—more than any other NT book. Four of the occurrences are in 1 Enoch's quotation (vv. 14-15), whereas the other two serve as catchwords, linking the quotation to the appeal (v. 4) and the apostolic prophecies (v. 18). The term is frequently used within the context of judgment for any evil deed, i.e., ἀσέβεια "godlessness," (1 En 10:20). This word undoubtedly sums up Jude's charge against the false teachers. Bauckham rightly explains the comparison being drawn in the use of this word: "The ungodly behavior of the false teachers (ἀσεβεῖς) is (1) in relation to God the Father a perversion of

---

82. Baukham argues strongly for such a remarkable influence by 1 Enoch (Bauckham, *Jude, 2 Peter*, 10).

83. Kelly, *A Commentary on the Epistles*, 250.

84. Bauckham, *Jude, 2 Peter*, 36-37.

his grace, and (2) in relation to Christ, a denial of his lordship."[85] He goes on to argue, the idea of denial of God by conduct is attested also in 1 Enoch (38:2; 41:2; 45:2; 46:7; 48:10; 67:8, 10).[86]

3) v. 4, "[They] deny our only Master and Lord, Jesus Christ," reflects its parallel in 1 Enoch (48:10), "They denied the Lord of spirits and his Messiah." The parallel is both in wording and sense if we consider that Jude is charging the false teachers of denying both God the father and Christ.[87]

4) v. 7, Jude's use of οὗτοι, which introduces each section of interpretation in his commentary, has often been compared to the standard formula ("This is . . ." "Those are . . .") used in the interpretation of apocalyptic dreams and visions as in 1 En 46:3.[88]

5) v. 8, ἐνυπνιαζόμενοι, the present passive participle of ἐνυπνιάζομαι, "on the strength of their dreams" may refer to 1 En 99:8, where the sinners of the last days "will sink into impiety because of the folly of their hearts, and their eyes will be blinded through the fear of their hearts, and through the visions of their dreams." Not only this verse, but "concern with false teachers is a feature of the Epistle of Enoch"[89] as it is with Jude.

6) v. 8, σάρκα μὲν μιαίνουσιν, "they defile the flesh": 1 Enoch repeatedly refers to the sin of the fallen watchers as "defiling themselves" with women μιαίνεσθαι "to defile themselves": 1 En 7:1; 9:8; 10:11; 12:4; 15:3, 4. Jude, therefore, seems to be identifying the sin of the false teachers as corresponding to that of the second and third types in vv. 6 and 7.

7) v. 9, besides Michael, archangel (ἀρχάγγελος) is a common expression for either 4 (1 En 40) or 7 (1 En 20:7) leading classes of angels in

---

85. Bauckham, *Jude, 2 Peter*, 40.

86. Bauckham, *Jude, 2 Peter*, 40.

87. Kelly, (*A Commentary on the Epistles*, 252) argues for understanding the denial towards both God and Christ (see the discussion above, #2) based on Jude's acquaintance with 1 Enoch from which he cites this expression.

88. Bauckham, *Jude, 2 Peter*, 45. Cf. Dan 5:25–26; Zech 1:10, 19–20; 4:10, 14; Rev 7:14; 11:4; 14:4.

89. Nickelsburg, *1 Enoch 1: A Commentary*, 86.

1 Enoch. Michael is included in either case, and often taking the leading role (cf. Asc. Isa. 3:16: "Michael the chief of the holy angels").[90]

8) v. 11 is a woe-oracle. In later Judaism, this genre "developed an increasingly imprecatory character, becoming a prophetic pronouncement of Judgment on sinners. This is the function of the large number of woes (32, more than in any other ancient Jewish work) in 1 Enoch 92–105."[91]

9) In vv. 12–13, Jude employs a series of four images from nature,[92] which likely parallels either 1 En 2:1—5:4 and/or 80:2-8. While in the former text, the four images are positively mentioned in the same sequence as in Jude,[93] in the latter text, only three of the images are referenced for the disobedient as in Jude.[94] Osburn contends that Jude here has in mind only 1 En 80:2-8 and 67:5-7 and not 2:1—5:4 for two reasons: (1) the context of 80:2-8 is in a section that treats the impending punishment of the ungodly; and (2) the order of Jude precisely parallels that of Enoch.[95] However it seems likely that both passages in 1 Enoch have inspired Jude's series of metaphors since both passages are formulated against lawlessness, which Jude also condemns. Jude, therefore, "represents the lawlessness of nature, prophesied for the last days, by selecting an example from each of the four regions of the world, and sees them as figures of lawless teachers who are also prophesied for the last day."[96]

---

90. Even if Jude's citation in v. 9 is potentially from *Testament of Moses*, it is more likely he is familiar with Michael from his close acquaintance with 1 Enoch.

91. Bauckham, *Jude, 2 Peter*, 77–78.

92. Reicke notes that the images are from each of the four regions of the physical world: cloud in the air, trees on the earth, waves in the sea, and star in the heavens (Reicke, *The Epistles of James*, 207).

93. However, the point emphasised in Enoch is that of violating the created order through sin, symbolically, thus, denotes a more proper functioning of creation according to God's order.

94. John P. Oleson argues that the missing fourth symbol in Jude comes from a pagan account of the birth of Aphrodite in Hesido's Theogony (Oleson, "An Echo of Hesido's Theogony," 492–503). But this is rejected by Osburn because "the presence of such a disgusting Hellenistic legend in the midst of a section dominated by quotations of and allusions to Second Temple Jewish apocalyptic literature (vv. 5–16) is decidedly strange" (Osburn, "1 Enoch 80:2-8," 299).

95. Osburn, "1 Enoch 80:2-8," 297.

96. Bauckham, *Jude, 2 Peter*, 91.

1 Enoch in Jude and Other Early Christian Texts

Enochic Themes and Motifs in Jude[97]

1) ***Theophany and Judgment:*** As examined in the quotation above (vv. 14–15), the motif of theophany in a judgment context is common to both 1 Enoch and Jude. In both texts, the Lord appears to execute judgment, ποιῆσαι κρίσιν κατὰ πάντων. By changing the subject of 1 En 1:9—who is God—into κύριος, who is Jesus, Jude reshapes the tradition to fit "the new historical situation in view of his eschatological purposes and Christological understandings."[98]

2) ***Ungodly and Judgment:*** Essentially, the deep crisis depicted in 1 Enoch is the perversion of the right order—the pious are convicted that this epoch was one of apostasy, and as a result eschatological judgment is inevitable.[99] In a similar fashion, Jude passionately exhorts his audience to struggle against the false teachers, who pervert the right teaching. As in Enoch, judgment is inevitable for these ungodly ones. In both texts, the Lord comes to deal judgment on the ungodly.

3) ***Eschatological Judgment:*** In Jude, just as in 1 Enoch, judgment is certain, yet, it will come in the future. The examples of judgment form the past used by Jude serve to point forward to the eschatological judgment that must inevitably follow. Nickelsburg notes that "the great judgment that looms in almost every major section of 1 Enoch and many of its subsections is the final judgment, which will occur at the end of the old age and before the beginning of the new."[100] Likewise, Jude's use of "great day" to describe the day of judgment illustrates his view of eschatological judgment.

4) ***The Figure of Enoch:*** Enoch is the ideal figure in 1 Enoch[101] and this concept is appropriated and adapted by Jude. Jude explicitly appeals to the prophetic authority of Enoch. In the whole of the NT only Jude refers to Enoch as the seventh generation from Adam who prophesied from of old to the present. Thus, both works—1 Enoch and Jude—are united in their characterization of the figure of Enoch.[102]

---

97. Jude's Angelology, which mainly comes from Jude's acquaintance with 1 Enoch, is consciously excluded here as it will be dealt with separately below.
98. Osburn, "The Christological Use of 1 Enoch," 340.
99. Charles, "Jude's Use of Pseudepigraphical," 140.
100. Nickelsburg, *1 Enoch 1: A Commentary*, 55.
101. The figure of Enoch in 1 Enoch will be discussed elsewhere.
102. The expression "the seventh from Adam" occurs twice in 1 Enoch (60:8, 93:3).

In summary, themes from 1 Enoch are evident in Jude in many ways. Notable amongst these are the theophany-statement, the common focus on apostasy, their eschatological orientation as well as the citations permeating Jude. In addition to these technical devices which demonstrate the strong influence of Jewish traditions on Jude's strong usage, the frequent mention of angels and the traditions which are reflected in Jude's angelology are all developed in manner which is indicative of Jude's strategic usage of Jewish material. With this in mind I will now turn to look at angels as a motif in Jude.

Angels in Jude: Specific Elements Connected to 1 Enoch

This section is intended to show that besides the overall dependence of Jude on 1 Enoch, the close parallel between Jude's angelology and that of Enoch reveals not only his dependence, but also the special status of the Enochic collection in Jude. Even though angelic beings are referred to elsewhere in the NT, Jude's angelology is exceptionally well developed and closely reflects the angelology discovered in STL. Jude's apparent interest in angels has led some to conclude that Jude is nearly obsessed with angels.[103] This is evident from Jude's (1) ontological and functional usage of angels, (2) categorizing of fallen and unfallen angels, (3) usage of developed imagery for angels like δόξα (v. 8), ἀστήρ (v. 13), and ἅγιος (v. 14), besides ἄγγελος (v. 6), and (4) a dualistic usage of Ὁ . . . Μιχαὴλ ὁ ἀρχάγγελος versus ὁ διάβολος (v. 9), all in line with a developed angelology of the Second Temple period, especially that of 1 Enoch. The five references identified above (vv. 6, 8, 9, 13, 14,) and the context surrounding them which will be discussed in detail, all come together to indicate the extent to which angelology is an important focus in Jude.

The exegesis of the five texts related to angels below will be presented under three categories. (1) The fallen angels—explicitly mentioned in v. 6 and implicitly referenced in v. 13—will mainly be discussed from an ontological point of view and their function in that particular context. In other words, the original position and the final fate of (fallen) angels are treated as understood in Jude. (2) The "ten thousands of his holy ones" (v. 14) and "the glorious ones" (v. 8)—representing the 'unfallen' angels—are also discussed in regard to ontology and function. (3) The text related to Michael

---

103. Benton, *Slandering the Angels*, 13.

and the devil (v. 9) discloses the dualistic angelology of *Jude* and Michael's special status in his angelology.

Fallen Angels

There are two texts in Jude referring to the fallen angels, both in usage and terminology: one explicit (v. 6) and the other implicit (v. 13). These references have both points of similarity and difference. In terms of similarity we can note the common dependence on 1 Enoch and the depiction of the fate of the fallen angels in relation to the "deepest darkness," to varying extents: (1) until the judgment day (v. 6) and (2) forever (v. 13). On the other, we can note that the parallels to 1 Enoch are more obvious in v.6 which also offers detailed descriptions about the fallen angels, absent in the latter verse. Moreover, while in v. 6, the most common designation for angels is ἄγγελος, v. 8 has a less frequent term for angels, δόξαι.

THE EXAMPLE OF THE FALLEN ANGELS (JUDE 6)

Context

Jude 6, as seen in the structure, is part of "text" 1 (vv. 5–6)—a midrash on four prophecies on the judgment of the false teachers (vv. 5–19). It is one of the "three Old Testament types"[104] sandwiched between the two other scriptural references—seemingly equally authoritative—which all refer to the false teachers and affirm the certitude of the judgment. The fallen angels, in the same manner as the other two groups of people—unbelieving Israel and Sodomites—serve as types of sin and judgment. For Jude, these groups, all function as scriptural types.

Jude 6 and 1 Enoch

Besides the direct quotation from 1 Enoch in verses 14–15,[105] Jude's extensive use of 1 Enoch in v. 6 signifies the significance of this text, not only for the author, but also most likely his anticipated readers. The story of the fallen angels is at the centre of the first three historical types, preceded

---

104. Bauckham ("Jude, Epistle of," 1098), in his analysis, refers v. 6 as the second OT type equally with the other two as summaries of the Scriptures.

105. For the discussion on the quotation, see below.

and succeeded by two other types from OT texts. The story reveals that the angels who had enjoyed heavenly prestige are not less but more in danger of judgment since they failed to keep that status. Including the other two types, they are "typological prophecies of the eschatological judgment at the Parousia which threatens apostate Christians in these last days."[106]

The parallels between texts from 1 Enoch and Jude 6 demonstrate not only Jude's acquaintance with 1 Enoch, but also his primary dependence upon it.[107] Here are some of the parallels:

Jude 6[108]	1 Enoch 12:4; 10:6; 10:4 (Geʻez)[109]	1 Enoch 12:4; 10:6; 10:4 (Greek)[110]
ἀγγέλους τε τοὺς μὴ τηρήσαντας τὴν ἑαυτῶν ἀρχὴν ἀλλὰ ἀπολιπόντας τὸ ἴδιον οἰκητήριον εἰς κρίσιν μεγάλης ἡμέρας δεσμοῖς ἀϊδίοις ὑπὸ ζόφον τετήρηκεν	. . . ለትጉሃን ሰማይ እለ ኀደጉ ሰማየ ልዑለ ወምቅዋመ ቅዱሰ ዘለዓለም . . . (12:4)	. . . τοις εγρηγοροις του ουρανου οιτινες απολιποντες του ουρανον τον υψηλον, το αγιασμα της στασεως του αιωνος . . . (12:4)
	ወበዕለት ዐባይ እንተ ኩነኔ ከመ ይትሀየው ውስተ ፍዕ (10:6)	και εν τη ημερα της μεγαλης της κρισεως (10:6)
	. . . እስር ለአዛዝኤል በእዴሁ ወበገቡ ወደይ ውስተ ጽልመት (10:4)	Δησον τον Αζαηλ ποσιν και χερσιν, και βαλε αυτον εις το σκοτος, (10:4)

The parallels shown above (translations in footnotes) demonstrate that Jude develops the leitmotif of angels by utilizing references from 1 En 6–19, which is "the earliest [account] of the fall of the Watchers."[111] The

106. Bauckham, *Jude, 2 Peter*, 63.

107. Kistemaker, *Exposition of the Epistles*, 379; Kelly, *A Commentary on the Epistles*, 257; Watson, *The Letter of Jude*, 488.

108. The English translation of v. 6 reads: "And the angels who did not keep their own position, but left their proper dwelling, he has kept in eternal chains in deepest darkness for the judgment of the great Day."

109. Translation: . . . Say to the Watchers of heaven who have left the high heaven, the eternal holy place . . . (12.4) And on the day of great judgment he shall be cast into fire . . . (10.6) . . . bind Azazel hand and foot and cast him into the darkness . . . (10.4).

110. Knibb's (*The Ethiopic Book of Enoch*) translation of these texts is: ". . . the watchers of heaven who have left the high heaven and the holy eternal place"; (12:4) "and that on the great day of judgment he may be hurled into the fire"; (10:6) "Bind Azazel by his hands and feet, and throw him into the darkness" (10:4).

111. Bauckham, *Jude, 2 Peter*, 51.

conflation of several texts from these chapters goes on to elucidate further Jude's close familiarity with the book.[112] As will be discussed in the next chapter, 1 Enoch stresses that the judgment for the watchers was inevitable. Likewise, Jude, using the watchers as a type of the false teachers, presupposes the certainty of judgment.

Exegetical Notes on Jude 6

1) ἡ ἑαυτῆς ἀρχή: The use of ἀρχή here is disputed. Some suggest that it conveys a meaning of "priesthood"—an estate given by God.[113] Other suggestions include "beginning"[114] "dominion"[115] or "position of authority."[116] One thing that all these potential translations have in common is that the terms denote a higher place for angels from an ontological point of view. The angels' position is one of "heavenly power or sphere of dominion, which the angels exercised over the world in the service of God."[117] Furthermore, the term is employed mainly as it has been understood in the Second Temple Period literature in relation to angels.[118] It can further be noted that the use of the definite article in the phrase ἡ ἑαυτῆς ἀρχή and its parallel τὸ ἴδιον οἰκητήριον signifies the place given by God to the angelic beings, which is superior to human beings.[119] Thus, ἀρχή here points to the exalted position and authority the angels occupied.[120] The two nouns, in synonymous

---

112. With several varying forms, the tradition of the fallen angels is well known in other Second Temple Period literature, yet none of them has as close a parallel as 1 Enoch to Jude. Cf. *Jub* 4:15, 22; 5:1; CD 2:17—19:1QApGen 2:1; *T. Reu.* 5:6–7; *T. Naph* 3:5; *2 Bar* 56:10–14. Other related texts in 1 Enoch are 21; 86–88; 106:13–15, 17.

113. Green, *The Second Epistle General*, 165.

114. Manton, *Jude*, 112. Manton favour's "beginning," as the more literal interpretation, is based on his suggestion that they left their "first position," which is related to the fall of the angels.

115. Kelly, *A Commentary on the Epistles*, 265. Kelly opts for this translation based on other similar NT titles such as "principalities" and "powers" in Rom 8:38; Col 2:15, or even "world-rulers" as in Eph 4:12.

116. Kistemaker, *Exposition of the Epistles*, 377.

117. Bauckham, *Jude, 2 Peter*, 52.

118. Cf. *Jub* 2:2; 5:6; 1 En 82:10–20; 1QM 10:12; 1QH 1:11. Note especially that ἀρχή is employed to denote a rank of angels in *T. Levi* 3:8; *2 En* 20:1 and as cosmic powers in Rom 8:38; Eph 1:21; 3:10; 6:12; Col 1:16; 2:15.

119. Kistemaker, *Exposition of the Epistles*, 380.

120. The exaltation is further strengthened by the expression ἀπολιπόντας, a verb

parallel, stress the two aspects of the position of angels: "stipulated responsibilities ([ἀρχή], 'dominion') and a set place [οἰκητήριον].[121]

2) εἰς κρίσιν μεγάλης ἡμέρας: The angels were kept "for the judgment of the great day," which is parallel to 1 En 10:12 where Michael is bidden to bind the fallen angels "for seventy generations in the valley of the earth, until the great day of their judgment." The adjective "great" is uncommon with "judgment" in biblical texts, where, "the great day of the Lord" is more usual (Joel 2:11, 31; (=Act 2:20) Zeph 1:14; Mal 4:5; Rev 16:18). Jude's use of the phrase is consistent with 1 Enoch, though both expressions are common in 1 Enoch (cf. 1 En 22:11; 54:6; 84:4). Here also Jude's dependence on 1 Enoch is evident.[122]

3) δεσμός: the language of chains is one of the remarkable expressions in 1 Enochic tradition of the fall of angels.[123] The extent of the punishment is intensified with an expression ὑπὸ ζόφον[124] where, besides the chains, the very darkness of the place enhances the misery.

4) ἀϊδίοις: The chains are called "eternal"—αἰώνιος—(v. 7), but they are also expected to last until the day of judgment. This is a difficult expression since both permanence and a time limit are being simultaneously expressed. The apparent discrepancy comes from Jude's wording of Enoch's different texts together. Jude's basic text here is 1 En 10:5, where Azazel is bound forever (εἰς τοὺς αἰῶνας) until the judgment. Bauckham notes that "forever" here must mean "for the duration of the world until the Day of judgment," which stresses unrelenting nature of the imprisonment—excluding any possibility of escape, until that day.[125] The everlasting chains could also indicate the hopeless

---

taken from the paralleling texts in 1 En 12:4; 15:3, which recounts that the angels left the high, holy and eternal heaven. Note also 1 En 15:7. "The spirits of heaven, in heaven is their dwelling."

121. Blum, "Jude," 390.

122. Kelly, *A Commentary on the Epistles*, 257; Green, *The Second Epistle General*, 165. Green further explains that Jude's dependence on 1 Enoch here is in both the subject matter and form of expression. He refers to frequent expression of "until the judgement of the great day" in 1 En 10:6; 14:1; 22:4, 10, 11; 97:5; 103:8.

123. 1 En 13:1; 14:5; 54:3–5; 56:1–4; 88:1; cf. Jub 5:6; 2 Bar 56:13.

124. For a discussion on ζόφον, see below on the discussion of v. 13.

125. Bauckham, *Jude, 2 Peter*, 53. Similar use of the expression can be attested in 10:12, where the fallen angels are bound to a complete period of time—seventy generations—but, here also, until the eternal judgement. See also 14:5: "imprisoned all the days of eternity"; Jub 5:10 (evidently dependent on 1 En 10): "they were bound in the depths

situation of the fallen angels. The chains are everlasting "because the wicked angels stand guilty forever, without hope of recovery or redemption."[126]

The Purpose of Jude 6 in Its Context

ἀστέρες πλανῆτα (v. 13) as Fallen Angels: In his literary plan, Jude portrays the false teachers in two categories of historical types: (1) vv. 5–10 (text + interpretation) groups—serving as types signify the false teachers as sinners to be judged, and (2) vv. 11–13 (text + interpretation) individual sinners—types signify the false teachers who are characterized as ones who lead other people to sin. V. 11 is the "text" for the second category, individual types, including Cain, Balaam and Korah, where vv. 12–13 are its interpretation. The ἀστέρες πλανῆτα in v. 13 is connected to the second type, τῇ πλάνῃ τοῦ Βαλαάμ, with a catchword πλάνη, which literally means "wandering" from the right path.[127]

ἀστέρες πλανῆτα, which literally means "wandering stars," is an image taken from 1 Enoch. It is maintained that the noun πλανήτης occurs only in Jude 13 in the sense of a wandering star or planet, indicating their irregular movement as violating "the order of the heavens and which was attributed to the disobedience of the angels controlling them."[128] The apparent allusion here seems to be to the passages in 1 Enoch[129] where the watchers are represented as seven stars "which transgressed the command of the Lord from the beginning of their rising because they did not come out at their proper times" (18:15), and further, the fall of the watchers is represented as the fall of the stars from heaven (86:1–3).[130] If Jude uses the concept of wandering stars in this sense, then he is once again, as in v.6, comparing

---

of the earth forever, until the day of great condemnation."

126. Manton, *Jude*, 18.

127. For the discussion on the meaning of the word, see Günther, "Πλνάω, Lead Astray. Deceive," 457.

128. Gunter, "Πλνάω, Lead Astray. Deceive," 459. Cf. 1 En 82 for the image that the heavenly bodies are controlled by angels.

129. 1 En 18:13–16; 21:3–6; 83–90. For the relations with passages see below.

130. Bauckham, *Jude, 2 Peter*, 89; Kelly, *A Commentary on the Epistles*, 274; Green, *The Second Epistle General*, 176; Perkins, *First and Second Peter*, 153; Sidebottom, *James, Jude and 2 Peter*, 90; Moffatt, *The General Epistles*, 239; Moo, *The Epistle to the Romans*, 261.

1 Enoch as Christian Scripture

the fallen angels with false teachers, and indicating that the judgment is inevitable. Green, further notes a contrast and peculiarly fitting allusion to Enoch: "for whereas the wicked angels lost their heavenly home by disobeying God, and fell to destruction, Enoch gained heaven by obeying God."[131]

Some more reasons to support the assertion that Jude borrowed this image from 1 Enoch are (1) in Jewish apocalyptic thought heavenly bodies are controlled by angels (1 En 82); (2) in 1 En 18:13–16; 21:3–6, the fallen angels are represented as seven stars "which transgressed the command of the Lord from the beginning of their rising because they did not come out at their proper times" (18:15);[132] (3) the imagery is taken up in the later Dreams (1 En 83–90), which represents the fall of the watchers as the fall of stars from heaven, in its allegory of world history (86:1–3); (4) in 88:1 and 3, the archangels cast the stars down into the darkness of the abyss and bind them there; (5) until the judgment of the End, when they will cast them into the abyss of fire (90:24).[133] In addition to the clear correspondence with Enochic imagery we can also note parallels in vocabulary.

ὁ ζόφος τοῦ σκότους: as Kelly maintains, the vocabulary use here is directly related to v. 6 above in both the wording and the idea.[134] To be sure, the darkness in 1 Enoch (88:1; cf. 10:4–5) and Jude 6 describes the temporary fate of the fallen angels, until the last judgment, whereas here, the darkness is the eternal destiny of the wandering stars. Moreover, in 1 Enoch the place of final damnation is usually represented by fire.[135] Bauckham argues that Jude prefers the image of darkness here because it is a more appropriate fate for stars.[136]

Just like the fallen angels in v. 6, here also the wandering stars of v. 13—who are the fallen angels—are kept (τηρέω the same verb as in v. 6) in the deepest darkness forever. Jude concludes this paragraph with the same note that he makes at the end of every section and sub-section—judgment.[137]

---

131. Green, *The Second Epistle General*, 177.
132. Kelly, *A Commentary on the Epistles*, 274; cf. 21:16.
133. Bauckham, *Jude, 2 Peter*, 89.
134. Kelly, *A Commentary on the Epistles*, 274.
135. In Jewish thought, the idea of imprisonment in eternal darkness is also known: Tob 14:10; 1 En 46:6; 63:6; *Pss. Sol.* 14:9; 15:10; cf. Matt 8:12; 22:13; 25:30. Sometimes the two images were combined: 1 En 103:8; 108:14; *Sib. Or.* 4:48; 1QS 2:8; 4:13; 2 En 10:2.
136. Bauckham, *Jude, 2 Peter*, 90.
137. Moo, *The Epistle to the Romans*, 261.

1 Enoch in Jude and Other Early Christian Texts

Unfallen Angels

As seen above, Jude's reference to fallen angels is primarily related to one of his major themes: judgment. In addition to these, Jude references another group of angels—"unfallen" angels. The archangel Michael and the holy and glorious angels referenced twice (vv. 8, 14) are prime examples of this group.[138] These references come together to illustrate Jude's angelology, which he shared with his source texts—1 Enoch and other apocalyptic literature from the Second Temple period.

However, this does not limit his inclusion of another group of angels. Moreover, his usage of various terms in all the occurrences indicates his developed angelology in line with his background references—1 Enoch and other apocalyptic literature. Besides the archangel Michael, Jude refers twice to holy and glorious angels (vv. 8, 14). Both texts signify Jude's ontological usage of the terms, although a functional nuance is not entirely absent from the latter text. My discussion below will be limited to the two terms δόξαι and ἅγιαι, in the two texts.

---

138. Designations given to angelic or heavenly beings in Scriptures seem to serve in at least two distinct ways: ontological and functional. That is, the terms designated to refer to angels, as employed in the Scriptures, denote either their being or function. T. H. Gaster, for instance, clearly maintains that the word "angel" is used with a twofold senses: a) a messenger from God, functional usage, and b) a spiritual being, an ontological usage (Gaster, "Angel," 128–29). This is nicely distinguished, according to him, in the earliest portions of the Bible: "while every divine messenger is regarded as a spiritual being, not every spiritual being is a divine messenger." In a broader sense, ontologically, angels are believed to be "heavenly beings, members of Yahweh's court, who serve and praise him." Bietenhard, however, argues that the most frequent usage of the term "angel," as it is used in the OT, is functional rather than ontological. As a matter of fact, many scholars would define and explain the usage of angels in the OT from the functional point of view (Bietenhard, "Αγγελος," 101). Many scholars would define and explain the usage of angels in the OT from the functional point of view (H Bietenhard, "Αγγελος"). A number of other scholars, agree with Bietenhard, understand the usage of angels in the OT from a functional point of view. The functional designation, according to these scholars, is connected to their duty which is "to execute God's universal will in heaven and on earth. They promote divine goodness, and they are mediators of God's love and good will to man" (Founderbruk, "Angel," 163). For a detailed discussion on the five categories of functions of angels, see Founderbruk, "Angel," 163–64; Gaster, "Angel," 129; von Rad, "Typological Interpretation," 77.

1 Enoch as Christian Scripture

δόξα, ης, ἡ (δόξαι as Angelic Beings)

Terminology

The basic dictionary meaning of δόξα is "glory," "honor," "radiance," or "reputation," where the concept of glory or honor are most common.[139] In the OT, this glory is basically found only in God, though in some texts angelic beings manifest it to some degree (Ezek 8:2; 1:7; 13; Dan 10:5–6). However, in the Second Temple period the concept of glory is further applied to entities in the heavenly realm: God, his throne, and the angels.[140] Among other more frequent usages, the term δόξα is used to refer to angelic powers, in continuation of Ezekiel's vision of the glory of heavenly beings, where the radiance of the angels is stressed.[141] Thus, the attribution of Jude's δόξαι as angels is well attested.[142]

δόξαι in Its Present Context

Tracing back to attestations in the Dead Sea Scrolls and in apocalyptic and Gnostic literature, the term δόξαι in Jude 8 is understood to mean angels.[143] In addition to these earlier attestations, interpretations of Jude in the early Church Fathers also understand Jude's δόξαι to be angels. Bauckham argues, this is a correct designation as angels, "they participate in or embody the glory of God."[144] Other commentators also argue along the same line. For instance, Kelly makes use of OT texts (LXX Exod 25:11; Exod 24:16–17; 33:18–23; Ps 19:1, and also other texts from Second Temple Period literature cited above) to support this idea.[145] He further notes that the author of Jude, as a Jewish Christian, who shared: "the intense interest in angels

---

139. Hegermann, "Δόξα, Ης, 'Η," 344.

140. Aalen, "Δόξα," 45. In the Dead Sea Scrolls, it is used for angels (1QH 10:8), also in other early literature (2 En 22:7, 10; Asc. Isa. 9:32) (Hillyer, *1 and 2 Peter, Jude*, 250).

141. Aalen, ("Δόξα," 46) discusses five other usages of the term in the NT.

142. See also Hegermann, "Δόξα, Ης, 'Η," 345, for a similar connotation of the concept which goes back to the selection of δόξα as the correct word to translate *kābôd* in the LXX.

143. Bauckham, *Jude, 2 Peter*, 57.

144. Bauckham, *Jude, 2 Peter*, 57. Cf. T. Jud. 25:2; T. Levi 18:5; Heb 9:5.

145. Kelly, *A Commentary on the Epistles*, 263.

which characterized later Judaism, the writer has a properly deferential attitude towards the glorious ones."[146]

If δόξαι refers to angels, then why do the false teachers slander them? This could potentially be explained in relation to the Second Temple Period background wherein—angels' function as givers, guardians, and watchers over the Law of Moses and to uphold the created order.[147] So the opponents of Jude, being antinomians,[148] desiring complete freedom, "slander"[149] angels and refuse to accept their authority connected to the Law. As Bauckham notes, "their 'slandering' of angels was a way of detaching the Law from God and interpreting it simply as an evil."[150]

ἐν ἁγίαις μυριάσιν αὐτοῦ (v. 14)[151]

As has already been noted, the context of 1 Enoch and the parallel text, Deut 33:2-4, where ἅγια μυριάς is employed, is that of theophany. This fits in with the primary themes in Jude as these passages describing God's giving of the Law at Sinai and his theophany with the presence of "myriads of angels," reference "the very beings that Jude's opponents 'slander' (v. 8) by their antinomian mindset."[152] It is also argued that not only Jude, but also other NT writers, in their eschatological doctrine, are influenced by the language of an attendant angelic company in their depiction of Christ's

---

146. Note also an alternative translation, "the angels" or "the heavenly beings" or "the glorious angels in heaven" given by Robert G. Bratcher (*A Translator's Guide*, 176–77). See also Dick Lucas and Christopher Green (*The Message of 2 Peter*, 189), where they argue for "celestial beings" as angels. However, some interpretations, such as "God's authority" (Wiersbe, *Be Alert: 2 Peter 2*, 164); "godly leaders" or "elders" (Cedar, *James, 1, 2 Peter, Jude*, 252–53) lack ground for their suggestion. Others, like Blum ("Jude," 391), who suggests "all spiritual forces—good or evil," and Reicke (*The Epistles of James*, 201) who interprets as "those in positions of power whether angels or men"; in their interpretation, demonstrate the ambiguity of the term, if not in this context.

147. For angels as mediators of the Law of Moses, a common Jewish belief, see *Jub* 1:27–29. Cf. Act 7:38; 53; Heb 2:2; Gal 3:19.

148. For identification of the opponents as antinomians see: Bauckham, "Jude, Epistle of," 1100; Watson, *The Letter of Jude*, 475; Barclay, *The Letters of John and Jude*, 186–87.

149. Note the catchword contrast (βλασφημέω) between the false teachers in v. 8 and 10 and the devil in v. 9 (βλασφημία).

150. Bauckham, *Jude, 2 Peter*, 59.

151. I will only deal with this phrase as it develops in Jude's angelology, the quotation from Enoch will be dealt with elsewhere.

152. Lucas and Green, *The Message of 2 Peter*, 207.

second coming. Thus the "holy ones" are identified with the holy angels, the heavenly army of the Divine warrior, as in Zechariah 14:5, which is likely the main background to the early Christian expectation that the Lord at his Parousia would be accompanied by a retinue of angels.[153] Jude's use of the "holy ones" to refer to angels, as it is used in 1 Enoch, therefore, signifies both Jude's highly developed angelology and his strong dependence on and high regard for 1 Enoch.

Michael versus the Devil (v. 9)

In addition to Jude's implicit classification of his angelology in two clear categories—fallen and unfallen, as categorized in 1 Enoch—the appearance of the archangel Michael and his opponent, the devil, offers a complete insight into the highly developed angelology permeating this text. While it is possible to raise several questions in relation to Jude 9, I will limit my discussion here to its source, its purpose within the literary context and the role of the archangel as portrayed.[154]

The Background and Source of Jude 9

The story of Jude's quotation in v. 9 goes back to Moses's death in Deut 34:5-6: "Then Moses, the servant of the Lord, died there in the land of Moab, at the Lord's command. He was buried in a valley in the land of Moab, opposite Beth-peor, but no one knows his burial place to this day." A number of legends, inspired by this account, grew up around the death and burial of Moses, one of which is the story in the *Testament of Moses*.[155] Unfortunately the part of this text which is quoted by Jude is not discovered in extant versions, which means that it needs to be reconstructed from fragments in the number of other works which refer to it. One such

---

153. Bauckham, *Jude, 2 Peter*, 97. C.f. Matt 16:27; 25:31; Mark 8:38; Luke 9:26; 2 Thess 1:7.

154. For a detailed discussion of the verse, the status of the source material in Jude, and the history of its interpretations, see: Tromp, *The Assumption of Moses*, 270-85; Bauckham, "Jude, Epistle of," 235-80; Bauckham, *Jude, 2 Peter*, 65-76; Priest, "Moses, Testament of," 920-22; Andersen, "Moses, Assumption of," 295-96.

155. Bauckham, *Jude, 2 Peter*; Lucas and Green, *The Message of 2 Peter*, 192-93. The debate as to whether this text is best identified as the Testament or the Assumption of Moses, and whether these texts are one and the same is dealt with by Bauckham, "Jude, Epistle of," 236-37.

reconstruction of the original story, as told in the *Testament of Moses*, proffered by Bauckham is as follows:

> Joshua accompanied Moses up Mount Nebo, where God showed Moses the land of promise. Moses then sent Joshua back, saying, "go down to the people and tell them that Moses is dead." When Joshua had gone down to the people, Moses died. God sent the archangel Michael to remove the body of Moses to another place and to bury it there, but Samma'el, the devil, opposed him, disputing Moses' right to honourable burial. Michael and the devil engaged in a dispute over the body. The devil slandered Moses, charging him with murder, because he slew the Egyptian and hid his body in the sand. But Michael, not tolerating the slander against Moses, said, "May the Lord rebuke you, Satan!" At that the devil took flight, and Michael removed the body to the place commanded by God. Thus no one saw the burial-place of Moses.[156]

The earliest example of this kind of contest between the devil and an angel is found in Zech 3:1–5, from which Michael's words to the devil, "May the Lord rebuke you!" in Jude's source are derived. Similar disputations are recorded in some Second Temple Period literature (see Jub. 17:15—18:16; 48, CD 5:17–18), a tradition to which Jude 9 alludes.[157] Jude is thus here drawing upon a common source shared with other literature from the period.[158]

Thus, that Jude here draws upon from the *Testament of Moses* is well supported and evident.[159]

Jude 9 in Context

The purpose behind Jude's use of this quotation here is not an easy question. However, as already indicated in the analysis of Jude, we can note that it is of only secondary importance, in that it is used to support the interpretation of "text" 1.[160]

---

156. Bauckham, "Jude, Epistle of," 238f.; Bauckham here makes some modifications from his previous work (Bauckham, *Jude, 2 Peter*, 72–73).

157. For further discussion see Bauckham, "Jude, Epistle of," 245–49.

158. Hillyer, *1 and 2 Peter, Jude*, 248–49; Sidebottom, *James, Jude and 2 Peter*, 88; Green, *The Second Epistle General*, 169.

159. For a similar argument see Hillyer, *1 and 2 Peter, Jude*, 248–49; Sidebottom, *James, Jude and 2 Peter*, 88; Green, *The Second Epistle General*, 169.

160. Bauckham explains that "the use of such a secondary text in the course of the

1 Enoch as Christian Scripture

In Jude's use, v. 9 is connected to vv. 8, 10 by the catchword βλασφημέω (8, 10) / βλασφημία (9) ("they slander"/"slander"). Jude's midrashic interpretation involves a type from the Scriptures which is applied on the antitype of his day. The story in v. 9 is introduced during the course of the interpretation of the types of vv. 5–7. In the scheme, v. 8 and v. 10 describe the slandering of the false teachers, the antitypes for the types in vv. 5–7, whereas the slander on v. 9 serves as mere support for the argument in v. 8. This is further evident in v. 10 in that it does not simply interpret v. 9, but rather takes up the interpretation begun in v. 8. Thus, with the catchword connection v. 9 relates to the final clause of v. 8. Moreover, v. 10 takes up the application of the types in its first clause, οὗτοι, as in v. 8, and ends the exposition by making it clear that judgment is inevitable.[161]

The agent of slander in v. 9 divides scholars. Some interpret "Michael did not bring a slanderous accusation against the devil," which is further applied to mean, "If the greatest of the good angels refused to speak evil of the greatest of the angels, surely no human being may speak evil of any angel."[162] Even if this interpretation sounds obvious, it is nonetheless odd in the context because the use of the catch word "slander" would draw a false contrast between Michael and the false teachers. Therefore, it seems more convincing that Michael did not dare to condemn the devil for slander, is more appropriate because the point here is that Michael invokes God's authority as the only one who could judge the slanderous devil.[163] This argument has further support from Jude's original source—as reconstructed above—where it is clear that "the devil slandered Moses." The point here is (1) the false teachers slander (as in v. 8) even the good angelic guardians of the Mosaic Law much like the devil slandering Moses and (2) Michael appeals to the Lord's judgment which Jude also applies to the false teachers.

---

interpretation of another text can be parallel in the Qumran Commentaries, as can the incorporation of implicit allusions to other texts in the course of the interpretation of a given text, a practice which Jude adopts in vv. 12–14, where there are allusions to Ezek 34:2; Prov 25:14; Isa 57:20; 1 En 80:6" (Bauckham, "Jude, Epistle of," 1099).

161. Bauckham, *Jude, 2 Peter*, 44.

162. Hillyer, *1 and 2 Peter, Jude*, 249; So: Moo, *The Epistle to the Romans*, 245; Barclay, *The Letters of John and Jude*, 211; Kelly, *A Commentary on the Epistles*, 264; Barnet, "The Epistle of Jude," 334.

163. Watson, *The Letter of Jude*, 489–90; Bauckham, *Jude, 2 Peter*, 60.

1 Enoch in Jude and Other Early Christian Texts

Michael in 1 Enoch as Understood in Jude

First Enoch serves not only as "a highly elaborate paradigm for the development of intertestamental angelology"[164] but also establishes the prominence of Michael. In 1 Enoch Michael appears 18 times as Ὁ ἄγγελος ὁ μέγας. Michael achieved an incomparable stature in later Judaism so that among the seven (four) archangels, he is considered to be the chief and is said to have "(1) mediated the giving of the Torah (cf. Gal 3:19), (2) stood at the right hand of God's throne, (3) mediated prayers of the saints, (4) offered the souls of the righteous who died, and (5) accompanied them in to paradise."[165]

Although it can be argued that both Danielic and Enochic traditions concerning Michael's angelic functions were taken up and expanded in apocalyptic literature, Jude's characterization of Michael's role as the primary opponent of the devil and as an eschatological hero echoes closely 1 Enoch. Even if Jude here quoted from *Testament of Moses*, it is undoubtedly primarily and mainly shaped by 1 Enoch.[166] Thus Jude's quotation which includes one of Michael's roles, defending God's people from the devil, is not primarily designed to make an argument on his major theme; but rather seems to emanate from Jude's high regard for angelic beings and apocalyptic literature drawing from 1 Enoch. In other words, Michael's prominence among the angels, which Jude recognizes, and the significance of 1 Enoch in shaping Jude's use of scripture supports the conclusion that the *Testament of Moses* at a secondary level.

---

164. Charles, "The Angels, Sonship," 172.

165. Charles, "The Angels, Sonship," 172; See Nicholl, for a detailed discussion and a thorough textual referencing on Michael's prominence among the archangels in Jewish Christian thought. He describes Michael as the most important one, charged with the task of defending Israel and of interceding for it. Michael, as Nicholl writes, was often regarded as a military angel and as having a significant eschatological role, the primary opponent of Satan/Belial, whom he defeats at the end. "It is also likely that in Qumran Michael was the Angel of Light, the Prince of Light and the Angel of His Truth, who fought for the sons of light against the sons of darkness, who are led by the Angel of Darkness" (Nicholl, "Michael, The Restrainer Removed," 37).

166. Michael's role as a primary opponent against Satan and mediator between God and man seems to reach its peak in the *Testament of the Twelve Patriarchs*: T. Dan 6:2; T. Levi 5:5–6.

1 Enoch as Christian Scripture

Summary

Central to the purpose of this chapter is the intention to show that Jude, besides being uniquely influenced by 1 Enoch, uses 1 Enoch as Scripture. In other words, Jude is not only permeated, and as a result shaped by 1 Enoch, but also accords it scriptural authority in its usage.[167] Furthermore, all the evidence indicates that Jude uses 1 Enoch as inspired Scripture which prophesied about his own time.[168] This status of 1 Enoch in Jude is not unique to Jude. It is preceded by at least the Qumran Community and Enochic circle itself.[169] Jude is also followed by some apostolic fathers who regarded 1 Enoch as scriptural. This leads us to a discussion in the ensuing chapter on the overview of 1 Enoch's status in a broader context of the Second Temple Judaism and Early Christian Periods until its disappearance in the West.

---

167. Going one step further, Cory D. Anderson ("Jude's Use of the Pseudepigraphal," 48) argues that "Jude's belief in the inspiration and authority of the pseudepigraphical book of 1 Enoch played an influential role in the writing of the Epistle of Jude, in that it caused him to read 1 Enoch with an eschatological and christological hermeneutic."

168. However, this does not mean Jude gives or does not give "canonical" status to 1 Enoch. Either would be misleading. For instance, Bauckham maintains that while "Jude regarded the prophecies in 1 Enoch as inspired by God, it need not imply that he regarded the book as canonical scripture." Essentially Bauckham maintains the scriptural status of 1 Enoch though his expression "canonical" is inadequate since that was not an issue in Jude's use of 1 Enoch. However, in his later work, it seems that Bauckham has changed his position on this point (Bauckham, *Jude, 2 Peter*, 96). He writes "[p]recisely what kind of authority it had by comparison with the canon we cannot tell; nor need he have done" (Bauckham, *Jude and the Relatives*, 231). See also: Rowston, "The Most Neglected Book," 557.

169. A closer look at the Dead Sea Scrolls will show the influence of Enoch and also several shifts away from Enoch at the same time. For a discussion on this see chapter 4 of Stuckenbruck's recent publication (*The Myth of Rebellious Angels*).

ADDENDUM II
Scriptural vs. Canonical

SEVERAL REASONS FOR ACCEPTING 1 Enoch's authoritative and scriptural status in Jude are proffered.¹ Predominant amongst these are:

(1) NT authors and Apostolic Fathers who quote from Jewish "pseudepigrapha" do not differentiate between "apocryphal" and "recognized" books of the OT.² However, Bauckham, although he admits the existence of such early Patristic attestations, contends that they are very rare.³

(2) As a consequence of such uses, regardless of rarity, it is possible to argue that the precise boundaries of the "canon" of the Early Church were yet to be fixed.⁴ On the other hand, Bauckham argues that at the time of NT there was a fairly stabilized "canon" alongside the other books which were given a subordinate status and any of which "might occasionally be quoted as inspired writings by a writer who recognized it as such . . . or who knew that within the limited circle for which he was writing it was generally valued."⁵ Bauckham applies this hypothesis to the case of 1 Enoch in Jude.

---

1. Gunther, "The Alexandrian Epistle of Jude," 550.

2. Adler is careful not using the term "canonical," rather he prefers the more general term "recognized," probably thinking that "canonical" could be anachronistic (Adler, "The Pseudepigrapha in the Early Church," 211–28).

3. Bauckham, *Jude and the Relatives*, 227-28.

4. Evans, "The Scriptures of Jesus," 185. Evans further notes that because of the lack of such a boundary it would be impossible to determine the canon of the Scriptures for anyone in the first century AD.

5. Bauckham, *Jude and the Relatives*, 231.

1 Enoch as Christian Scripture

(3) The way Jude introduces his quotation from 1 Enoch shows that Jude considered 1 Enoch to be scriptural.[6]

(4) In addition to the formula, "Jude's hermeneutic included the principle that inspired Scripture speaks of the last days in which the interpreter is living," as is evident "in the use of the text of 1 Enoch 1:9" directed against the false teachers of Jude's day.[7]

(5) 1 Enoch was considered as Scripture or inspired by the early church and apostolic fathers. It is maintained that "at the time when Barnabas wrote, Enoch was held to be an inspired book; it retains this reputation, more or less, throughout the second century."[8]

(6) Some Church Fathers held 1 Enoch as inspired Scripture not only because of the book itself, but, more importantly because Jude considered it to be Scripture.[9]

Another important argument for the scriptural status of Enoch is that this status arises from within the "self-understanding" of the book itself. Nickelsburg argues that "the editor(s) of 1 Enoch presented their apocalyptic corpus as itself being Scripture—revealed, authoritative, and life-giving in its function."[10] He establishes Enoch's self-assertion as Scripture in two major ways: in its use of other scriptural material and the internal evidence of how the Enochic corpus identifies itself.

First, Nickelsburg assumes that the Jewish authors of 1 Enoch knew much of the Hebrew Bible and observes three ways in which they understood their relationship to the Scriptures.[11] (1) 1 Enoch never *explicitly* refers to any source of the Hebrew Bible; rather biblical tradition is woven into its own wording, phrasing and motifs. (2) The Enochic authors made broad and varied use of the material in the Scriptures, employing a variety

---

6. VanderKam, "1 Enoch, Enochic Motifs," 34–36. VanderKam argues that not only the prophecy of Enoch, but also the content of Enoch which Jude used and accepted, entails scriptural authority of Enoch.

7. Dunnett, "The Hermeneutics of Jude," 289.

8. Bigg, *A Critical and Exegetical Commentary*, 309. This is evident in their use of 1 Enoch. For a detailed discussion on the use of 1 Enoch by Early Church Fathers see: VanderKam, "1 Enoch, Enochic Motifs," 36–60; Nickelsburg, *1 Enoch 1: A Commentary*, 67–95; VanBeek, "Enoch among Jews and Christinas," 111.

9. Tertullian used *1 Enoch* in this sense as maintained by VanBeek, "Enoch among Jews and Christians," 110.

10. Nickelsburg, "Scripture in 1 Enoch," 333.

11. Nickelsburg, "Scripture in 1 Enoch," 334–37.

of techniques, interpreting the tradition "toward a common end: moral exhortation governed by an eschatological perspective."[12] (3) Because of Enoch's gradual development which embodies traditions over three centuries, it is not always clear whether a particular Enochic text is dependent on a biblical text or a parallel form of a tradition, and whether an Enochic author considers his source to be Scripture. Therefore, Nickelsburg concludes:

> The lack of any explicit appeal to Scriptural authority is counterpoised with the claim that the Enochic books are the deposit of a revelation given long before the birth of the Bible's first author, Moses, and intended for earth's last generation. This diminution of the authority of the Tanakh and celebration of Enochic authority are linked to the function of the Enochic corpus: it is revealed scripture intended to constitute the eschatological community of the chosen who will endure the final Judgment and receive the blessings of eternal life.[13]

Second, Nickelsburg asserts several points suggesting that 1 Enoch considers itself as Scripture. (1) The generic form of 1 Enoch took the form of a testament ascribed to Enoch, namely that "the corpus ends with a self-conscious reference to itself as the embodiment of heavenly wisdom, gotten by Enoch and revealed to the eschatological community of the righteous as Enoch's testimony."[14] (2) There is an explicit, central and repeated claim in 1 Enoch to be a revelation from God.[15] (3) The Enochic corpus claims Enoch's revelation is the embodiment of the heavenly wisdom that has the power to give life.[16] (4) Enoch's authority supersedes that of the Torah, for the Enochic authors, because they believed the ancient seer and sage received revelation not found in the Tanakh. For them Enoch "had foreseen their time, its problems, and its critical place at the end of history and he received a pointed and explicit message of judgment and salvation that was directed to the people of the last generation."[17] Thus, the corpus and

---

12. Nickelsburg, "Scripture in 1 Enoch," 334 also 337–42.
13. Nickelsburg, "Scripture in 1 Enoch," 342.
14. Nickelsburg, "Scripture in 1 Enoch," 344.
15. This is especially true in chapters 92–105 where "the author claims to be imparting divine revelation" in a way similar to prophetic corpus. See: Nickelsburg, "The Apocalyptic Message," 326.
16. The relationship is with the notion of wisdom in the book of Sirach where heavenly wisdom has become resident in the Mosaic Law. See Nickelsburg, "The Apocalyptic Message," 345.
17. Nickelsburg, "The Apocalyptic Message," 347.

1 ENOCH AS CHRISTIAN SCRIPTURE

its message were presented by its compilers, and accepted by some others as well, as authoritative revelation. Moreover, its self-conscious references to its written character justifies describing it as Scripture at least in these contexts.[18]

The discussion of Jude's use of 1 Enoch so far clearly shows that Jude uses 1 Enoch not only as authoritative, but also as scriptural.[19] Whether Jude includes 1 Enoch in the "canon" of the Scriptures is an irrelevant question to ask since that was not a question Jude would have asked. It is, therefore, anachronistic for us to be asking the same question because Jude predates the close of the Hebrew Bible and the Western preoccupation with reliance on a fixed body of books as the canon rather than on a set of basic principles (which enable the church to interpret this conglomerate of differing texts). However, scholars differ on the status Jude gives to 1Enoch. The discussion here, therefore, focuses on the different positions taken by modern scholars and some external evidence relevant to the question.[20]

First, those who reject the authoritative status of 1 Enoch in Jude point to at least two reasons for their rejection: (1) The Old Testament "canon" is already "closed" in the first century and 1 Enoch was not included.[21] However, this position is not only questioned[22] but also rejected by many who

---

18. Nickelsburg notes that the fact that 1 Enoch was not accepted as part of the Jewish canon of the Rabbis should not pre-empt the question of its status as canonical Scripture in some circles. Clearly the text itself claims to be definitive revelation constituting the eschatological community, to whom, the text was Scripture (Nickelsburg, "The Apocalyptic Message," 346).

19. For a discussion on what constitutes "(the) Scripture(s)" and the take of this study, see above, chapter 3. In this study, the word "Scripture/scriptural" is employed to designate early Jewish and Christian writings, which are authoritative and inspired, but not necessarily "canonical." To be more specific, this study assumes that for Jude, 1 Enoch is among the inspired Scripture as this concept is understood in the NT (2 Tim 3:16).

20. Part of the disagreement on 1 Enoch's status in Jude among scholars arises from the extent to which they give attention to Jude's use of 1 Enoch. Some simply base their arguments on only the quotation in Jude 14–15 whereas others make theirs based on a thorough discussion of various ways (as discussed in this chapter) that Jude's embodiment of 1 Enoch is evident.

21. Moo, *The Epistle to the Romans*, 273. Moo further notes "1 Enoch has never been given official canonical status by any religious body," an argument some others could also hold. But this claim is made in either wilful or unknowing ignorance that 1 Enoch enjoyed a canonical status in the EOTC from its introduction at an early period to date. This will be discussed in the following chapter.

22. McDonald and Sanders warn that caution is required in discerning what ancient writers concluded about the divine status of earlier literature that they cited. They further questioned "perhaps the notion of an unclosed biblical canon is present even though the

maintain that the canon was "unclosed" during this period.²³ Some of the evidence for the openness of the OT canon at Jude's time is found in (a) the usage of extracanonical literature by different Jewish groups including, the Qumran community, NT authors and early Church Fathers, without making clear distinction between "canonical" and "non-canonical" Scriptures; (b) the difference of opinions among early Fathers on the extent of the OT "canon"; (c) the divergence in LXX codices, and (d) the fact that after AD 70, Judaism and Christianity went their separate ways and thus established the bounds of the "canon" relatively independently of one another.²⁴

In conclusion, all the evidence indicates that Jude uses 1 Enoch as inspired Scripture which prophesied about his own time. However, this should not invite conflation of scriptural status with canonical status. Asking whether Jude gives or does not give "canonical" status to 1 Enoch would be misleading.²⁵ Such an assertion requires a re-examination of the difference between inspired Scripture and canonical Scripture. But these scarcely differ for Jude, if indeed Jude had a sharply defined concept of "canon."

Thus, Jude uses 1 Enoch as authoritative Scripture without necessarily considering its "canonical" status in the same way as it came to be understood in the later periods.²⁶

---

ancient writers did not yet have a term available to identify it" (McDonald and Sanders, *The Canon Debate*, 5).

23. For instance, D. Moody Smith argues that because the OT canon was not yet closed by the Jews at the time when many NT books were being written and some fluidity in Christian usage even after the "canon" was closed, it is incorrect that NT writers have a closed canon (Smith, "The Use of the Old Testament in the New," 4).

24. Dunbar, "The Biblical Canon," 309.

25. For instance, Bauckham maintained that while "Jude regarded the prophecies in 1 Enoch as inspired by God, it need not imply that he regarded the book as canonical scripture." Essentially Bauckham maintains the scriptural status of 1 Enoch though his expression "canonical" is inadequate since that was not an issue in Jude's use of 1 Enoch (Bauckham, *Jude, 2 Peter*, 96). However, in his later work, he seems to nuance his position noting, "[p]recisely what kind of authority it had by comparison with the canon we cannot tell; nor need he have done" (Bauckham, *Jude and the Relatives*, 231). For a similar position see also Rowston, "The Most Neglected Book," 557.

26. This applies, in fact, to other New Testament authors as well.

4

1 ENOCH IN OTHER EARLY JEWISH AND CHRISTIAN TEXTS

Introduction

IN THIS CHAPTER, I will discuss the use and status of 1 Enoch in early Jewish and Christian literature. The influence and status of 1 Enoch within early Jewish and Christian literature is an area of consensus within the field of study.[1] My purpose here will particularly be to identify the extent to which 1 Enoch was known both amongst Jews and the earliest Christians and its influence on the NT and some other Second Temple Period literature. I will then go on to look at the process by which it fell out of popularity and eventually almost disappeared amongst both Jews and Christians. Through this overview I hope to better demonstrate the historical and social factors that contributed to the disappearance of 1 Enoch from the "Scriptures" other than through its appropriation in other texts that retained their scriptural status.

To this end, I will begin by looking at the influence of Enoch in one particular Jewish community—the group identified as the Qumranites

---

1. It is more than a decade since authoritative scholars on Enochic studies began to gather biennially under an umbrella group called "Enoch Seminar." The Seminar was made up of, "a group of scholars highly trained in Second Temple Judaism and Christian origins, and most experts on the books of Enoch (= 1 Enoch)" (Charlesworth, "Summary and Conclusions," 436). It is among such a circle of scholars that the influence of 1 Enoch on early Judaism, including Christianity, is agreed upon.

1 Enoch in Other Early Jewish and Christian Texts

before going to look at the Church Fathers in the first four centuries of Christianity.

The Use and Influence of 1 Enoch in Judaism

The "Qumran" Community

We can assess the influence and status of 1 Enoch within early Judaism in at least two ways: influence on groups and influence on literature. The preservation and use of 1 Enoch, demonstrated in extant findings suggest that a Jewish group at Qumran[2] not only "considered parts of 1 Enoch to be authoritative,"[3] but also accorded them scriptural status.[4] The wider use or circulation of 1 Enoch among the community is evident in that, to some extent, they were shaped and influenced by it.[5] The possibility of "some continuity between the sect and the movement attested in Enoch" is thus something that can credibly be supposed.[6] Nickelsburg qualifies the relationship between the community behind the corpus of Enoch and Qumran community as a kind of parent-child status. He summarizes the issue as follows:

> Although there is no evidence that any of the Enochic text was composed at Qumran, the fragments from Cave 1 and Cave 4 indicate that the Enochic texts were favourites to the community . . . Furthermore, references to community formation in CD 1 and 1QS 8 parallel some of the details in the Apocalypse of Weeks and

---

2. The identity of the Qumran community has been a matter of extensive debate. However, many would agree that they most likely represented an off shot of the Essenes. For a discussion on the identity of the group see: VanderKam, "Identity and History of the Community," 487–533; Fitzmyer, *The Dead Sea Scrolls*, 249–60.

3. VanBeek, "Enoch among Jews and Christians," 95.

4. Flint, "'Apocrypha,' Other Previously Unknown Writings," 62–66. Flint draws this conclusion after discussing a number of criteria which may determine a writing to be viewed as Scripture. These include, formal indications of scriptural status, claims of Divine authority and Davidic superscriptions, the appeal to prophecy, number of manuscripts used (which indicates the popularity), translation into Greek, and quotations, allusions and dependence of the community's work on the literature in question. 1 Enoch is one of the prominent works which would fit these criteria.

5. VanderKam, *The Dead Sea Scrolls Today*, 155–56. In the same line John J. Collins argues that "there is no doubt that the Enochic writings helped shape the worldview of the sect" (Collins, "How Distinctive Was Enochic Judaism?," 33).

6. Collins, *The Apocalyptic Imagination*, 146.

suggest that the Qumran Community was a latter-day derivation of or successor to the community or communities that authored and transmitted the Enochic texts.[7]

The high regard and influence of 1 Enoch among the Qumran Community is also evident when considered against relative to the use of the Hebrew Scriptures.[8] This in of itself is arguably evidence for the rather exceptional authoritative nature of 1 Enoch. This is further supported by the wide circulation—evident from the significant numbers of copies discovered in extant manuscript fragments—and its inclusion in the relatively small group of books translated into the vernacular, Greek. In this connection, Eugene Ulrich lists six verifying criteria indicative of the standards to which "canonical" Scriptures would have to adhere among the Qumran community.[9] According to these criteria it is evident that 1 Enoch and Jubilees had claims of such canonicity next, only, to the Torah and the Prophets.[10]

Furthermore, the theology of the Qumran community, which shares significant commonality with that of 1 Enoch, serves as indirect confirmation of the influence of this literature on the Qumran community.[11] Some examples of these parallels are as follow: (1) The theology of angels and demons at Qumran maintains a clear echo of the imagery of 1 Enoch. In addition to the broader story of the Enochic story involving the angels, the

---

7. Nickelsburg, *1 Enoch 1: A Commentary*, 65.

8. Daniel J. Harrington notes, that in regard to the superior status of 1 Enoch among the Qumran Community, this book "had much greater use and influence than any of the apocrypha or Old Testament Writings apart from Psalms" (Harrington, "The Old Testament Apocrypha," 197).

9. Ulrich, "The Jewish Scriptures," 116–17.

10. After examining the level of scriptural or "canonical" status of various corpora, based on the criteria he set for canonicity of a work among the Qumran Community, Ulrich concludes that the Torah and the Prophets, including Psalms and Daniel, followed by 1 Enoch and Jubilees, could be part of their "canon," while "Job and possibly Proverbs might qualify." The rest of the OT books might have been known but may or may not have been considered as part of the Scriptures (Ulrich, "The Jewish Scriptures," 117).

11. Here, we need to make note of the dating of 1 Enoch if only to establish that at least parts of 1 Enoch are recognized as pre-dating the founding of the community. For further and more detailed discussion on the dates, see: Stegemann, *The Library of Qumran*, 142–62. Likewise, Charlesworth notes that "the members of the Enochic Seminar agreed on the probable date of the earliest composition among the books of Enoch. . . . conceivably [they originated] as early as the end of the fourth century B.C.E." (Charlesworth, "Summary and Conclusions," 446.

1 Enoch in Other Early Jewish and Christian Texts

four archangels, who are also called "angels of the presence," the impotence of human beings against the power of evil, and as a result, the need of angelic intercession, are additional parallels. (2) Other themes such as the end time, final judgment, the resurrection of the dead, and time of salvation, which are common to both the community and 1 Enoch, also suggest a shared eschatologically-oriented theology.[12]

After the landmark discovery of the Dead Sea Scrolls, which included the comparatively large number of Enochic manuscripts, it is argued that the number of the fragments in itself can be evidence for "the authority the book enjoyed for a time in Jewish circles, at least amongst the groups that lie behind [them]."[13] However, this should not automatically be taken to mean that the Enochic literature is purely a sectarian work as it has clearly enjoyed a much broader influence among other Jewish circles,[14] as will be demonstrated from the following look at some Jewish texts from the Second Temple period.

1 Enoch in Other Jewish Writings of the Second Temple

An important element of the significance of the Enochic tradition in Judaism can be noted in its influence on a substantial body of Jewish writings of the Second Temple Period. 1 Enoch enjoyed authoritative status not only among some Jewish groups but also in some Jewish literature.[15] Nickelsburg identifies more than a dozen examples of Jewish literature—including

---

12. Stegemann, *The Library of Qumran*, 201–10. Nickelsburg proposes three major outcomes that affected the Qumran community as a result of Enochic literature influence: (a) "They informed and undergirded the community's high eschatological consciousness; (b) they informed and supported the community's dualistic cosmology; and (c) they were consonant with Qumranic claims to possess special revelation (Nickelsburg, *1 Enoch 1: A Commentary*, 78).

13. Knibb, *Essays on the Book of Enoch*, 19. The significance of 1 Enoch amongst the Qumran community extended to the high regard to other works inspired by it. A prime example of this is the book of Jubilees. Besides the biblical tradition, according to Henry W. Rietz, "*the most important* [italics mine] traditions inherited by the Qumran Community include 1 Enoch and Jubilees." As literary evidence, he further notes that, "[of] the documents found at Qumran but not composed there, excluding documents later collected into the Tanakh, Jubilees leads the list of extant copies with at least fifteen manuscripts" (Rietz, "Synchronizing Worship," 111).

14. For a similar position and supporting evidence see, Knibb, *Essays on the Book of Enoch*, 19.

15. VanBeek, "Enoch among Jews and Christians," 93.

the *Wisdom of Jesus Ben Sira, Pseudo-Eupolemos, The Book of Jubilees, The Genesis Apocryphon, The Aramaic Levi Document, The Wisdom of Solomon, 2 Baruch, 2 and 3 Enoch,* Philo, and Josephus—which are influenced, directly or indirectly, by 1 Enoch, to various degrees.[16]

Jubilees is the most outstanding example of the reception and appropriation of 1 Enoch among Jewish writings of the period.[17] The reliance of this work on 1 Enoch, alongside the expected attention and regard to the conventional Mosaic tradition is quite remarkable.[18] Jubilees refers to the Book of the Luminaries, the Book of the Watchers, the Animal vision,[19] and the Apocalypse of Weeks, the four parts of 1 Enoch discovered in

---

16. Nickelsburg, *1 Enoch 1: A Commentary*, 71–81. In addition to the literature from Qumran, including Jubilees and The Genesis Apocryphon, VanBeek adds the Testaments of Reuben and Naphtali and Targum pseudo-Jonathan to his list of Jewish literature influenced by 1 Enoch (VanBeek, "Enoch among Jews and Christians," 93–100). In most of these writings, the watchers story, the most prominent narrative of 1 Enoch, shows up several times—most particularly in Qumran literature.

17. Larson, "The LXX and Enoch," 84–89. The possibility that both works belong to a common group and tradition, as opposed to *Jubilees* being directly dependant on *Enoch*, is discussed by Ida Fröhlich. Fröhlich argues, "[the] authors and readers of both Enochic collection and Jubilees may have belonged to the same religious group. Differences between the two works reflect the particular interests of their authors" (Fröhlich, "Enoch and Jubilees," 147).

18. Boccaccini notes that the major "enigma of Jubilees"—as he refers to it is its synthesis or synchronization of both the Enochic tradition and the Mosaic tradition, arguably at the same level of dignity, authority, or inspiration. Boccaccini summarizes the various positions adopted by scholars of the field into four major categories, based on the papers presented on the Fourth Enoch Seminar, at Camaldoli, 8–12 July 2007. These include: (1) those who "claimed that Jubilees was a direct product of Enochic Judaism with some Mosaic influence—Mosaic features were simply subordinated to Enoch ideology. [2] . . . Jubilees was a conscious synthesis of Enochic and Mosaic tradition, yet remaining autonomous from both. [3] . . . Jubilees was essentially a Mosaic text with some Enochic influence—in the confrontation it was Moses who prevailed. [4] . . . [and those who] questioned the very existence of a gulf between Enochic and Mosaic traditions as competing forms of Judaism at the time of Jubilees" (Boccaccini, "Preface: The Enigma of Jubilees," xvi).

19. Jacques van Ruiten, on the contrary, argues that the assertion by VanderKam that Jubilees is dependent almost on all existing parts of 1 Enoch, including the Book of Dream Vision, is not plausible as both Jubilees and the Book of Dream Vision might have used "a common tradition, which is probably to be found in the Book of the Watchers" (Ruiten, "A Literary Dependency of Jubilees on 1 Enoch," 93). VanderKam responds, convincingly, to Ruiten's arguments stating that it is impossible to "minimize the significance of the fact that Jubilees underscores that Enoch left written works behind," supporting his position with textual evidences (VanderKam, "Response: Jubilees and Enoch," 164).

1 Enoch in Other Early Jewish and Christian Texts

fragmentary manuscript witnesses at Qumran.[20] Themes such as the figure and call of Enoch, the solar calendar,[21] are some of the motifs developed in this literature. It is believed that Jubilees was not only possibly "the earliest attestation of the Enoch traditions apart from the Enochic corpus itself,"[22] but also refers to the corpus "as authentic and authoritative divine revelations."[23]

Although not to the same extent as the Book of Jubilees and the literature of the Qumran Community, there is other minor evidence that 1 Enoch was in use or was known among other Jewish communities or their literature. Among these, the *Testament of Reuben* 5 is significant for taking up the story of the Watchers.[24] The *Testament of Naphtali* 3.5—4.1,[25] similarly, mentions the watchers story in a manner which clearly indicates that the writer of the Testament[26] had encountered the writings of Enoch. VanBeek further mentions that *Targum Pseudo-Jonathan*, a book possibly dated in the early fifth century, has clearly mentioned the story of the watchers from 1 Enoch, which indicates the continued use of the book among some Jewish groups as late as the time of Augustine.[27]

Two points, however, which need to be clearly established in regard to the connection between the Qumran community and 1 Enoch: (1) The significance or influence of 1 Enoch surmised from the uses discussed need to be understood in relation to other authoritative Scriptures in a pluralistic context; and (2) it bears noting that from the evidence we have to date, the community at Qumran did not seem to have had a list of books in the sense

---

20. VanderKam, *Enoch: A Man for All Generations*, 110–21; VanderKam, *The Book of Jubilees*, 305; 331.

21. For instance, Uwe Glessmer, maintains that 1 Enoch is not only "the oldest source material for the 364-D[ay] C[alendar] T[radition], but also generally for Jewish texts with explicit calendrical contents" (Glessmer, "Calendars in the Qumran Scrolls," 233.

22. Nickelsburg, *1 Enoch 1: A Commentary*, 72.

23. Jackson, "Jubilees and Enochic Judaism," 411.

24. Unlike 1 Enoch and Jubilees, where the watchers are responsible for sin, the Testament of Reuben shifts the responsibility to the women, who allured the watchers.

25. VanBeek, "Enoch among Jews and Christians," 99. VanBeek, notes that the Testament of Naphtali was one of the texts discovered at Qumran.

26. It should be noted that in recent studies many hold the *Testaments of the Twelve Patriarchs* to be Christian in their present form.

27. VanBeek, "Enoch among Jews and Christians," 100.

of a clearly defined body of authoritative Scriptures, or something like "a canon" according to the modern understanding of this concept.[28]

The authoritative status and influence of 1 Enoch was not limited to Jewish groups. I will now turn to look at the reception of this work amongst Christians who seemed to have been significantly attracted to it—as evidenced by its use until about the time of Augustine, who openly denied the possibility of the story of the angels—the core story of 1 Enoch.[29]

The Influence of 1 Enoch in Christian Writings

The influence of 1 Enoch on the NT writers, the Apostolic and Church Fathers, has been noted by several contemporary scholars who have studied this text. R. H. Charles, at the beginning of the last century, wrote that "the influence of 1 Enoch on the New Testament has been greater than all the other Apocrypha put together."[30] Ephraim Isaac supports this, as follows:

> There is little doubt that 1 Enoch was influential in moulding New Testament doctrines concerning the nature of the messiah, the son of man, the messianic kingdom, demonology, the future, resurrection, final judgment, the whole eschatological theatre, and symbolism. No wonder, however, that the book was highly regarded by many of the earliest apostolic and Church Fathers.[31]

The reception and appropriation of Enochic literature among early Christians can be seen in two general periods: (1) in the New Testament and other early Christian writings, and (2) in the writings of the Church Fathers. VanderKam describes the use of Enoch in these periods in terms of its influence on (1) the literature, (2) the motifs, especially the angel story, and (3) the person of Enoch himself.[32] Such appropriation can be identified in two different types of references: (a) direct quotations and explicit

---

28. Eileen Schuller, after persuasive discussion on this point, reaches the plausible conclusion that the "high theology" developed in the Dead Sea Scrolls, through various books, "could co-exist with considerable textual pluriformity and diversity. For whatever reason, there seems to have been no impetus to make lists, to count books, to define explicitly what is to be included and excluded" (Schuller, "The Dead Sea Scrolls and Canon," 310).

29. VanBeek, "Enoch among Jews and Christians," 111.

30. Charles, *The Book of Enoch or 1 Enoch*, xcv.

31. Isaac, "Ethiopic Apocalypse of," 10.

32. VanderKam, "1 Enoch, Enochic Motifs," 33–101.

1 Enoch in Other Early Jewish and Christian Texts

allusions and (b) echoes (indirect allusions) to the writings or the figure of Enoch.[33]

Enoch in the NT and Other Early Christian Writings

NT Writings

The most apparent appropriation of 1 Enoch in the NT is discovered in Jude and 2 Pet 2:4. Having discussed the significant use of Enochic literature in Jude above, I will begin here by looking at 2 Peter.

As noted by VanBeek, 2 Peter alludes to 1 Enoch through its use of Jude 6.[34] He argues, "2 Peter puts the story of the flood for the destruction of the ancient world and the salvation of Noah directly after the story of the watchers."[35] It may even be possible—especially since the priority of Jude over 2 Peter is debatable—that 2 Peter is independently alluding to the Book of the Watchers. Vanderkam, for his part, affirms this perspective noting that "[t]here can be no doubt that the same Enochic section which underlies Jude 6 also inspired this passage although, unlike Jude (one of his sources), the writer never names Enoch as the authority on which his words rest."[36]

In additions to these two texts, there are several other allusions to 1 Enoch in the New Testament. VanBeek notes such allusions in 2 Pet 1:19, 20, 21; 3:2, all suggesting the authoritative status of 1 Enoch.[37] Other allusions can be discovered Rev 14:20 to 1 En 100:3; Rom 8:38, Eph 1:21, Col 1:16, "angels . . . principalities . . . powers," to 1 En 61:10, "angels of power and . . . angels of principalities," and 1 Pet 3:19-20 // 1 En 19:1.[38] All these

---

33. Adler, "Enoch in Early Christian Literature," 271.
34. VanBeek, "Enoch among Jews and Christians," 100–101.
35. VanBeek, "Enoch among Jews and Christians," 101.
36. VanderKam, "1 Enoch, Enochic Motifs," 63. It bears noting that Bauckham contradicts this view arguing that it is unlikely the author of 2 Peter was familiar with the text of 1 Enoch as it seems the echoes of 1 Enoch discovered in Jude seem to be lost in 2 Peter 2.4 (Bauckham, *Jude, 2 Peter*, 247).
37. VanBeek, "Enoch among Jews and Christians," 102–13. He particularly focuses on the use of the phrase τὸν προφητικὸν λόγον (the prophetic word) in 1:19.
38. For a discussion of the reception of the figure of Enoch as discovered in Rev 11 see below.

instances of the reception and appropriation of 1 Enoch in the writings of the New Testament demonstrate the influence of this corpus during this period.[39] The influence of 1 Enoch is also discovered in the formulation of the theological conceptions of the Gospels—especially in relation to the development of Christological terminology. These include titles such as "Son of Man," "Son of God," "the Anointed One," "the Chosen One," "the Messiah," which are used and developed in 1 Enoch—and other Second Temple Period Literature. These terms were later adopted by the Gospel writers with a Christological nuance to potentially suggest the influence of 1 Enoch in general, and the Book of Parables in particular, or at the very least a common background of ideas.[40] Shirley Lucass, convincingly notes and rightly writes that:

> the writers [of the New Testament] sought to portray Jesus as Messiah in the terms they did, and in many instances these were terms which, for them, were derived directly from the Hebrew Scriptures themselves. Therefore, the type of Messiah portrayed in the New Testament, for them, is rooted in antecedent Jewish tradition.[41]

Church Fathers

The use and influence of 1 Enoch among the Apostolic and Church Fathers is more evident than in the New Testament, as demonstrated by the many allusions, references, and even direct quotations of 1 Enoch.[42] Such use is attested in (a) *Barnabas* 4:3 // 1 En 89:61–64; 90:17 and *Barnabas* 16:5 // 1 En 89:45–77; (b) Justin Martyr's *2 Apologia* 5 // 1 Enoch's account of the angels, (c) Clement of Alexandria's *Stromata* 5.1.10,2 // 1 Enoch's angelic account. Moreover, among the Church Fathers, Tertullian, Origen,

---

39. Dalton, *Christ's Proclamation to the Saints*, 175.

40. For an extended discussion of such a development from 1 Enoch (and some other Jewish writings) to the NT writers, and the continuity and innovative use of such terms by the NT writers, see Lucass, *The Concept of the Messiah*, 144–87.

41. Lucass, *The Concept of the Messiah*, 187. By Hebrew Scriptures here Lucass is referring to writings from the Second Temple period, later identified as pseudepigraphical as well as those affirmed as biblical. (See in particular Lucass, *The Concept of the Messiah*, 144–57.)

42. VanBeek, ("Enoch among Jews and Christians," 106) boldly writes, "several of the Apostolic and Church Fathers saw *1 Enoch* as authoritative."

1 Enoch in Other Early Jewish and Christian Texts

Athenagoras, Irenaeus, Cyprian, and Tatian all are noteworthy for their use of 1 Enoch—particularly that of the story of the angels.[43]

Epistle of Barnabas (AD 70–100)

Likely from the same century as much of the NT material, Epistle of Barnabas[44] is believed to have originated in Egypt—possibly in Alexandria—where the authoritative status of 1 Enoch seems to have acknowledged more even at this early stage.[45] Composed in Greek, this text seeks to establish that Jewish Scriptures as witnesses for the Christian in apparent polemics against Jews. Towards this end, the author references and elaborates upon different passages from the Hebrew Scriptures including Enoch. Two references to 1 Enoch in the Epistle are particularly significant in that they seem to indicate that he considered it to be authoritative Scripture. These can be inferred from instances such as, *Barn.* 16.5 where he uses the formula: λέγει γάρ ἡ γραφή ("for scripture says") and again his use of γέγραπται γάρ ("for it is written") in 16.6—both formula indicating the use of Scripture.[46]

Justin Martyr, Athenagoras, and Irenaeus (2nd Century)

In chapter V of his *Second Apology* addressed to the Roman Senate (AD 150–157), Justin Martyr references the story of the fallen angels.

> God ... committed the care of men and of all things under heaven to angels whom He appointed over them. But the angels transgressed this appointment, and were captivated by love of women, and begat children who are those that are called demons; and besides, they afterwards subdued the human race to themselves, partly by magical writings.[47]

---

43. All of these, and even some more literature, and their usage and dependence on 1 Enoch, are thoroughly discussed in VanderKam, "1 Enoch, Enochic Motifs," 36–88. See also Adler, "Enoch in Early Christian Literature," 271–73 and VanBeek, "Enoch among Jews and Christians," 106–11.

44. Holmes, *The Apostolic Fathers*.

45. Nickelsburg, *1 Enoch 1: A Commentary*, 87.

46. For a more detailed analysis of the textual character and content of the use of Enoch in the Epistle of Barnabas, see: VanderKam, "1 Enoch, Enochic Motifs," 36–40.

47. Roberts et al., eds., *Ante Nicene Fathers*, 190.

Athenagoras of Athens, in his *Plea for the Christians*, addressed to Marcus Aurelius Anoninus and Lucius Aurelius Commodus makes similarly references of the story of the fallen angels.

> For this is the office of the angels—to exercise providence for God ... [but] ... others of those who were placed about this first firmament these fell into impure love of virgins, and were subjugated by the flesh, and he became negligent and wicked in the management of the things entrusted to him. Of these lovers of virgins, therefore, were begotten those who are called giants.[48]

These two writers both utilize the Enochic story in polemics with pagans to explain both the existence of powerful pagan Gods and the existence of sin in the world.[49]

Irenaeus, a contemporary of Justin Martyr and Athenagoras, is another early Church father who references Enochic material. Writing from Asia Minor, Irenaeus (ca. 130–200), in his writings, specifically refers to Enoch (see more below) and the story of the Watchers. Irenaeus uses this story to explicate:

> the black arts of magic, Ever by tricks such as these confirming the doctrines of error, Furnishing signs unto those involved by thee in deception, Wonders of power that is utterly severed from God and apostate, Which Satan, thy true father, enables thee still to accomplish, By means of Azazel, that fallen and yet mighty angel—thus making thee the precursor of his own impious actions.[50]

In Book IV he references the Watcher's story twice. First, he does so in relation to the Flood which was "for the purpose of extinguishing that most infamous race of men then existent, who could not bring forth fruit to God, since the angels that sinned had commingled with them."[51] The second reference—"angels who transgressed and became apostates"[52]—is peculiarly interesting because it is formulated in relation to the Holy Spirit and his inspiration of the prophets.[53] From this use, which is juxtaposed

---

48. "Athenagoras of Athens: A Plea for the Christians."

49. Nickelsburg suggests that the theological implications of this use of the Watcher's narrative may account—at least partially—as to why 1 Enoch was ultimately rejected by later Christian discourse (Nickelsburg, *1 Enoch 1: A Commentary*, 87–88).

50. Roberts et al., eds., *Ante Nicene Fathers*, vol. I, 340.

51. Roberts et al., eds., *Ante Nicene Fathers*, vol. I, 516.

52. Roberts et al., eds., *Ante Nicene Fathers*, vol. I, 330.

53. So, VanderKam, "1 Enoch, Enochic Motifs," 42–43.

1 Enoch in Other Early Jewish and Christian Texts

with several other scriptural texts, including Eph 1:10; 6:11; and Phil 2:10–11, it seems fair to conclude that Irenaeus considered the account of the Watchers to have been equally inspired work.

Tertullian of Carthage

In the works of Tertullian of Carthage (ca. 155–ca. 240), which seek to defend its scriptural authority, we discover the first evidence that the authority of 1 Enoch is being questioned.[54] *On the Apparel of Women* directly addresses doubts arising from 1 Enoch not being included in the canon of the Hebrew Scriptures: "I am aware that the Scripture of Enoch, which has assigned this order (of action) to angels, is not received by some, because it is not admitted into the Jewish canon either."[55] Tertullian assumes 1 Enoch was omitted, possibly because it could not have survived the deluge if it was written by the Patriarch and argues Noah could have easily preserved the writings of his great grandfather. Elsewhere, Tertullian also stresses the inspiration of Enoch by the Holy Spirit; "the Holy Spirit foreseeing from the beginning, fore-chanted, through the most ancient prophet Enoch . . ."[56] Tertullian also makes much of the person of Enoch as we will see in more detail below.[57]

Clement of Alexandria

Clement of Alexandria (ca. 150–ca. 215) references the story of the Watcher's in his *Comments on the Epistle of Jude* noting that Jude verifies the prophecy.[58] In Stromata V Clement references directly to the story of the fallen angels, claiming that they were responsible for the perverted knowledge stolen by the Greek philosophers:

---

54. Nicklesburg notes that Tertullian was arguably the one Church Father most acquainted with 1 Enoch: "More than any other early church theologian, Tertullian of Carthage indicates knowledge of 1 Enoch and defends its authenticity and inspiration" (Nickelsburg, *1 Enoch 1: A Commentary*, 89).

55. Roberts et al., eds., *Ante Nicene Fathers*, vol. IV, 15 .

56. Roberts et al., eds., *Ante Nicene Fathers*, vol. III, 70.

57. Another Carthagian, Cyprian, likely followed his predecessor, Tertullian, on the debate surrounding 1 Enoch (Nickelsburg, *1 Enoch 1: A Commentary*, 89–90). Nickelsburg further notes that there are some treatises falsely ascribed to Cyprian that refer to 1 Enoch as Scripture, using an introductory formula "as it is written."

58. Roberts et al., eds., *Ante Nicene Fathers*, vol. II, 159.

> ... the philosophers of the Greeks are called thieves, in as much as they have taken without acknowledgment their principal dogmas from Moses and the prophets.... that the angels who had obtained the superior rank, having sunk into pleasures, told to the women the secrets which had come to their knowledge ...[59]

The reference here is likely from 1 En 16:3 which speaks of the Angels making known to women the 'worthless mystery' that they had in their possession causing women and men to cause evil to increase on the earth.[60]

Origen

Origen (ca. 185–ca. 254)—an immediate successor of Clement in Alexandria—uses in 1 Enoch in a manner that Nickelsburg summarizes as follows: (1) Origen considers the writings "to be the authentic products of the patriarch and [(2)] he cites them as Scripture; [(3)] however, he also indicates that others in the church [did] not hold this position."[61] Origen's own perception of the book seems to evolve and shift. We can note his initial use of it in, for example, *de Principiis* (3.3) and (4.35) he uses the book of Enoch as additional corroboration, alongside other Scripture, to support his theological discussion. This, however changes in *Against Celsus* where he seeks to deny claims his opponent has made about the subject of angels: "... derived, without seeing its meaning, from the contents of the book of Enoch; for he does not appear to have read the passages in question, nor to have been aware that the books which bear the name Enoch do not at all circulate in the Churches as divine, although it is from this source that he might be supposed to have obtained the statement, that "sixty or seventy angels descended at the same time, who fell into a state of wickedness."[62] Origen's perception of 1 Enoch thus seems to change as a matter of expediency.

---

59. Roberts et al., eds., *Ante Nicene Fathers*, vol. II, 446.
60. So: VanderKam, "1 Enoch, Enochic Motifs," 47; Charles, *The Book of Enoch*, 37.
61. Nickelsburg, *1 Enoch 1: A Commentary*, 90.
62. Roberts et al., eds., *Ante Nicene Fathers*, vol. II, 567.

1 Enoch in Other Early Jewish and Christian Texts

Julius Africanus

Julius Africanus (ca. 160–ca. 240) marks a notable development in the interpretive history of 1 Enoch amongst Christians. In fragmentary piece of his writings, Africanus understands "Sons of God" to reference the sons of Seth and the daughters of Cain, instead of "angels of heavens," corresponding to the "watchers, the sons of heaven."[63] He does not completely discount the veracity of the Enochic story, however, as he goes on to note, that even:

> if it is thought that these refer to angels, we must take them to be those who deal with magic and jugglery, who taught the women the motions of the stars and the knowledge of things celestial, by whose power they conceived the giants as their children, by whom wickedness came to its height on the earth, until God decreed that the whole race of the living should perish in their impiety by the deluge.[64]

Athanasius

By the time we get to Athanasius in the fourth century (ca. 296–373), the shift towards considering the Enochic literature as apocryphal seems to be, more or less, complete—although some debate lingered. Although Athanasius does not refer to Enochic literature in his *Festal Letter* (367), listing canonical and apocryphal texts, he nonetheless seems to engage the debate in his final words categorically denying the veracity of pseudepigraphal texts:

> but they are an invention of heretics, who write them when they choose, bestowing upon them their approbation, and assigning to them a date, that so, using them as ancient writings, they may find occasion to lead astray the simple.[65]

Athanasius main opposition—stated as his rationale for writing his canon—to these texts seem to be that they are used to lead the ignorant and the simple astray. Interestingly, however, Athanasius does not address the possible use of apocryphal and/or pseudepigraphal materials in texts which he accepts as canonical, such as Jude.

---

63. Nickelsburg, *1 Enoch 1: A Commentary*, 92.
64. Nickelsburg, *1 Enoch 1: A Commentary*, 92.
65. Schaff, ed., *The Nicene and Post-Nicene Fathers*, vol. IV, 552.

1 Enoch as Christian Scripture

Augustine of Hippo

Augustine of Hippo (354–430) represents another and even more influential voice establishing the apocryphal status of the Enochic literature. Augustine's treatment of 1 Enoch demonstrates both his doubts about the veracity of the story of the Watchers and his desire to exonerate Jude's use of parts of this literature. In *De Civitate* XV he rejects the Enochic elaboration on the basic story discovered in Gen 6:1–4.

> Let us omit, then, the fables of those scriptures which are called apocryphal, because their obscure origin was unknown to the fathers from whom the authority of the true Scriptures has been transmitted to us by a most certain and well-ascertained succession.[66]

Even so Augustine concedes that some parts of this literature is of needs inspired as it was appropriated in Jude—"We cannot deny that Enoch, the seventh from Adam, left some divine writings, for this is asserted by the Apostle Jude in his canonical epistle." He ultimately concludes however: "these writings have no place in that canon of Scripture which was preserved in the temple of the Hebrew people by the diligence of successive priests; for their antiquity brought them under suspicion . . ."[67]

This last argument indicates Augustine's appropriation of previous arguments, against the scriptural inspiration of the Enochic literature, refuted in the past by Church Fathers like Tertullian. He also utilizes the interpretive paradigm discussed here in relation to Africanus to demonstrate that the "sons of God" as discovered in Genesis 6 are "according to the flesh the sons of Seth," not to be confused with the Watchers.[68]

---

66. Schaff, ed., *The Nicene and Post-Nicene Fathers*, vol. II, 305.

67. Schaff, ed., *The Nicene and Post-Nicene Fathers*, vol. II, 305. For a complete discussion of the reasons why the Enochic literature was rejected from the OT canon, see Reed, *Fallen Angels and the History*, 194–205.

68. Jerome, like Augustine, rejects the canonicity of 1 Enoch because he finds the story of the Watchers as heretical—especially as it had become associated with the "heretical" Manicheans. Unlike Augustine, Jerome is not inclined to concede inspiration to any part of Enoch on the basis that it is quoted by Jude. He sees this, instead as cause to doubt Jude (Nickelsburg, *1 Enoch 1: A Commentary*, 94).

1 Enoch in Other Early Jewish and Christian Texts

1 Enoch in the Church Fathers: Summary[69]

The following are the factors influencing the reception of 1 Enoch in the Church Fathers and their different perspectives on its scriptural authority: (1) The use of Enoch in polemical interaction by pagan anti-Christian polemics to attack Christianity. (2) Overt contradictions between Enoch and other more traditionally accepted Scripture and its interpretation—e.g., the doctrine of sin and the narrative in the first chapters of Genesis. (3) The exclusion of 1 Enoch from the Jewish "canon"—which in relation to the OT was an influential standard. (4) The questionable authorship and provenance of the writings in the antediluvian period. As a result of these, and other factors which came to bear to varying degrees in different periods and contexts and for different Church Fathers.

An important point that comes out through our brief review, is that Enochic literature was excluded from the emerging canon of the Christian through a gradual process which saw its diminishing authority among influential Christian thinkers. Moreover, this process did not occur evenly or simultaneously—as noted by Reed the writings attributed to Enoch continued to circulate.[70] He rightly describes this process as "progressive marginalization" of the Enochic works "occur[ing] concurrently with a shift in the consensus among learned Jews and Christians about the identity of the "sons of God" in Gen 6:1–4."[71]

It also needs mentioning that the rejection of Enoch was more complete and faster within the Western church relative to the Eastern Church.[72]

---

69. In addition to examples of direct appropriation by Christian interpreters, there are other writings presented as Jewish literature but which are likely to have originated or been edited and preserved, among Christians, who were directly influenced by or dependent on 1 Enoch. A primary example of this category are the two other books named after Enoch, 2 (Slavonic) Enoch and 3 (Jewish) Enoch. These two writings, ascribed to Enoch do not only follow the traditions discovered in 1 Enoch, rather they further develop the tradition to include different stages of religious practice and understanding discovered in the post Second Temple Period. The angel story is also widely used in Gnostic circles in relation to evil and its origin.

70. Reed, *Fallen Angels and the History*, 152.

71. Reed, *Fallen Angels and the History*, 206.

72. The reception of 1 Enoch alongside other scriptural texts in the Ethiopian Church to be discussed below is likely an example of the continued influence of this corpus in the East relatively late.

5

1 ENOCH IN THE EOTC
Reception and Transmission of Scriptures[1]

Introduction

THE HISTORY OF ENOCHIC literature in Ethiopia is the story of the reception and transmission of Scriptures in Ethiopia. This history is characterized by several questions that contemporary scholars have sought to answer: (1) When and from which versions were the Geʻez translations made? (2) Were the OT writings received in Ethiopia before the introduction of Christianity? (3) Alternatively, were the scriptures brought to Ethiopia during the fourth century, when Christianity was the official religion of the government at Aksum? (4) Or with the coming of "the Nine Saints"? (5) Or even later only in the thirteenth and fourteenth centuries, when the church underwent a major internal reformation?

These questions have been asked and answered diversely. I will attempt here to summarize the various positions to identify the most credible account of the reception and transmission of scripture and the development of the canon of the EOTC to establish the process by which 1 Enoch was introduced and appropriated in the Ethiopian milieu. There are five major points in the history of Christianity in Ethiopia that are understood as likely periods for the translation of the Scriptures into Geʻez. These periods

---

1. Parts of this chapter has been published separately, here: Asale, "The Ethiopian Orthodox Tewahǝdo Church Canon," 202–22.

are: (1) Pre-Christian translation of the Hebrew Scriptures; (2) the fourth century AD, when Christianity was accepted as the state religion; (3) the fifth to sixth centuries AD—typically believed to be the time of the arrival of "the Nine Saints,"—characterized by wide spread evangelism and consolidation of the church structure; (4) the fourteenth to fifteenth centuries AD, when the church underwent a major reform; and (5) the modern time translation works in the nineteenth and twentieth centuries.

This identification of the transmission of scripture with the reception, development, and reformation of Christianity requires that we also look at the history of the EOTC. Traditionally the church traces Judeo-Christian religion in Ethiopia to the time of King Solomon of Israel. According to this tradition the visit of the Queen of Sheba—identified as a Queen of the Aksumite Kingdom—resulted in the transplantation of the religion and hence of the scriptures of Israel to Ethiopia.

Theoretically this means that some portions of the Hebrew Bible, at least the Pentateuch, a text also used by the Falasha[2]—the Beta Israel of Ethiopia, or Ethiopian Jews—could have been translated into Ge'ez, at this time. While this is a rather intriguing and persevering claim[3,] it is unlikely since Ge'ez was not yet a written language before the Christian Era.

Most contemporary scholarship accepts that, contrary to this tradition of the EOTC,

> Bible translation into Ethiopic (Ge'ez) prob[ably] began in the 4th–5th cent[uries], basically from Greek, but with some influence from Syriac and possibly also Hebrew. From the 14th cent[ury] there were revisions based on the Arabic texts. Almost all Ethiopic biblical manuscripts date from the 13th/ 14th cent[uries] or later.[4]

An important contribution, with regards to the large lacuna in manuscripts witnesses, has been the recent archaeological discovery which

---

2. Even if Ethiopian legends strongly claim a very early date for the Falasha arrival in Ethiopia, dating it back to Menelik I's visit and return from Jerusalem, the dating of their coming to Ethiopia is much disputed.

3. This position is particularly argued for on the basis of Acts 8, where the Ethiopian eunuch is said to be reading from the Book of Isaiah, which is seen as proof—probably existed in Ethiopia as early as the Christian era, or even before.

4. Cross and Livingstone, *The Oxford Dictionary*, 569. It is additionally noted here that, "The extent of the canon of the EOTC is unclear in detail, but most lists of books said to comprise the canon include (in addition to the OT, NT, and most of the Deuterocanonical Books) various other items such as Jubilees, 1 Enoch, and the Ethiopic Didascalia."

1 Enoch as Christian Scripture

revealed that there exist well-preserved biblical manuscripts in Ge'ez from as early as the fourth century.[5] A report from the archaeologists in relation to a particularly important find discloses that:

> What could be the world's earliest Illustrated Christian manuscript has been found in a remote Ethiopian monastery. The Four Gospels were previously assumed to date from about 1100 AD, but radiocarbon dating conducted in Oxford suggests they were made between 330 and 650 AD. This discovery looks set to transform our knowledge about the development of illuminated manuscripts. It also throws new light on the spread of Christianity into sub-Saharan Africa.[6]

This could also serve as a possible challenge to the consensus that translation of scripture in Ethiopia did not precede the fourth and fifth centuries as the existence of illuminated manuscripts indicate scribal expertise and a well-established religion in this period,[7] from at least the period to which these manuscripts are dated. This in turn indicates that during the time of King Ezana of Aksum or the coming of St. Frumentius, the first bishop of the EOTC, in the early fourth century, Christianity was potentially being practiced in Ethiopia to some extent even if it was not endorsed by the state. This discovery thus undermines the previous academic consensus that Christianity was introduced to Ethiopia only during or after the fourth century.[8]

Another argument raised by some scholars against the possibility of Bible translation into Ge'ez before the time of Ezana—the second quarter of the fourth century—is the claim that Ge'ez was not a written language before this period. This argument too, is convincingly countered by archaeological evidence which demonstrates that some of the kings before Ezana used Ge'ez to inscribe their coinage.[9]

---

5. This is not very surprising as, has been noted by Mikre Sellassie, there has hardly been sufficient palaeographical or archaeological studies done in the field in Ethiopia (Gebre-Amanuel, "የቅዱሳት መጻሕፍት ታሪክ በኢትዮጵያ፦" 165).

6. "Discovery of Earliest Illuminated Manuscript." For a detailed report on the archaeological discovery and the carbon dating process at Oxford see EOTC, *Ethiopian Church: Treasures and Faith*.

7. It needs to be noted that the existing manuscripts do not claim at all to be translations—they are probably transcriptions of older manuscripts.

8. So, Henze, *Layers of Time*, 32–34.

9. For instance, King Wazeba, one of the Aksumite kings before Ezana, began to use Ge'ez instead of Greek on his coins (Henze, *Layers of Time*, 31).

1 Enoch in the EOTC

While these elements pose interesting questions for further research, the most reliable piece of evidence as it stands now is that the most likely period of the initial period of the formal translation of Scripture in Ethiopia is during the period when Christianity first became the state religion of the Aksumite Kingdom during the reign of King Ezana in the first half of the fourth century. St. Frumentius, the first bishop of the Ethiopian Church, who is believed to have been ordained by St. Athanasius, head of the Alexandrian Patriarchate, is credited with instigating these initial translation efforts. Part of the circumstantial evidence supporting the idea of translation activity in this period are the two major changes that are not noted in the Geʻez language. The first of these changes is the reversal of the direction of writing, becoming left to right instead of right to left as it had been prior to this period, which perhaps reflects an influence from Greek. The second important change to the language is the introduction of vowels.[10]

In as much as this may be acknowledged as the initial period of the translation of Scripture into Geʻez there are several important elements that are not known. Most significantly, while this ordination of Frumentius is understood as the foundation of the historical relationship between the Coptic Church and the EOTC,[11] it is not clear whether this meant he followed the canon of St. Athanasius or whether the newly established church of Ethiopia even subscribed to a specific canon. It seems more convincing to assume that a wide range of Jewish and Christian writings—Greek as well as Syrio-Arabic and Coptic texts—were translated at this time with little regard to the issue of canon—particularly since the question of canon was far from being settled at the time.

The third turning point in the history of reception, transmission, and translation of Scriptures in Ethiopia is believed to have been the arrival of "the Nine Saints" from Syria in the fifth to sixth centuries. These missionaries widely propagated the faith and consolidated the church in many aspects. Pankhurst believes that "the Nine Saints," besides introducing monasticism and a Christian education system in Ethiopia, were involved in "translating, or re-translating the Bible, mainly from the Greek, into Geʻez."[12] While the historical identity of the so called Nine Saints, and the character of their sojourn in Ethiopia is yet to be conclusively established,

---

10. Pankhurst, *The Ethiopians*, 25.

11. The EOTC was officially under the See of Mark, for sixteen hundred years, until it became an autonomous Patriarchate in the mid-twentieth century.

12. Pankhurst, *The Ethiopians*, 37.

1 Enoch as Christian Scripture

there is general consensus that the translation of Scripture into Ge'ez was at this time influenced by the arrival of a group (nine or otherwise) of non-Chalcedonian monks possibly fleeing persecution.[13] It is believed the base text for this translation process was the LXX as their base text with some reference to the Syriac text. This, however, should not be taken to mean that indigenous scholars were not already in possession of Scripture nor that the process of translation was solely conducted by a group of expatriates.

Indeed, the evidence of the writings retained by the EOTC, including and especially 1 Enoch, indicate that the local traditions of translation may have been influential. Thus, it is important to note that there is no indication of an attempt—a successful one at least—to designate a list of authoritative scriptural books. Rather, the evidence indicates that the translators of this period translated both "canonical" and "pseudepigraphical" books without making any distinction. The survival of 1 Enoch in the Ge'ez serves as evidence for this, in as much as it had, more or less, disappeared from the list of authoritative writings amongst most Christian communities by this time. It is, of course, possible that this work was translated into Ge'ez prior to this period. Even so that it continued in use suggests that it had already acquired or will quickly acquire importance as part of the sacred books of the EOTC.

Another major period of literary activity in the history of Ethiopia is the fourteenth century, known as a time of literary renaissance. After the so-called "dark age"[14] that marks dynastic transition in Ethiopian history, there was both political and religious reform in Ethiopia. During this period, the Ge'ez version underwent a major revision, this time based on an

---

13. This group is also credited with exerting significant influence on the development of the Miaphysite theology so instrumental in the formulation of EOTC identity.

14. There are three major features which characterize the period known as "the dark age" in Ethiopian (Christian) history, a period from the late seventh to the early thirteenth centuries. First, as the kingdom of Aksum weakened, the ports were captured by Islamic Arabs and the inland roads were blocked by internal rivals, which also blocked all trade routes, resulting in both economic and political crisis. Second, as a result of the political crisis and internal rifts, the Coptic Church refused to send patriarchs for about a century, meaning that the Ethiopian Church was completely isolated and left without legitimate leadership. As there was no one authorized to ordain priests and the existing generation was biologically decimated, the church's pastoral and liturgical ministry was endangered. Finally, the invasion of Queen Judith marked the first political and religious persecution of the Ethiopian state and church. With the destruction of the religious and historical heritage, this assault marked the climax of "the dark age."

1 Enoch in the EOTC

Arabic translation,[15] which was itself probably based on a Hebrew text. In other words, the LXX-based Geʻez translation was revised using a Hebrew-based Arabic, which made the Geʻez version a hybrid of the LXX and MT.[16] This influence was evident during the recent translation process from the LXX-based Geʻez text into Amharic.[17] Mikre Sellassie Gebre-Amanuel, a leading EOTC scholar and translation expert, notes that, at times, the Geʻez is much closer to the MT than the LXX because of the Arabic influence in the fourteenth century.[18]

The issue of canon is also addressed through canonical lists in this period. One such is discovered in the *Fetḥa Nagast*, the Law/Justice of the Kings—which served as the canon law for State and Church well into the middle century.[19] In this legal code it is mentioned that there are eighty-one "divine books which must be accepted by the holy church," though only seventy-three (or seventy-four) are actually listed. On the basis of this tradition, which the *Fetḥa Nagast* claims to be of apostolic origin, the Ethiopian Church affirms the "canon" of Scriptures as comprising eighty-one books. There is, however, no record to indicate how and when the church adopted this number. Nor does there seem to be a tradition about a council or officially proclamation supporting this decision. Another interesting element that seems to characterise the canon of the church to this day is that, while the number eighty-one is agreed upon, there is no one list with all 81 books—although 1 Enoch is included in all existing lists.[20]

From the fifteenth until the twentieth centuries, the Ethiopian church faced many challenges, both from external bodies and within itself. Most notable factors shaping the church at this time include (1) political and

---

15. Knibb, "Bible Vorlage: Syriac, Hebrew, Coptic, Arabic," 565.

16. Knibb, also notes that Syriac versions also had significant influence on the early Geʻez translations which makes the Geʻez version a fusion of all those other texts (Knibb, "Bible Vorlage: Syriac, Hebrew, Coptic, Arabic," 565).

17. For a more detailed discussion of the Millennium translation of the Amharic Bible based on the Geʻez and LXX texts—undertaken by the EOTC and the Bible Society of Ethiopia (BSE)—and the controversy around the translation, see. Asale, "A Millennium Translation Based on the Geʻez and LXX," 49–73.

18. Gebre-Amanuel, "የቅዱሳት መጻሕፍት ታሪክ በኢትዮጵያ፡" 171.

19. Tzadua, *The Fetha Nagast*, xv–xvi. It is believed that it was compiled around 1240 by an Egyptian Christian writer in Arabic and later translated into Geʻez and expanded with numerous local laws.

20. For a detailed discussion of different perspectives on the Ethiopic canon, see Asale, "The Ethiopian Orthodox *Tewahǝdo* Church Canon," 202–22.

1 Enoch as Christian Scripture

dynastic shifts resulting in the Imperial centres;[21] (2) less than friendly relationship with the Coptic Church—which itself was under constant pressure from Egyptian Muslim governors;[22] (3) failed attempts by the Jesuits to Catholicize Ethiopian Christians;[23] (4) violent theological controversies;[24] (5) invasion by the Muslim sultanate of Adal, are but a few examples of the historical events which seriously shook the church.[25]

In spite of, or possibly as a consequence of, these challenges this period is notable for being a period of significant literary production—this seems to have been particularly inspired by the theological controversies. Simultaneously the church managed to copy, transmit, and retain scriptural books at various monasteries, remote from danger and other challenging circumstances.

The indigenous commentary tradition which offers insight into the more fluid perception of canon in the Ethiopian Church can also be traced to this period. This tradition was developed as a direct result of theological debates which persistently troubled the church and which councils—such as the fifteenth century EOC Council at Däbrä Məṭmaq failed to fully rectify. The commentary tradition was fully realized during the Gondarene era (sixteenth–eighteenth centuries). The Andəmta schools focused on commentary on the *asərawu* "main" books, (biblical corpus) and the *awaləd* "progeny" or "derived" texts, (doctrinal and theological books including

---

21. The major shifts were from Aksum to Zagwe/Lalibäla, from there to Gondär, and then finally to Šäwa. For a detailed discussion on such power shifts, see: Munro-Hay, *Ethiopia, the Unknown Land*, 19–36.

22. For a detailed discussion of the difficult relationship between the Ethiopic Church and the Coptic Church, see: O'Leary, *The Ethiopian Church*, 47–49; Lule Melaku, የኢትዮጵያ ኦርቶዶክስ ተዋሕዶ ቤተክርስቲያን ታሪክ፡ 49–59፡ Gorgorios, የኢትዮጵያ ኦርቶዶክስ ተዋሕዶ ቤተክርስቲያን ታሪክ, 74–83.

23. The largely failed attempts by the Jesuits to Catholicize Ethiopia were strongly and violently contested, resulting in long lasting consequences. Taddesse Tamrat notes: "The Jesuit experience was very bitter for the Ethiopian Church, and it naturally led to the creation of very strong antipathies towards anything European for a long time" (Tamrat, *Church and State in Ethiopia 1270–1527*, 29). Similarly, Patrick Gilkes notes that the Portuguese "attempt to convert Ethiopia to Roman Catholicism created havoc; . . . and it had the effect of encouraging the empire's already strong xenophobia" (Gilkes, *The Dying Lion: Feudalism*, 1).

24. Jones and Monroe, *A History of Ethiopia*, 88–96; Crummey, "Church and Nation."

25. These challenges are mainly connected to external attempts at expansion which resulted in the invasion of both the country and the church. For a detailed discussion of the major wars fought at this time, see Pankhurst, *The Ethiopians*, 37.

the writings of the Church Fathers).[26] This interpretive tradition, which has been compared to the Jewish midrashim interpretive method,[27] is open for alternative or contending meanings. It is in this context and tradition of openness that Scriptural texts were received and interpreted without the clear distinction of "Canon" versus alongside some "pseudepigraphical" writings.[28]

As we can see from this brief look at the history of the reception, translation, and transmission of Scriptures in Ethiopia, influence from a wide range of sources including, the Alexandrian Coptic Church, Syrian missionaries and texts, and later, from an Arabic textual and theological legacy, is evident alongside the indigenous history of translation and interpretation. The overview of this history further indicates that the EOTC scriptural tradition is most likely a conglomeration of all these influences and as a result open to them all. It is amidst such competing textual traditions that some of the texts, such as 1 Enoch, gain prominence as they became central for various practical traditions such as angelology, amulets, astrology, dualism, medicine, and many other aspects in the lives of both the laity and the clergy.[29]

Summary

In summary, the Geʻez translations of the Scriptures serve as an ancient witness to biblical and other texts. Although the translation process has been very complex, it is clear that the main text for the Geʻez Bible is the LXX with, at times, influences from the MT, the Syriac,[30] and at a later age from the Arabic. The earliest translation was likely made in, or even before, the fourth century, with major translation work following in the fifth and sixth centuries, and another major revision taking place as late as the fourteenth and subsequent centuries. However, the production of an authoritative list of books to be included remained lacking or unclear or incomplete, with

---

26. Cowley, "The Beginnings of the Andəmta," 1–16; Cowley, "Old Testament Introduction," 133–75; Cowley, *Ethiopian Biblical Interpretation*; Cowley, *The Traditional Interpretation*.

27. See, Cowley, *The Traditional Interpretation*.

28. An example of the reception of 1 Enoch in the Andəmta commentary can be seen below in the Addendum to this chapter.

29. See discussion in the chapter below.

30. Whether the Syriac origin is MT or LXX is not known and needs further study.

variations. In other words, the canon of Scriptures was never fixed definitively in the long history of the church, which affords equal authority to both "canonical" and some "pseudepigraphical" works.

6

1 ENOCH IN THE EOTC
Literary and Cultural Appropriation

Introduction

IN THIS CHAPTER, I will look at the reception of 1 Enoch in the literature, theology and cultural framework of the Ethiopian people. By doing so I hope to indicate the extent to which this text has served to shape and inform the traditions and self-understanding of a unique Christian tradition and community. I will first begin by looking at the Andəmta commentary to one chapter of 1 Enoch and the reception of Enoch in the Ethiopian Synaxarium (Sénkéssar) as examples of the interpretation of this text in the EOTC. It bears noting here that 1 Enoch is interpreted in the Andəmta schools as one of *asərawu* "main" books—i.e. as a biblical book in its own right. I will next look at the appropriation of 1 Enoch in important theological constructions before moving on to look at its influence on larger cultural constructions.

Chapter IV [Chapters 13-15 in English Translations] of the Andəmta Commentary to Ethiopic Enoch[1]

Roger Cowley notes that the *Andəmta* commentary (AC) corpus initially developed as an Ethiopian oral commentary on biblical and Patristic texts, most probably beginning from the time the texts were translated into the Ge'ez language.[2] The distinctive social history reflected in the commentary material suggests that the oral tradition, expanded and augmented, reached its most definitive form in the Gondärine period (ca. seventeenth century).[3] According to Cowley, the AC tradition is largely continuous with Antiochene exegesis, although some of its contents reflect material from the Alexandrian tradition.[4] He notes, however, that this material has been shaped by Ethiopian scholars and is not particularly influenced by the hermeneutical theories or doctrinal debates influencing the sources.[5] The AC tradition assimilates elements it has appropriated from external sources in "an excellent example of inculturating texts . . . in distant contexts into one's own *Sitz im Leben*."[6]

The AC is recognized for its use of the distinctive "*andəm*" formula—literally meaning for one, or firstly serving to function as alternatively or on the one hand/the other hand to list different potential interpretations—which introduces successive interpretations. The commentary utilizes a common structure made up of the Ge'ez text (*zär* or *nəbab*), the Amharic translation of the text (*zäybe*) and the commentary (*tərgwame*) consisting of illustrative stories (*tarik*), explanation (*hatäta*) and application.[7]

---

1. For an analysis of Chapter II of the Andəmta to Ethiopic Enoch see Ralph Lee, "The Ethiopic 'Andəmta' Commentary," 179-200.

2. Cowley, *The Traditional Interpretation*, 23.

3. Cowley, *The Traditional Interpretation*, 23. For example the OT commentary tradition claims to contain records of the line of oral transmission beginning from the time of the mythical Menelik I (ca. 3000 BC) up to modern times.

4. Cowley, *Ethiopian Biblical Interpretation*, 382. Cowley suggests that it is possible to trace the development of the oral tradition through annotations in the manuscripts (Cowley, "The Beginnings of the Andəmta Commentary Tradition," 1-16).

5. Cowley, *Ethiopian Biblical Interpretation*, 382.

6. Pedersen and Abraham, "Andəmta," 258.

7. Cowley, *Ethiopian Biblical Interpretation*, 379.

Text[8]

1. *Before all these things Enoch was hidden. Because this pre-ceded what came before he lived in Paradise for seventy years before all this.*[9]

2. *None of the children of man knew of him while he was in the place of his hiding. And none knew whether he lived or died.*

    Because if a man stands firm in the faith and his good works overflow he will live with the Archangels and the hosts of the angels in deed and life.

3. *And in the months when his doings were hidden he was with the Angels and saints who were diligent in their Praise* (ቅዳሴ).

4. *And I Enoch began to praise the exalted Lord*—who made the cosmos, who governs the cosmos, who took me around and showed me the cosmos and who will bring the cosmos to an end. *I began to give thanks to God who reigns over the four corners of the world.*

5. *Angels, who are diligent in their Praise, call I Enoch a scribe* [of righteousness], *who inscribes the law on the hearts of men.*

6. *They said to me: Enoch, [you] who inscribes the law on your heart; to those who are diligent to sin, who lost their heavenly honour which remains glorified eternally.*

7. *Speak to the children of Seth, who fallen; who have done as the children of Cain do, they said to me.*

    Those who have rejected his majesty, the Mountain of righteousness and heavenly deeds, their eternally separate and exalted place, being lost with women, performing the deeds of the children of Cain.

8. *They took wives for themselves and great condemnation fell upon them in this world.*

9. *They will not know love, harmony* [Peace with God?] *nor will there be the forgiveness of sins for them in this world.*

---

8. The translation here is a dynamic translation by the author based on the printed edition of the Ethiopic Andəmta, Anonymous, Addis Ababa, 2003.

9. The text of Enoch is displayed here in italics—I have organized text and commentary separately for ease.

10. *They will not feel joy in their children because they will witness the death of the children whom they love. They will weep loudly at the destruction of their children.*

11. *They will plead eternally, forgiveness, love, and harmony* [Peace with God] *will not be done for them.*
    [They will] *beg to live for five hundred years; an age of forgiveness and mercy they will not know.*

12. *It is to say I went. I Enoch went to Azazel (and said) love and harmony [Peace with God] will not be done to you.*

13. *For a severe sentence has been uttered for your destruction.*
    You shall have no peace. Bind him above for **Andəm** a severe sentence has been passed and you shall have no rest or mercy.

14. *Because you have taught injustice and the way of curses; taught the things of sin and injustice, to the children of men rest, mercy and forgiveness will not be done unto you, I said.*

15. *At that time, I went to them and spoke to them as one.*

16. *And they were all afraid; fear and trembling possessed them.*

17. *They pleaded with me to write on their behalf, to God who is in heaven, they asked me to write a memorial of their petition, that I may take up before him a testament of their petition to be for the redemption of their sins.*

18. *For* [having come down from the Righteous Mountain and taken women in marriage] *they are from this onward prohibited from speaking with God; they dare not lift their eyes to look toward heaven because of the shame of the sin for which they have been condemned.*

19. *At that time, I wrote a testament of the entirety of their petition on behalf of their humanity. That it may be for the redemption of their sins and an age of forbearance; before they brought their pleas to me I wrote the deeds of this and the other one.*

20. *And I went and sat by the waters; and these were the waters in the country to left and to the right of Hermon.*

21. *I spoke the memorial of their petition until sleep overpowered me.*

For where suffering is multiplied mystery is revealed and grace abounds, I said this one had sinned thus and the other one has sinned thus until sleep overpowered me.

22. *And behold a dream came to me and visions were revealed to me.*

23. *I saw a vision of affliction* [There are visions of peace and visions of mercy] *that I would tell to curse the children of Seth who had been of heavenly honour.*

24. *And awakening, I came to them. They were sitting at Eubelseyael, between Lebanon and Seneser, weeping together with their faces covered.*

25. *And I proclaimed, before them all the vision I had seen while I slept.*

26. *I began to speak this word which had the things of truth, to* [those] *who had been in the holy mount teach the children of Seth, diligent in their sin.*

    As it was said to speak to the heavenly watchers and to reprimand the heavenly watchers.

27. *Just as the honoured and exalted Creator commanded me to tell them in that vision, this book is inscribed with the reprimand and truth [addressed] to [those who are] diligent in their sins, the children of Seth who were since ancient time.*

    Andəm this is truth which reprimands the children of Seth.

28. *What I utter today, with the tongue of the flesh and the conscious, I saw in my sleep. He that gave speech to mankind that they speak; who created them that they are in their hearts aware of the things of knowledge, endowing them with cognition.*

29. *Because the exalted God had created and endowed me with cognition that I may teach the children of Seth in the holy mount, I saw what I was to speak, as I slept.*

30. *I inscribed you petition on your behalf.*

31. *And he showed me thus in my sleep; I saw that your petition will not be fulfilled in all the ages of this world.*

32. *The final tribulation has been proclaimed on you and the petition that you have brought will not be granted.*

33. *From this forward, until the passing of this world you will never more ascend to your exalted honour.*

You will not ascend to the righteous Mountain, to the presence of his majesty and the deeds of heaven from this day until this world should pass.

34. *This has been proclaimed to the world to bind you for all eternity;*
   Andəm it was spoken that you may be bound on the earth for all eternity.

35. *Before this you witnessed the destruction of your beloved children.*
   Before your death you witness the death of your beloved children.

36. *They will not be a remnant unto you but they will perish by the sword before you.*
   There are not as children to you, because a child is the legacy of the father, **Andəm** it says they will perish by the sword before you.

37. *Your petitions on your own behalf and your petitions on their behalf will not be fulfilled.*

38. *All this has come upon you as you are frustrated in your sorrow. And you speak no truth from the book that I have written for [to] you.*
   But all this will come upon you as you plead and weep. From the book that I have written there is no truth that you can claim this was done for us.

39. *And such a vision was revealed to me.*

40. *Behold clouds call to me in a vision and the mist calls to me.*
   (He sees clouds summoning him because it is a vision.) **Andəm** angels are calling to him and he called them clouds because clouds are light and they too are light. **Andəm**, clouds are majestic and they too are majestic. Still again those who preside over the clouds are calling me. A mist is calling me; (It is a vision so he sees the mist summoning to him). **Andəm**, he says the mist is calling to him because angels are calling to him. He calls them mist because mist is immeasurable and they are immeasurable. **Andəm**, those who preside over the mist are calling me.

41. *Lightening and stars hasten me on [and] pressed me.*
   Because it is a vision, **Andəm** he means to say the angels drive him on and so [because they are angels] he calls them stars. Stars are bright and they [Angels] too are bright, stars are majestic as they are majestic and **Andəm** he means they preside over the stars. He also

called them lightning because it is awesome and they are awesome. **Andəm** it is bright and so they are bright and **Andəm** he is agitated by those who preside over the lightning.

42. *And the winds cause me to fly in my dreams, they hasten me. (Angels) bore me to the heavens above the earth.*

    Because it is a vision he says the winds cause him to fly. **Andəm** he means the angels are in charge of the winds which are immeasurably powerful. **Andəm** he means that those who preside over the winds speed him on and hasten him.

43. *I entered the gates until drew near to a wall made of crystal stone.*
44. *A wall of fire encircles it and it terrified me.*

    The walls of the building are tongues of fire.

45. *And I entered through the encircling fire and approached a great house made of crystal stone.*
46. *The walls of that house made from crystal stones are smooth like wooden board.*

    The walls are like a board prepared for writing, pleasingly smoothly cut, and pleasing.

47. *And the pavement is crystal; and the ceiling like lightening and stars.*

    [It was] like the path of the stars and the lightning. The mix of colours, was like of the stars and the stars and lightings have been placed [upon it?] regularly.

48. *Between the outer gate and the house are the fiery cherubim. They have skies of water.*

    Because he sees the house and walls beneath the heavens he refers it as their sky. **Andəm** what he had called the pavement he referred to as their sky and what he had referred to as crystal he again referred to as water. He says sky because the cherubim are to be found there.

49. *The walls are encircled by intense fire; and the portal blazes with fire.*
50. *I entered that house and, because it is fire, it is warm; because it is crystal it is cold.*

    Andəm it is hot like fire because it is fiery. It is cold as ice because it is of icy crystal.

51. *There is no comfort, joy, and life, whatsoever, within it. Terror overwhelmed me and trembles seized me. Disturbed and trembling I fell down on my face. And in my dream, I saw such a vision.*

52. *Behold there is a house even greater than this house.*

53. *and all its entrance were open before me and it was made in the shape of fire.*

54. *It exceeded in every regard; in glory, in magnificence, in honour; its magnificence and its magnitude surpasses all to an extent that I am not able to describe it to you.*

55. *Its floors are fire; and above were lighting and the pathway of the stars; and its limits were blazing fire.*

56. *And therein I saw the lofty throne of God.*

    Andəm he says the throne of the magnificent to mean he saw a great throne.

57. *Its appearance is as frost; while its covering is like a brilliant sun. And the words of the cherubim resounded.*

58. *And beneath the great throne streams of blazing fire issued.*

    Andəm from his glory emanates affliction for sinners and the blessing of the Holy Spirit. They cannot look upon his face.

59. *And the Lord of Glory sit upon it. His robe shines brighter than the sun; and is whiter than snow.*

    He sees him sitting on the throne clad in his royal splendour.

60. *Not one of the angels could enter into his presence and look upon his magnificent and glorious countenance. What man, of flesh and blood, is able to see that he may see that fire?*

61. *There is a blazing fire surrounding him; and before him is a great pillar of fire.*

    These [the surrounding fire] are the angels. **Andəm** this [the pillar of fire] means that before him is an angel making intercession.

62. *Of the angels that surround him there is not one that draws near to him and myriads of myriads of angels are before him.*

63. *But unnecessary is to him counsel that is not of his nature.*

1 Enoch in the EOTC

He says persevere; but he needs no counsel. He is moved because he is God, Creator, and Lord (ፐነተ 12:12). And so he does not delight in counsel alien to his nature. He has no need of counsel from others.

64. *And yet the angels that are near him depart not from him, either by day or night.*

Should you remember that he had said there was no one who draws near it is because when he says they never depart from him he witnesses to their service and when he says no one draws near he means that there is no one who has studied and come to know his nature.

65. *And I had approached thus far trembling; with my face, veiled.*

66. *And the Lord called with his own mouth and said to me "Enoch draw close and obey my holy words."*

This is a command to pay heed and to obey.

67. *He raised me and brought me forward even unto the entrance, but I kept my face down with my eyes directed on the ground.*

He raised him up because he had fallen. He saw such a vision which was a preview of what is to come later. The fire is the providence of God and the former house is the world of the righteous of the Old Testament. He said therein are angels because they are never apart from the providence of God. He said a hot fire to signify the Old Testament righteous protected by the providence of God. And the chill of the crystal signifies that the souls of the righteous are in the hands of God and no suffering has come upon them (ፐነተ 3:1) because they are in the world and the delight of heaven is not in it. The latter house is the house of the righteous of the New Testament and he said it is superior because these are servants who are closer [to God] and greater in glory. He said it was open, meaning that no one who perseveres in faith and abounds in good deeds will be turned away (ዕተ. 6:36). Therein also is the throne of God because he indwells and lives within them. He said covered to signify that they [the righteous of the OT] lived behind the veil of the Old Testament. He said I look down to signify that their 5500 years sojourn in Gahanna. (At that time souls will be sent to Gahanna? Qerlos 4). **Andəm** he said it was hot because it was the abode of creatures he had seen at first; he said it was cold because He allows them to partake of the glory that is his nature. **Andəm** it is hot because of the grace they partake and he said it was cold because they bear a hundred-fold or thirty-fold. Still again he said hot and cold meaning that a place which is neither too hot nor too cold is loved by all signifying that he will bequeath heaven to his those he loves. He said frost because the comfort and joy of this world is not to be found in heaven. He said he who is the creator of the world is greater to signify that the creator of the world is greater than the creation of the world.

68. *He said to me: "Enoch, a man of righteousness who inscribes the law in the hearts of men; hearken to my words and do not fear.*

69. *Come hither and heed my words. Go and tell the children of Seth who are diligent in sin; who have sent you that you may intercede for them.*

70. *By rights, you ought to have interceded for men, but it is not right for a man to intercede for you.*

    But men intercede for you who are angel.

71. *Say to them; 'Wherefore have you left the holy mount; even the heavenly kingdom which endures eternally?'*

    Why have you departed from your exalted place, the Mountain of Righteousness, and from the glory of the deeds of heaven?

72. *You went into the women and you defiled yourselves with the children of Cain.*

73. *You took to yourselves wives and acted like the children of Cain. And you begat tall children,* meaning giants.

74. *You, being, incorporeal, glorified and possessing a life which is eternal (the Holy Spirit) you polluted yourself with women.*

    Andəm you who seek to be spiritual should be alive spiritually and in the Holy Spirit and **Andəm** you who are living spiritually and in the Holy Spirit defiled yourselves with women.

75. *You have begotten from them in carnal acts of the flesh. And you became besotted with the things of flesh and blood; just as they do the things of flesh and blood you acted like them.*

76. *These, however, die and perish. Because they are destined to die, I gave to them women that they sow their seed and beget children by them.*

Andəm that they may impregnate them and sow their seed I gave to them women. I gave them women that they may have children by them.

77. *Life in this world is lived thus.*

78. *But you were, before this, incorporeal, made alive in the Holy Spirit who endures eternally from generation to generation:*

    Andəm You are alive in the spirit, alive in the Holy Spirit, you were spiritual.

79. *Because incorporeal angels dwell in the heavens; for this reason, I did not give you women as wives.*

    Therefore, I did not ordain the things of women or appoint wives to you. Those born of the children of Seth ought to have lived in exaltation on the Mountain of Righteousness.

80. *Still yet the giants who were born of the will be known as evil offspring on the earth.*

    The children of Seth born of spirit and flesh will be evil spirits.

81. *On earth shall be their habitation.*

82. *For they had been born of their fathers, who had descended from the holy mount; evil offspring were born of the children of Seth:*

    Andəm because they were born from their relatives the children of Seth their habitation was said to be on the earth. **Andəm** because they are born of the children of Seth—from the evil children of Seth who descended from the Mountain of Righteousness to bear offspring.

83. *These who had formerly been the source of purity these will be in this world evil offspring and they will be called evil offspring.*

84. *Incorporeal angels who live in the heavens their habitation will be in the heavens; and people who were born in this world their habitation will be on earth.*

    Those who were exalted in heavenly deeds formerly dwelled on the Mountain of Righteousness. Those who are born of the children of Cain dwell on this earth.

85. *The giants who reach as high as the clouds will perish completely; and they will war amongst themselves; they will destroy mankind from the earth.*

86. They will afflict mankind and they [mankind] will not find food to eat. They will drink all the water and they will not thirst. They shall be concealed and will not be known.

87. He said they will drink blood thus they will not thirst. **Andəm** they will drink the water of destruction and not thirst; **Andəm** they have no spiritual thirst? They are concealed because they have no good deeds and they will not rise up in enmity against men or women. They will never again rise up in enmity because they have come forth in the time of their destruction.

Some Notes on Chapter IV of the Andəmta Commentary to Ethiopic Enoch

The text and commentary discovered in this chapter is significant on several fronts. The first such element is the identification of the Sons of God and the Watchers with the Children of Seth (ዪቀቀ ሴት). This demonstrates the development of similar interpretive traditions witnessed in Church fathers like Julius Africanus—whether by reception and appropriation or separate, but likeminded, theological gloss of aspects of the Enochic narrative perceived as problematic in Christian thought.

The Andəmta commentary utilizes this to promote the prominent theme of ascetic separation which seems to inform theological thinking of the period, including the commentary to 1 Enoch.[10]

This framework, identified throughout the commentary, however seems to have distinctive emphasis in different sections. As noted by Lee, in Chapter II (1 En 6–9 in English translations) of the Andəmta for example: "The 'angels' are understood to be holy men, living pure lives at the foot of the holy mountain. The children of Cain are culpable in leading the pure children of Seth astray, although there is some indication too that the holy men were not being as pure as they should have been . . ." Chapter IV seems to focus a bit more on the guilt of the Children of Seth—the holy men who had abandoned the holy mount. This change in tone probably fits the setting of this section which is quite literally happening before the divine throne of judgment where the petition for mercy brought by Enoch

---

10. Ralph Lee notes a similar framework in his translation and comments on Chapter 2 of the Andəmta commentary to 1 Enoch (Lee, "The Ethiopic 'Andəmta' Commentary," 197).

on behalf of the fallen is being adjudicated. Ultimately, however, the angels are condemned by their actions; their failure to adhere to the higher degree of purity required of "angels" who would come before God. By embracing the desires of the flesh and sharing their wisdom with the children of Cain they are twice damned.

Here we can see the use of the narrative of 1 Enoch to promote and to develop the ascetic framework which is characteristic of many aspects of the traditions and theological formulations of the EOTC.

Reception of Enoch in the Ethiopian Synaxarium [Sénkéssar]

The Sénkéssar, the Ethiopian Synaxarium—like other similar works of the Christian tradition—describes the hagiographical notices to be read during divine office to commemorate the day of the death of the saints and martyrs of the church. It is arguably amongst the most influential works in the EOTC, in that it is read as part of the daily liturgy of the church, thus serving to inform the understanding of the laity significantly.

It is believed that the original form of the Sénkéssar was translated in the fourteenth century from the Coptic Synaxarium.[11] Gérard Colin and Alessandro Bausi note that this original translation was later revised in the sixteenth century (1563–1581) augmented the original version with texts from various sources such as the Apocryphal Acts of the Apostles;

> Yet the most original additions are those commemorating Ethiopian saints, resuming longer Gädl, but sometimes also recalling older traditions not elsewhere recorded. Commemoration days and characters (including Jesus Christ, the Virgin etc.) from the O.T. and N.T. narratives (with strong influence of apocryphal traditions) are also included."[12]

Not unexpectedly, one of the apocryphal traditions that is taken up and developed in the Sénkéssar is that of 1 Enoch. Below I will briefly look at the appropriation and development of characters and motifs from Enoch in the Sénkéssar to demonstrate another influential instance of the literary reception of Enoch in the EOTC.

---

11. Colin and Bausi, "Sénkéssar," 622.
12. Colin and Bausi, "Sénkéssar," 623.

1 Enoch as Christian Scripture

Sénkéssar 1st of *Meskerem* (11th September)

To be read on the first day of the Ethiopian Calendar year, the Sénkéssar for this date commemorates "the festival of Raguel, the angel, one of the nine archangels, who informed Enoch concerning the fire which burneth, and the destruction of the world; and he is the angel of lights. May the intercession of this angel be with us all."[13]

Sénkéssar for 8th of *Hedar* (17th November)

Another commemoration from the Sénkéssar for *Hedar* 8th (November 17th) is similarly dedicated to:

> Afnin the Archangel, one of the nine and ninety archangels, who together with Surafel guard the throne of glory. Of him Enoch said that he goeth round that house; and Surafel, and Kirubel, and Afnin, "These are the [angels] who never sleep, and who guard the throne of His glory," Salutation to this Trinity of Angels who guard the throne of God.[14]

Sénkéssar for 13th of *Hedar* (22nd November)

In addition to these angels which are mentioned by name, the Sénkéssar also commemorates the "myriads of myriads" of angels—mentioned in our discussion of the Enochic Andəmta above:

> who make intercessions for all the world, and of whom Enoch speaks, saying, "I was in the waters, and the winds and the clouds carried me up and brought me into a house which was built with a tongue of fire, and I saw there thousands of thousands." And he also says, "I saw the children of the angels standing upon flames of fire and their apparel was as white as snow."[15]

These references to the angelic characters of 1 Enoch serve to indicate one important source of the development of the angelology as we shall see below.[16] Importantly these dedications cannot help but fix these figures

---

13. Budge, *Synaxarium*, 5.
14. Budge, *Synaxarium*, 128.
15. Budge, *Synaxarium*, 136.
16. The importance of Angelic beings, such as Michael, Gabriel, Rufael, Uriel, Raguel,

of the divine court in the everyday imagination of the laity by portraying them as approachable figures mediating human divine relations. Enoch himself here serves as a figure of authority cited to establish the credentials of these figures as the holy angels. The implicit counterparts to these figures, especially within the framework of the Enochic narrative, are of course the fallen angels which in turn serve to inform the demonology of the community.

Sénkéssar for the 1st of *Tahisas* (10th December)

In this commemoration Enoch is cited as an apocalyptic figure, alongside Elijah [Elias] who will come "to rebuke the False Christ, and they shall perform miracles before him."[17] This prophecy is claimed to have originated with "John of the Apocalypse" although no such mention can be discovered in Revelation. The basis of this claim in Revelation, however is supported by an additional reference in the commemoration of the ascension of Elijah in the *Sénkéssar* for the 6th of *Tirr* (14th January) which identifies Elijah and Enoch with the eschatological witness who "shall rebuke the false Christ, and they shall kill his people, and their bodies shall be cast out for three days and a half, and then they shall be raised up, and the resurrection of the dead shall take place."[18] It is likely this reference reflects an old Christian tradition which identifies the two un-named witnesses in Revelation 11:3–13 with Elijah and Enoch who return to challenge the anti-Christ.[19]

Sénkéssar for the 2nd of *Tirr* (10th January)

The figure of Enoch is used in a slightly different capacity in the commemoration of Abel. Here he is identified as the eternal scribe who records the activity of mankind: "And this curse was exceedingly heavy upon Cain, and

---

Remiel, and Phanuel in EOTC can also be seen in that, churches are founded in their names and tabots are dedicated in their honour. Moreover, in addition' to the instances in the *Sénkéssar* that we discuss here many angels have feast days celebrated in their honour, to mention a few we can note: To mention the major ones, while the feast of Michael is celebrated on *Tirr* 12 (January 20), follows right the colorful celebration of *Timket*, Epiphany, the feasts of Gabriel are celebrated on *Tahsas* 19 (January 28), *Megabit* 30 (April 8), and *Sene* 12 (June 19).

17. Budge, *Synaxarium*, 178.
18. Budge, *Synaxarium*, 267.
19. Stone and Bergren, *Biblical Figures Outside the Bible*, 115.

at length his seed was destroyed from off the face of the earth by the waters of the Flood, because of Abel. And Enoch saith, 'I heard the blood of Abel crying out, and accusing his brother.'"[20]

Sénkéssar for the 25th of *Hamle* (1st August)

Finally, we turn to the commemoration of the translation of Enoch on the 25th of *Hamle*. This section of the *Sénkéssar* recounts large sections of the narrative of 1 Enoch. It begins by telling of the occasion of the commemoration:

> And on this day they [angels] carried away Enoch, the son of Jared, the son of Mahalaleel, the son of Cainan, the son of Henok (Enos), the son of Seth, the son of Adam, with the rushing of stars, and of lightening and of winds, and they took him up above the heavens and seated him between two spiritual beings.[21]

The *Sénkéssar* then goes on to describe Enoch's subsequent role as the eternal scribe and a Priestly figure who "will answer on behalf of the righteous." He is also characterized as a fearful figure executing judgment upon both humanity: "He Judgeth Dan which is on the right hand of the Arabs, and he reciteth the memorials of their petitions until the sleep of a dream calleth him, and visions of all are upon him; and they revile the watchers of heaven."[22] In this instance he seems to be portrayed as a proto-messianic figure although the *Sénkéssar* does not confuse him with Christ himself, as it also notes that Enoch prophecies; ". . . concerning Christ, 'With the Head of Days was going another, and His face was like the face of a man, and it was fitted with grace like one of the holy angels.'"[23]

The *Sénkéssar* also affirms Enoch as having foreseen the Church and the Christian community through the references to the sheep in the *Animal Apocalypse*:

> God brought sheep into a new house, which was larger and higher than the one before it, and He set them in the front one, which was veiled, and all the pillars thereof were new, and the beauty

---

20. Budge, *Synaxarium*, 254.
21. Budge, *Synaxarium*, 319.
22. Budge, *Synaxarium*, 319.
23. Budge, *Synaxarium*, 319.

thereof was new, and greater than that of the former house which was rejected, and all the sheep were in the midst thereof.²⁴

These characterizations all come together to highlight important features of the figure of Enoch; as patriarch, righteous scribe, judge, messianic prophet and eschatological witness.

The Influence of 1 Enoch on the Development of Angelology and Demonology in the EOTC

Arguably, one of the features that would be regarded as contributing to the unique character of the EOTC is its highly developed and elaborate angelology. As noted above in our brief discussion of the *Sénkéssar*, high regard and veneration of angelic beings is a well-articulated mainstay of the teachings and daily worship of the Church.

According to the teachings of the EOTC, angels ontologically share some of the attributes of God, such as holiness, which necessitates that they be venerated and honoured to the degree demanded by such the quasi-divine status afforded them by being sharers in the attributes of God. In other words, the honour they receive or their functional identity derives from their very nature which shares a likeness to God himself.²⁵ It is of course important to note that this is no way suggests that the high angelology of the EOTC confuses the inherent ontological difference between uncreated and created, God and angels.

In describing the significance of this veneration in the EOTC Wondmagegnehu and Motovu, note that, "there exists a Holy Book known as The Homilies of the Angels which shows how angels are sent by God and come down from Heaven to help and guard the faithful and destroy the wicked by divine punishment."²⁶ They go on to summarize the main tenets of the precepts of the angelology of the church as follows:

> God in His goodness sends His angels and saves from evil the faithful who fear Him and believe in His name, and guards and helps them in the time of affliction. We pray to God that he will

---

24. Budge, *Synaxarium*, 319.

25. For a detailed discussion on the ontological and functional identity of angels from the perspective of the EOTC's point of view, see: EOTC, *The Ethiopian Orthodox Tewahǝdo Church Faith*, 1996.

26. Wondmagegnehu and Motovu, *The Ethiopian Orthodox Church*, 84. This study serves as an important resource for understanding the basic teachings of the EOTC.

send His holy angels to save us from all evil, and that in the time of trouble His angels will help us. They repel the demons from the church and guard the priest lest the devils snatch away the Flesh and Blood of our Master. So, also when the priests depart, one or more angels remain to guard the church and the tabot.[27]

According to the teachings of the EOTC, therefore angels are beings which descend and ascend between humans and God, to serve both. On the one hand, they are close aides and ministers of God, always ready to execute his orders. This we can note is reminiscent of the multitudes of multitudes that never depart from God's side witnessed in Enoch's Vision. In this capacity, they can be both messengers of mercy and of wrath. The angels also intercede on behalf of humans and help human beings by bringing prayers and offerings to God, a status accorded to them as a favour.[28] These functions also serve as additional basis for the veneration and honour that they receive.[29]

The cultural significance of the theological development and practical liturgical aspects of the angelology of the church can be seen in the importance of angels as characters in indigenous hagiographies.[30] Furthermore, according to Wondmagegnehu and Motovu in EOTC tradition, "[e]ach family has its own patron saint or angel whose feast it celebrates every year both in the church and at home when friends and neighbours are invited."[31] This use is predicated in elaborate—if not systematic—hierarchy of guardian angels, in their various orders and ranks. All this demonstrates the significance of angels—especially the highly popular few identified as Archangels such Michael, Gabriel, Raphael, and Uriel—in the religious and social life of the people.

It is inarguable that all of these expressions and functions of angels within the theology, praxis, and culture of the church are mainly developed on the basis of Enochic angelology, even though I will not seek to make an argument here that this is the exclusive source of inspiration.

---

27. Wondmagegnehu and Motovu, *The Ethiopian Orthodox Church*, 84.
28. EOTC, *The Ethiopian Orthodox Tewahǝdo Church Faith*, 57.
29. Haile, *The Mariology of Emperor Zär'a Yaqob of Ethiopia*, 15–60.
30. Nickelsburg, *1 Enoch 1: A Commentary*, 105.
31. Wondmagegnehu and Motovu, *The Ethiopian Orthodox Church*, 82.

1 Enoch in the EOTC

The Christology of the EOTC and the Place of 1 Enoch

Christology is inarguably one of the most important and controversial theological issues for the EOTC. Debates on this topic defined both the internal debate and external relations of the church for centuries.[32] Nickelsburg and Vanderkam note the distinctive influence 1 Enoch on the EOTC Christology, saying, "even at points where the Western Churches have relied on texts from the New Testament," the EOTC uses 1 Enoch as its recourse for its Christological formulation.[33]

One of the major Ethiopian works on the Christology of the EOTC, the fifteenth century *Metshafe Mi'lad*, "Book of the Nativity,"[34] for example, demonstrates extensive reference to 1 Enoch. "Enoch is frequently cited as a prophet, probably as the preeminent prophet, sometimes as the first prophet, and often in conjunction with Daniel (in the order, Enoch and Daniel)."[35] The Book of the Parables in particular is extensively used with significant portions of the text cited including 1 En 46; 48; 50–51; 60–63; 69; and 70–71, which are mainly used as proof texts to demonstrate that the glorified Son of Man reveals "Jesus' divine status as a member of the Holy Trinity."[36]

---

32. The significance of this is best noted in that the church characterizes itself as the *Tewahǝdo* church representing the group which was ultimately triumphant in the acrimonious Christological controversies of the seventeenth, eighteenth, and nineteenth centuries. The prolonged Christological controversy lingering for several centuries in the EOTC, among three schools, ጸጎች *Tsegoch* (three birth or grace), ቅባቶች *Qibatoch* (unction or anointment), ተዋሕዶዎች *Tewahǝdo* (unionists), was finally settled in the so-called Boru Meda Council or Debate in 1885, adopting the position of the ተዋሕዶዎች *Tewahǝdo* (unionists) as the official position of the church. For a detailed discussion on the debate of this Council, see Jembere, ዝክረ ሕቃውንት, 279–83. For a more detailed discussion of the Christological debate in the EOTC, see Melaku, የኢትዮጵያ ኦርቶዶክስ ተዋሕዶ ቤተ ክርስትያን ታሪክ, 137–38. For a systematic discussion on the Christological position of the EOTC, see Strauss, "Perspectives on the Nature of Christ in the Ethiopian Orthodox Church." A complete and detailed analysis of the Miaphysite Christology of the EOTC can also be discovered in Ayenew, "Influence of Cyrillian Christology in the Ethiopian Orthodox Anaphora," 2009.

33. Nickelsburg and VanderKam, *1 Enoch 2: A Commentary*, 78. The influence of the Book of the Parables on the formulation of New Testament Christology is generally accepted by New Testament Scholars.

34. This is a book with "a collection of homilies for the monthly observances of the nativity of Jesus, whose origins are attributed to the Emperor Zarʿa Yaʿqob Konstantin (1434–1468)" (Nickelsburg and VanderKam, *1 Enoch 2: A Commentary*, 78).

35. Nickelsburg and VanderKam, *1 Enoch 2: A Commentary*, 78.

36. As noted by Nickelsburg and Vanderkam the most frequently cited text is 1 En

1 Enoch as Christian Scripture

This thus reveals an important function of Enochic literature in terms of articulating the high Christology of the EOTC which seeks to emphasize the eternal divinity of the Son in line with the Miaphysite Christology which stresses the one-united nature (*mia-physis*) of Christ.[37] It should also be noted, however, that 1 Enoch is not the only source from whence the EOTC Christological stance is formulated; rather, it is one important source amongst several others that come together to shape this theology.

Enochic Influence on Spiritual and Socio-cultural Practices

Some of the most common popular religious beliefs and practices in Ethiopian society in general are tradition around magic, possession by evil spirits, and protective devices such as amulets.[38] These practices are by no means unique to the EOTC or to its adherents; but are rather, widely shared customs in every part of the nation and among almost all religious communities.[39] The major differences between different communities that is seen in this regard revolves around the different elements that go into practices and the varying range of anticipated outcomes and focus.[40] These practices all indicate programmatic efforts to address 'evil' which in the context of EOTC Christians presumes an ongoing battle between angels and demons seeking to influence the individual and communal destiny. This imagery draws upon the elaborate schemata discovered in 1 Enoch,

---

46:1(–4). For more references see, Nickelsburg and VanderKam, *1 Enoch 2: A Commentary*, 78–79.

37. Ayenew, "Influence of Cyrillian Christology in the Ethiopian Orthodox Anaphora," 20. In this thesis Abba Hailemariam M. Ayenew discusses the Miaphysite Christology of the EOTC in a detailed and illuminating analysis.

38. Besides belief in witchdoctors, magic, evil possession and exorcism, some other superstitions widely common in Ethiopia include belief in the power of the evil-eye, protective rituals—against sickness, drought, fertility etc—food taboos, the concept of sacred trees housing both benign and evil spirits, water-places, mountain-tops, etc. For a detailed discussion on these and others, see: Levine, *Greater Ethiopia*, 46–74.

39. Levine, *Greater Ethiopia*, 48. Levine notes, "Throughout Greater Ethiopia there are beliefs that certain physical symptoms are caused by named spirits which take possession of a victim.... The term zar, [which refers to a kind of spirit believed to possess persons until placated by physical offerings], is the most widely used name for this intrusive spirit: belief in zar possession appears among the Amhara, Tigreans, Felasha, Kimant ...," people groups predominately EOTC adherents.

40. For some examples of various kinds of practices of exorcism and alleviating the problem, see Levine, *Greater Ethiopia*, 48–49.

1 ENOCH IN THE EOTC

and which provides the practitioner with characters and settings to utilize in executing protective devices.

One of these protective devices are the amulets which in contemporary practice are associated with one of the enigmatic characters of the EOTC, the *debteras*. Although the *debtera*—understood in the popular sense—is an official position in the ecclesiastical hierarchy these characters still associate themselves with the church and provide their services to the adherents.[41] For our purposes the most interesting aspect of the *debteras* and the service they provide—mainly the writing and sale of amulets—is informed by Enochic imagery and angelology.[42] In as much as the amulets would be used for many various things, the content and imagery utilized from 1 Enoch is also diverse. Some of the more prominent elements from

---

41. Appleyard correctly describes this office and its role thus: "A peculiar office in the church hierarchy is that of the däbtära, an unordained officiant whose role in performing the liturgy is not unlike that to the Greek psaltēs. However, the däbtära also has the role of administrator, scribe and scholar, who may also use his skills in preparing amulets and in traditional medicine and divination, which sometimes imbues him with an ambiguous reputation, serving what have been called the "licit" and the "illicit" aspects of religion (Appleyard, "Ethiopian Christianity," 115–36). Getnet Tamene describes two categories of function they hold at one and the same time, activities which are within the realm of the church and activities outside the realm of the church. In his words:

> The däbtära occupy in the Ethiopian Church an intermediate position between the clergy and layman. They study spiritual subjects longer than priests, devoting about 20–30 years of their life time to acquiring religious knowledge. Ritual dances that are conducted by the däbtära at times of important religious ceremonies are accompanied with cultural musical instruments such as the drums of different sizes (käbäro, nägarit), which are made of a hollowed-out tree-trunk, good to indicate rhythm, and sistram (sänasel). . . . Out of churches, the däbtära also perform magical rituals, astrological activities, and provide amulets and medicines prepared from various herbs to scatter demons and to avert disease. . . . This attitude of superstitious and magical practices which is common among the däbtära puts them somewhere on the margin of Christianity in the hierarchy of the Ethiopian churches" (Tamene, "Features of the Ethiopian Orthodox Church and the Clergy," 98–99).

42. Niall Finneran notes that "[t]he more you look beneath the veneer of the Ethiopian Orthodox Church, the more apparent it becomes that Ethiopia is rich in folk belief and superstition . . ." He gives examples of evil eye, magic, amulets, and some other aspects related to these practices to indicate that the "Ethiopian Orthodox Christianity embraces a number of idiosyncratic beliefs . . ." (Finneran, "Ethiopian Evil Eye Belief," 427; 429). An official source of the church Gorgorios admits that some of his EOTC members practice sacrifices for ancestral spirits (መቄስ) during various Christian festivals, he condemns that such practices are non-Christian and as a result the church denounces them (Gorgorios, የኢትዮጵያ አርቶዶክስ ቤተክርስትያን ታሪክ፣ 122).

1 Enoch to be used in amulets are the angels and the watchers, especially the seven archangels and Shemihaza and Azazel/Azaz'el/Asael. While the archangels are used as protective elements and guardians, Shemihaza and Azazel/Azaz'el/Asael are used to attack the enemy and bring bad luck.[43]

Furthermore, in line with the dualistic theology of 1 Enoch—between evil spirits and good spirits or the watchers and angels—these traditional practices have clear dualistic character. For instance, Finneran notes that:

> [t]raditional dualistic notions of good and evil are also a vital component of the daily Christian belief [in Ethiopia]; the *Zar*, for instance, are spiteful malevolent spirits allied to the harmful and evil *Saytan* (ghouls), whilst the *Adbar* are generally benign protective nature spirits. It is in this realm of superstition, beneath a Christian veneer, that the belief of the evil eye still flourishes.[44]

This use indicates an important factor in the popular reception and appropriation of 1 Enoch.[45]

Enoch and Iconography in Ethiopia

Alongside the flourishing literary history of the Ethiopian church, we also can discover the flourishing of the art of painting and iconography which has had significant cultural impact. As has been noted Christian art in Ethiopia "continued to be reproduced there for a much longer period than any other centre of Christianity in Africa," it has not been well known in the outside world as the country remains remote and isolated from the Western world.[46] It bears noting that the recently discovered ancient Ethiopian Garima Gospels—dated to the fourth to sixth centuries—are illuminated

---

43. At a workshop and exhibition on Ethiopian Church's paintings of "yesterday and today," held at Addis Ababa University, Institute of Ethiopian Studies on 13th Dec. 2011, a few paintings and texts of amulets were displayed and reflected that both the paintings and the text have clear resemblance to the book of Enoch even if they are more of paraphrases and stories blended with other biblical texts.

44. Finneran, "Ethiopian Evil Eye Belief," 429.

45. This does not mean, however, that 1 Enoch is the only text used for amulets in Ethiopian tradition; rather, it is only one of the texts. Texts from the Psalms and other local writings, including *Tea'mere Mariam* (the Miracle of Mary), are especially common. For an extensive discussion of magical practices and prayers among the wider Ethiopian populous, see Ullendorff, "Hebraic-Jewish Elements in Abyssinian," 216–56.

46. Langmuir et al., *Ethiopia: The Christian Art*, 1.

1 Enoch in the EOTC

ones[47] revealing that art in the Ethiopian church is as old as its history. Judith Mckenzie notes that of the art discovered in the Garima Gospels. The white stags are reminiscent of the beasts and birds in heaven that become white in the Animal Apocalypse.

In addition to the ever-popular images of the Virgin Mary and the Apostles and Old Testament figures, the art and iconography of the church is permeated with images of angels, especially the archangels Michael and Gabriel, Apostles, saints, and martyrs.[48] It is in this context that we need to understand the place of Enoch himself in the flourishing of Ethiopian Christian iconography. As an Old Testament figure himself, Enoch is no different from other prominent OT figures, where his images are only marginal in the mainline painting of the church. In other words, Enoch is not one of the main figures in Ethiopian iconography, possibly because OT figures are not at the centre of the iconography as compared to the NT figures and stories from it. This does not mean, however, that Enoch is entirely absent from the scene of painting. To mention only a few, Enoch appears just once—out of more than 300 icons in the IES collection—and then only as tiny figure hardly identifiable as part of a major painting of the second coming of Christ.[49]

However, even if the figure of Enoch himself is rare in Ethiopian iconography, as compared with other prominent biblical figures—and especially relative to the general influence of Enochic literature in other aspects of the theology and traditions of the church—the general prevalence of Angels, as in other parts of the popular culture may indicate Enochic influence. For instance, the ceiling of the Church of Debre Berhan Selassie

---

47. For a detailed report on the entire process of the archaeological discovery and the carbon dating at Oxford see EOTC, *Ethiopian Church Treasures and Faith*.

48. As iconography is roughly a reflection of the popular culture of a given society, the Virgin Mary is at the centre of Ethiopian Christian painting tradition since the ascendency of her centrality around the life of the church in the fifteenth century, "thus epitomizing Ethiopia's devotion to the Mother of Christ" (Langmuir et al., *Ethiopia: The Christian Art*, 3). For example the subject of "the Covenant of Mercy," where a "composition represents an alleged promise given by Christ to His mother that 'whatever she asks will be granted,'" as maintained by scholars, shows a "belief in Mary's extensive power of intercession, [which is] important in Ethiopian religious thinking" (Langmuir et al., *Ethiopia: The Christian Art*, 5). Following the Virgin's icons, Christ's images are depicted in connection to His Birth (closely connected to Mary), Crucifixion, His Resurrection, Baptism, his second coming, and some others from the Gospel stories. Some of the scenes important to Ethiopian iconography related to Christ, are those depicting the Flight into Egypt, Christ's Entry into Jerusalem, or His teaching to the disciples.

49. Institute of Ethiopian Studies, *Ethiopian Icons: Catalogue of the Collection*, 136.

1 Enoch as Christian Scripture

at Gondar is decorated with row upon row of winged cherubs. According to Richard Marsh, these "may well have been inspired by words from the Book of Enoch."[50]

In the rich tradition of Ethiopian Christian iconography, therefore, the influence of 1 Enoch which may at first glance seem only minimal, is more significant when we take into consideration the depiction of the larger body of Enochic figures and imagery.

Other Areas of Enochic Influence

Beyond the spiritual and religious realm, Enochic echoes and allusions seem to resonate in diverse arenas.[51] Such potential areas of influence include geography, cosmology, philosophy, hymnology/music, astrology, local mythology, science, medicine, and so on. We will attempt to look at some of these aspects although it should be noted that each of these suggest rich and undoubtedly fruitful areas of future research.

1 Enoch—the Book of Watchers in particular—is characterized by a highly elaborate depiction of geography.[52] This is developed in relation to travel and cosmology. In the Book of Watchers, Enoch travels from mountain peak to mountain and across other mountains from east to west, from south to north, led by creatures like angels.[53] Nickelsburg makes an

---

50. Marsh, *Black Angels*, 34–37. Marsh argues that the painting is a direct reflection of the text of 1 En 71, where he quotes the entire chapter in conjunction with the painting.

51. In light of the close ties between culture and religion, there is undoubtedly large areas of overlap.

52. For a detailed discussion of the geography of 1 Enoch, with special attention to chapters 17–19, see the monograph by Bautch, *A Study of the Geography of 1 Enoch 17–19*.

53. According to Bautch, the genre of this section, i.e., 1 En 17–19, is both apocalyptic and nekyia, "a Hellenistic genre featuring accounts of journeys to the land of the dead" (Bautch, *A Study of the Geography of 1 Enoch 17–19*, 29). See also Brooke, Review of Kelley Coblentz Bautch, 266–70. While the genre proffered by Bautch is accepted by some, it is nonetheless contradicted strongly by others. e.g.; Scott suggests, "seen as a whole, 1 En. 17–19 is an example of the well-established periodos ges or 'around-the-earth journey' literature . . . the periodos ges offered ancient audiences a pleasingly synoptic view of the earth's circuit, embellished with curious details of its most exotic phenomena," a phenomenon amenable to the Ethiopian context (Scott, Review of Kelley Coblentz Bautch, 755). For a thorough discussion of this genre see: Romm, *The Edges of the Earth in Ancient Thought*, 26–31.

1 Enoch in the EOTC

interesting observation in regards to the spatial parallels between the book of Enoch and the Ethiopian interpretation of geography as follows:

> 1 Enoch's focus on the created material world, its sacred cosmology and geography and its flora and fauna, may have helped the book to exude a sense of familiarity. In a country of deep ravines and high mountain peaks[54]—some of them sacred[55]—the story of the watchers' descent onto Mount Hermon (ch. 6) and the accounts of Enoch's journeys to the great mountain ranges of the West and East[56] and the valleys of punishment would have led the reader's imagination through familiar terrain. Enoch's journeys through the spice orchards to the great tree of paradise would have resonated in a world where groves of trees were sacred. Many of the wild animals[57] that preyed on the Israelite sheep that populate Enoch's second dream vision were part of the everyday experience of many Ethiopians.[58]

As a matter of long tradition in the EOTC, churches are mainly built at the highest point in their respective vicinity, and where possible on the tops of hills and peaks of mountains. Another longstanding tradition is the sacred practice of pilgrimage between churches whereby clergy and "pious" members of the laity. Whether consciously or unconsciously, these two traditions come together to evoke the travels of Enoch in various directions and for various purposes, accompanied by an angel.

Another aspect of potential Enochic influence is that of hymnology and music. It is claimed that St Yared—the Ethiopian composer credited with being the father of the unique hymnology of the EOTC as found in the five hymnological books: ድጓ፥ Dəggua, ምዕራፍ፥ Məräf, ዝማሬ፥ Zəmāre, መዋሥእት፥ Mäwāset, እና ቅዳሴ፥ Qidase—was influenced by the Book of

---

54. As Nickelsburg ("The Book of Enoch," 617, n.54) notes, for summary descriptions of Ethiopian geography, see Mountjoy and Embleton, *Africa: A New Geographical Survey*, 326–29; Kaplan et al., *Area Handbook for Ethiopia*, 347–50. For some visual depictions of the terrain in Ethiopia, see Veitch, *Views in Central Abyssinia*; Pankhurst and Ingram, *Ethiopia Engraved*.

55. Ullendorff, *The Ethiopians*, 94.

56. For a detailed analysis of Enoch's travels to various mountains, including the seven mountains in the south, see the Bautch's discussion in section of his study entitled "Description of the Geography of 1 Enoch 17–19" (Bautch, *A Study of the Geography of 1 Enoch 17–19*, 33–156).

57. On Ethiopian wildlife, see Steven Kaplan, *The Monastic Holy Man*, 23–24; Pankhurst and Ingram, *Ethiopia Engraved*, 155–76.

58. Nickelsburg, "The Book of Enoch," 617.

1 Enoch as Christian Scripture

Enoch in the development of his music.[59] This influence is particularly identified in relation to compositions addressing the feasts of angels, martyrs and saints, he used 1 Enoch as his source.

Summary

In this chapter, I have attempted to demonstrate the influence of the reception and appropriation of 1 Enoch on the literature, theology, religious praxis and culture of the Ethiopian church. Understanding the literary and theological influence is particularly important when we take into consideration that this is the only literary and theological tradition which has preserved this text in its entirety. The limited insight garnered here, in this regard, is indicative of the possibility for more extensive research in this area.

In addition to the literary and theological influences, allusions and echoes of Enoch discovered in a wide range of elements from iconography to music and protective amulets to geography indicate that, 1 Enoch is arguably one of the texts that have exerted considerable influence on the development of culture in the Ethiopian context.[60] Such a conclusion, however, should not discount in any way other important texts which have had as significant impact on the worldview of the church.[61] Indeed, it is important to note that the history of 1 Enoch in Ethiopia is one which is told in its location as part of the entire body of Scripture and other related texts all coming together to interweave religion and culture in a unique manner.

---

59. For a discussion on the originality of Ethiopian Church music and the legacy of St Yared's creativity in the production of music from the 5th and 6th centuries onwards, see Reda Asres, ‹‹የኢትዮጵያ ኦርቶዶክስ ተዋሕዶ ቤተ ክርስቲያንና ጸዋትወ ዜማ››፤ 95–128.

60. Harden, *An Introduction to Ethiopic Christian Literature*, 20.

61. Such a broad and categorical claim proffered by Ephraim Isaac is refuted in Addendum one (Ephraim, "Ethiopic Apocalypse of."). It is very important to note other literary works such as the Kebre Negest which have had as much if not more influence on the entire spectrum of Ethiopian literature, religion and culture. Pierluigi Piovanelli, for example argues; "the Kebrä Nägäst played a major role in the shaping of the special Christian identity of Ethiopian society, in the creation of the biblical flavour that permeates every aspect of Ethiopian daily life and culture" (Piovanelli, "The Apocryphal Legitimization of a 'Solomonic' Dynasty," 7–44). This argument seems to seek to highlight the singular influence of the Kebra Nagast. Much as in the case of Isaac's arguments in relation to Enoch this is a misleading representation which discounts the wide and broad range of literature that come together in the Ethiopian tradition.

ADDENDUM III

The Influence of Enoch among Ethiopian Evangelical Christians

Introduction

IN THIS SHORT ADDENDUM, I will briefly look at the influence of 1 Enoch among Ethiopian Evangelical Christians. I look at this influence as part of my study into the larger cultural influence of Enoch in Ethiopia and more personally because this is the tradition from which I personally came to interact with this work. I will begin with a highly condensed summary of the history of Evangelical Christianity in Ethiopia[1] before moving on to look at the influence of Enochic literature on this group.

Evangelical Christianity in Ethiopia

As compared with the very ancient history of the EOTC, the introduction of Evangelicalism in Ethiopia is very recent. The oldest Evangelical Churches in Ethiopia are a little more than 100 years old.[2] Protestant missions in Ethiopia began in the seventeenth century, although it was not until the

---

1. For a detailed and authoritative study of the history of Evangelical Christianity in Ethiopia see, Eshete, *The Evangelical Movement in Ethiopia*.

2. For instance, the two largest Evangelical denominations in Ethiopia celebrated their establishments' anniversaries as national churches recently. The Ethiopian Evangelical Church Mekane Yesus (EECMY), a Lutheran denomination, celebrated the centenary of its inception and the 50th anniversary of its establishment as a national church in the last decade. The Ethiopian *Kale Hiwot* Church (EKHC), celebrated its 75th anniversary over the same period.

late nineteenth century when these efforts bore any significant fruit, which favoured them to root themselves in some parts of the country. Following the Ethiopian state's consolidation of power in the south and east of Ethiopia during the time of Emperor Menelik II (r. 1889–1913), missionaries—heretofore largely unsuccessful in the Northern highlands—were able to direct efforts in these areas. Mission works in these areas were consolidated by a decree which identified "Ethiopian Church Areas" and "Open Areas" proclaimed by the modernizing Emperor Haile Sellassie, in 1944.[3] Mission activities in these areas—primarily characterized by traditional religions—proved to be successful leading to the planting and development of the first missionary churches, which retained their close connection with the missionary sending denominations in the Western world.[4]

An important element of the evangelical beliefs and traditions inherited by the Ethiopian Evangelical Christians is the 66 books Protestant canon. This was particularly important as one of the primary tasks of missionaries has been the translation of the Bible into vernacular languages. This was radical innovation in Ethiopia both for the imposition of a sixty-six-book canon and for forgoing the long-standing tradition of Ge'ez as the sacred language of church literature, and liturgy. As a result of these and other theological and social factors the relationship between evangelicals and Orthodox Christians in Ethiopia has long been characterized by strong animosity.[5]

In spite of this history of conflict and the missionary influenced identity of Evangelical Christianity in Ethiopia, there are indications that this tradition has been indigenized mainly through its interaction with the EOTC. As a result, Evangelical Christianity in Ethiopia is influenced by and has adopted a number of EOTC practices and traditions. Significantly this includes the celebration, as a matter of course, EOTC feast days such as the finding of the Holy Cross. Moreover, the national use of the Julian Calendar and dates from the liturgical calendar for the celebration of Christian holiday's such as Christmas and Easter means that Ethiopian Evangelicals commemorate holidays with the Eastern Orthodox world.

3. Forslund, *The Word of God in Ethiopian Tongues*, 37.

4. The sustained connection between these churches and the founding denominations in Europe and America fuelled the suspicion with which Evangelicals churches and believers were regarded by the Communist military junta—the Dergue—1974–1991.

5. Such animosity seems to be slowly abating, at least officially amongst the representatives of the churches, helped by the establishment of interdenominational efforts such as the Bible Society of Ethiopia.

ADDENDUM III

1 Enoch among Ethiopian Evangelicals

The place of 1 Enoch among Ethiopian Evangelicals, at a traditional level, is no different from the place of other "pseudepigraphical" writings, which are part of the authoritative Scriptures of the EOTC.[6] As part of this literary body, 1 Enoch, is not only rejected, but is also very little known. This then raises the legitimate question as to how one could make a credible claim that a book, neither recognized nor read could possibly influence a religious tradition? The answer to this question would be two-fold; ecclesiastical and socio-cultural.

First from an ecclesiastical point of view, the influence of the centuries old EOTC on the newly established Ethiopian Evangelical churches is far from insignificant. First and foremost, some of the first influential leaders who crafted both the confessional and ministerial stances of the nascent indigenous Evangelical movements—especially in the western part of Ethiopia—and who later on wielded major influence on the movement at the national level, were originally ordained priests in the EOTC.[7] Even if they were keen to accept the core Evangelical concepts brought by the missionaries, where reading of the Scriptures and conformity to it are at the centre of their teaching, the national ordained clergy were strongly inclined to retain a number of EOTC traditions and practices. As noted above, an important example of this is the adoption of the religious and political calendar of Ethiopia.[8] This then leads to one indirect appropriation of 1 Enoch in as much as the liturgical calendar of the EOTC incorporates elements from this tradition. Additionally, a significant number of evangelical converts come from the EOTC, with the full complement of the tradition and spirituality which had previously framed their understanding of Christianity and Scriptures. Among these, perceptions can be discovered some that reveal the thoroughgoing influence of 1 Enoch on the larger culture. One example of this, which seems exert considerable influence on Evangelical Christianity in Ethiopia is a metaphysical dualism—between the

---

6. For a discussion on the place of various scriptural books and the concept of "canon" around both the EOTC and the Ethiopian Evangelicals see above, Addendum II and Asale, "The Ethiopian Orthodox Tewahǝdo Church Canon," 202–22.

7. Among these influential leaders, Qes Gebre-Ewostateos and Qes Badima Yalew are notable (Bakke, *Christian Ministry: Patterns and Functions*, 107–24).

8. According to Forslund, Evangelicals did not find any reason, and in fact no other substantial choice, other than following the EOTC calendar for their liturgical and other purposes (Forslund, *The Word of God in Ethiopian Tongues*, 62).

two spiritual realms, the good angels who serve good and the fallen angels (watchers or demons in contemporary parlance). This in turn contributes to the strong emphasis on spiritual warfare between the evil spirits and the good spirits in matters that affect the lives of individual believers. In addition, even if the concept of sin at the confessional level is extracted from the standard evangelical handbook, the idea that sin can be a result of the influence of evil spirits imposing their wills on human beings is one which is shared between Orthodox and Evangelicals in Ethiopia.[9]

Secondly, from a socio-cultural point of view, most of the spiritual or cultural practices mentioned above under the subtopic "popular religion," i.e., tradition of magic, possession by evil spirits and hence exorcism, and some other traditional beliefs, are in one way or other common among Evangelicals in Ethiopia, as a shared cultural mind-set of Ethiopians. The strong belief in evil spirit possession and exorcism which are widely practiced spiritual cultures both among Orthodox and Evangelicals in Ethiopia, owes nothing to the influence of missionary planted evangelical Christianity. And although the different traditions maintain distinctions in form and procedure,[10] the practice and nomenclature of evil possession and exorcism is much the same and partly in line with 1 Enoch's angelology and demonology.[11]

---

9. Amongst the innumerable anecdotal evidence that can be cited in this regards we can raise as an example the sermon preached at a church of the Ethiopian Evangelical Church Mekane Yesus, witnessed by Forslund, in which the origin of sin from various and distinct evil spirits. The fable used to illustrate this point is as follows: "The first spirit is a lion which causes people to be proud (ኩራ). The second one is a male goat which leads people to (commit) adultery (ሰሙነ ዝሙት). The third one is a swine which leads people to stealing (ስረቅ). The fourth one is a tortoise which makes people lazy (ስንፍ). The fifth one is a beetle (ጥንዚዛ) which makes people greedy (ገቡዕ). The sixth one is a snake which makes people cunning (ተንኮለኛ). The seventh and the last one is a leopard which makes people angry and quarrelsome (ተጣላ)"(Forslund, *The Word of God in Ethiopian Tongues*, 217).

10. It is important to note two significant points around this practice of evil spirit possession and exorcism among Evangelicals. On the one hand, these practices are possibly blended from three different sources—(1) traditional EOTC background, (2) Ethiopian traditional religious practices, and (3) conglomerated to some related biblical texts. On the other hand, even if both faith communities have similar concepts and objectives, they do it in different forms or procedures, reflecting, sometimes consciously, the distinction between the different traditions.

11. For instance, one of my seminary classmates, who has been famous practitioner of exorcism repeatedly witnessed that a number of women come to him and confessed that they had sex with an evil spirit, and only after he prayed for them would they be liberated. This is one of the stories commonly heard among charismatic ministers as

ADDENDUM III

Summary

This brief analysis indicates the extent to which the cultural and religious appropriation of 1 Enoch by the EOTC can potentially influence the beliefs and practices of other Christian traditions.

---

much as we can hear from EOTC exorcism stories.

7

CONCLUDING REMARKS

IN UNDERTAKING THIS STUDY, I set out to understand 1 Enoch in relation to its reception and appropriation in a thriving Christian tradition, the Ethiopian Orthodox *Tewahǝdo* Church. This is particularly significant in that the full text of 1 Enoch has been preserved only by the EOTC in Ge'ez. In doing this, I hoped to indicate the potential theological significance of Enochic traditions and the different manners in which this could enlighten into the meaning(s) of the text to the contemporary interpreter. I also sought to highlight the cultural influence of this text as one small contribution towards demonstrating common roots for the religious and social practice of all denominations in Ethiopia today.

With these aims in mind I began my study by looking at the earliest reception of 1 Enoch in the texts that make up the New Testament. By doing this I aimed to demonstrate that from the earliest history of Christianity, aspects of Enochic literature have been recognized as scripture. My study of the reception of 1 Enoch in Jude demonstrated that this, relatively short letter, is permeated with Enochic motifs and themes. In addition to a direct quote of 1 En 1:9 in Jude 14–15 we also discover the appropriation of themes such as the theophany-statement, a common focus on apostasy, and a decidedly eschatological orientation. The characterization of angels in Jude, with the depiction of two categories of angels—the fallen angels (the Watchers) and the "unfallen" angels (the holy angels)—also reflects a parallel to Enoch.

Having looked at Jude I then turned to look at the use of 1 Enoch in other Jewish and Christian texts. This study revealed that the influence

Concluding Remarks

and authoritative status of 1 Enoch is not unique to the Letter of Jude. Our look at Jewish literature from the Second Temple Period revealed the importance of 1 Enoch in the Qumran community which equaled that of the Torah and the Prophets. Its influence, to varying degrees on a wide range of other literature from this period—including the Wisdom of Jesus Ben Sira, *Pseudo-Eupolemos, The Book of Jubilees, The Genesis Apocryphon, The Aramaic Levi Document,* The Wisdom of Solomon, *2 Baruch,* 2 and *3 Enoch,* Philo and Josephus—served to demonstrate that 1 Enoch was far from a sectarian text.

Similarly, we are able to identify notable influence of Enochic literature in the Church Fathers. We began by looking at references to 1 Enoch in the Epistle of Barnabas, which are prefaced by formulaic expressions indicating the use of scripture. The authoritative status of 1 Enoch continues in its polemical use—against pagans (Justin Martyr, Athenagoras) and against Jews (Irenaeus)—in juxtaposition with other texts from the OT and NT in the second century. A similar perspective is also seen in Tertullian and Clement of Alexandria although in this period we see efforts to defend 1 Enoch or some parts of it—clearly against polemical critique. With the latter works of Origen we encounter the beginning of Christian rejection of 1 Enoch, which is later developed in Athanasius and fully articulated by Augustine. We noted that 1 Enoch was progressively marginalized in Christianity was primarily a result of its overt contradictions with other texts making up the accepted canon of the Hebrew Scriptures later accepted by Christians, its use by 'heretic' sects, use of some of its narrative in anti-Christian pagan polemics and its questionable provenance and authorship.

Following the overview of the reception of 1 Enoch in early Jewish and Christian contexts, I then moved on to look at the history of its transmission and reception in Ethiopia. We noted that the history of the transmission of 1 Enoch in Ethiopia is likely identical with the history of the transmission of other scriptural texts in Ethiopia. This history indicates that the Geʻez translations of the Hebrew Scriptures mainly relied on the LXX with, at times, influences from the MT, the Syriac, and at a later age from the Arabic. The earliest translation was likely made in, or even before, the fourth century, with periods of translation and revision in the fifth and sixth and fourteenth and fifteenth centuries. It is notable, however, that these efforts did not establish a list of authoritative texts as such—other than mandating the eighty-one-book canon. As a result, the EOTC uniquely ascribes equal authority to wider range of texts, including writings identified as apocryphal and pseudepigraphical in other Christian traditions.

We then moved on to look at the influence of 1 Enoch on specific examples from the literature, theology, and praxis of the church. This review helped us demonstrate the extent and depth of the influence of Enochic themes, motifs, and characters in important texts, theological expressions, and worship. This influence in turn widely influenced the construction of the Ethiopian worldview as reflected in various cultural elements.

This study of the reception and appropriation 1 Enoch demonstrates the extent and breadth of the historical influence of 1 Enoch. In addition, we were also able to see the extent to which this text has influenced the Christian tradition which has adopted it as authoritative scripture.

BIBLIOGRAPHY

Aalen, S. "Δόξα," In *New International Dictionary of New Testament*, 44–48. Carlisle, UK: Paternoster, 1986.

Adler, William. "Enoch in Early Christian Literature." In *Society of Biblical Literature, 1978 Seminar Papers*, edited by Paul J. Achtemeier, 1:271–75. Missoula, MT: Scholars, 1978.

———. "The Pseudepigrapha in the Early Church." In *The Canon Debate: On the Origins and Formation of the Bible*, edited by Lee Martin McDonald and James A. Sanders, 211–28. Peabody, MA: Hendrickson, 2002.

Anderson, Cory D. "Jude's Use of the Pseudepigraphal Book of 1 Enoch." *Dialogue* 36/2 (2003) 47–64.

Andersen, H. G. "Moses, Assumption of." In *The Zondervan Pictorial Encyclopedia of the Bible*, 295–96. Grand Rapids: Zondervan, 1967.

Appleyard, David. "Ethiopian Christianity." In *The Blackwell Companion to Eastern Christianity*, edited by Ken Parry, 115–36. Malden, MA: Blackwell, 2007.

Arcari, Luca. "A Symbolic Transfiguration of a Historical Event: The Parthian Invasion in Josephus and the Parables of Enoch." In *Enoch and the Messiah Son of Man: Revisiting the Book of Parables*, edited by Gabriele Boccaccini, 478–86. Grand Rapids: Eerdmans, 2007.

Asale, Bruk A. "The Ethiopian Orthodox Tewahǝdo Church Canon of the Scriptures: Neither Open nor Closed." *The Bible Translator* 67/2 (2016) 202–22.

———. "A Millennium Translation based on the Geʿez and LXX: A New Bible Translation in the Ethiopian Church and Its Controversy." *The Bible Translator: Technical Paper* 65/1 (2014) 49–73.

Asres, Reda (ረዳ አስረስ). «የኢትዮጵያ ኦርቶዶክስ ተዋሕዶ ቤተ ክርስቲያንና ጸዋትወ ዜማ»፡ በየኢትዮጵያ ኦርቶዶክስ ተዋሄዶ ቤተ ክርስቲያን ታሪክ ከልደተ ክርስቶስ አስከ 2000 ዓ.ም. 95–128፡ [አዲስ አበባ፡ ኢኦተቤክ], 2000.

"Athenagoras of Athens: A Plea for the Christians." Chapter XXIV. http://www.earlychristianwritings.com/text/athenagoras-plea.html

Ayenew, Hailemariam Melese. "Influence of Cyrillian Christology in the Ethiopian Orthodox Anaphora." PhD diss., University of South Africa, 2009.

Bakke, Johnny. *Christian Ministry: Patterns and Functions within the Ethiopian Evangelical Church Mekane Yesus*. Studia Missionalia Upsalinsia 44. Oslo: Solum, 1987.

Bampfylde, Gillian. "The Similitudes of Enoch: Historical Allusions." *JSJ* 15 (1984) 9–31.

Barclay, William. *The Letters of John and Jude*. Edinburgh: St Andrew Press, 1960.

Bibliography

Barnet, Albert E. "The Epistle of Jude: Introduction and Exegesis." In *The Interpreter's Bible*, edited by George Arthur Buttrick, 12:317–43. New York: Abingdon, 1957.

Barr, James. "Aramaic-Greek Notes on the Book of Enoch." *Journal of Semitic Studies* 24 (1979) 179–192.

Bauckham, Richard. *Jude, 2 Peter*. Word Biblical Commentary 50. Waco, TX: Word, 1983.

———. *Jude and the Relatives of Jesus in the Early Church*. Edinburgh: T. & T. Clark, 1990.

———. "Jude, Epistle of." In *ABD*, edited by David Noel Freedman, 3:1098–103. New York: Doubleday, 1992.

———. "A Note on a Problem in the Greek Version of 1 Enoch 1:9." *JTS* 32 (1981) 136–38.

Bautch, Kelley Coblentz. *A Study of the Geography of 1 Enoch 17–19: "No One Has Seen What I Have Seen."* Leiden: Brill, 2003.

Beckwith, Roger. "A Modern Theory of the Old Testament Canon." *VT* 41 (1991) 385–95.

———. *The Old Testament Canon of the New Testament Church and Its Background in Early Judaism*. Grand Rapids: Eerdmans, 1985.

Benton, John. *Slandering the Angels: The Message of Jude*. Grange Close: Evangelical Press, 1999.

Berger, Klaus. "Review of Michael Knibb's *The Ethiopic Book of Enoch*." *JSJ* 11 (1980) 100–109.

Bietenhard, H. "Αγγελος." In *New International Dictionary of New Testament Theology*, edited by Colin Brown, 1:101–3. Grand Rapids: Zondervan, 1979.

Bigg, Charles. *A Critical and Exegetical Commentary on the Epistles of St. Peter and St. Jude*. International Critical Commentary. Edinburgh: T. & T. Clark, 1902.

Black, Matthew. *Apocalypsis Henochi Graece*. Pseudepigrapha Veteris Testamenti Graece. Leiden: Brill. 1970.

———. *The Book of Enoch or 1 Enoch: A New English Edition*. Leiden: Brill, 1985.

———. "The Composition, Character, and Date of the 'Second Vision of Enoch.'" In *Text-Wort-Glaube: Studien zur Überlieferung, Interpretation und Autorisierung Biblischer Texte, Kurt Aland Gewidmet*, edited by Martin Brecht, 19–30. Arbeiten zur Kirchengeschichte 50 Berlin: de Gruyter, 1980.

———. "The Maranatha Invocation and Jude 14, 15 (1 Enoch 1:9)." In *Christ and Spirit in the New Testament: In Honour of Charles Fransis, Digby Moule*, edited by B. Lindars and S.S. Smalley, 195. Cambridge: Cambridge University Press, 1973.

Blum, Edwin. "Jude." In *Expositor's Bible Commentary*, edited by Frank E. Gaebelein and J. D. Douglas, 12:379–96. Grand Rapids: Zondervan, 1981.

Boccaccini, Gabriele, ed. *Enoch and Qumran Origins: New Lights on a Forgotten Connection*. Grand Rapids: Eerdmans, 2005.

———. *Enoch and the Messiah Son of Man: Revisiting the Book of Parables*. Grand Rapids: Eerdmans, 2007.

———. "James Bruce's 'Fourth' Manuscript: Solving the Mystery of the Provenance of the Roman Enoch Manuscript (Vat. et. 71)." *JSP* 27 (2018) 237–63.

———. *The Origins of Enochic Judaism: Proceedings of the First Enoch Seminar: University of Michigan, Sesto Fiorentiono, Italy, June 19–23, 2001*. Turin: Zamorani, 2002.

———. "Preface: The Enigma of Jubilees and the Lesson of the Enoch Seminar." In *Enoch and the Mosaic Torah: The Evidence of Jubilees*, edited by Gabriele Boccaccini and Giovanni Ibba, xiv–xxi. Grand Rapids: Eerdmans, 2009.

Bratcher, Robert G. *A Translator's Guide to the Letters from James, Peter, and Jude*. Help for Translators. London: United Bible Societies, 1984.

BIBLIOGRAPHY

Brooke, George J. Review of Kelley Coblentz Bautch, *A Study of the Geography of 1 Enoch 17–19: "No One Has Seen What I Have Seen."* In *Dead Sea Discoveries* 13 (2006) 266–70.

Budge, E. A. Wallis, trans. *Synaxarium: The Book of the Saints of The Ethiopian Orthodox Tewahǝdo Church*. Garland: Ethiopian Orthodox Tewahǝdo Debre Meheret St. Michael Church, 1928.

Carson, D. A. "John and the Johannine Epistles." In *It Is Written: Scripture Citing Scripture*, edited by D. A. Carson and W. G. M. Williamson. Cambridge: Cambridge University Press, 1988.

Cedar, Paul A. *James, 1, 2 Peter, Jude*. Communicator's Commentary. Waco, TX: Word Books, 1984.

Charles, J. Daryl. "The Angels, Sonship and Birthright in the Letter of the Hebrews." *JETS* 33 (1990) 171–78.

———. "Jude's Use of Pseudepigraphical Source-Material as Part of a Literary Strategy." *NTS* 37 (1991) 130–45.

———. "Literary Artifice in the Epistle of Jude." *Zeitschrift für die neutestamentliche Wissenschaft* 82 (1991) 106–24.

———. "'Those' and 'These': The Use of the Old Testament in the Epistle of Jude." *JSNT* 38 (1990) 109–24.

Charles, R.H. *The Book of Enoch or 1 Enoch*. Oxford: Oxford University Press, 1912

———. *The Ethiopic Version of the Book of Enoch*. Oxford: Oxford University Press, 1906.

Charlesworth, James H. "Can We Discern the Composition Date of the Parables of Enoch?" In *Enoch and the Messiah Son of Man: Revisiting the Book of Parables*, edited by Gabriele Boccaccini, 450–68. Grand Rapids: Eerdmans, 2007.

———. *O Livro de Enoque Etíope* ou *1Enoque*, with Ephraim Isaac and Orlando Iannuzzi Filho, 249–526. Sao Paulo, Brazil: Entre os Tempos, 2015.

———. "The SNTS Pseudepigrapha Seminars at Tübingen and Paris on the Books of Enoch." *NTS* 25 (1979) 315–23.

———. "Summary and Conclusions: The Books of Enoch or 1 Enoch Matters: New Paradigms for understanding Pre-70 Judaism." In *Enoch and Qumran Origins: New Lights on a Forgotten Connection*, edited by Gabriele Boccaccini, 436–54. Grand Rapids: Eerdmans, 2005.

Clark, David J. "Discourse Structure in Jude." *The Bible Translator* 55 (2004) 125–37.

Colin, Gérard, and Alessandro Bausi. "Sénkéssar." In *Encyclopaedia Aethiopica*, edited by Siegbert Uhlig and Alessandro Bausi, 622–23. Wiesbaden: Harrassowitz, 2011.

Collins, John J. *The Apocalyptic Imagination: An Introduction to Jewish Apocalyptic Literature*. Grand Rapids: Eerdmans, 1998.

———. "How Distinctive Was Enochic Judaism?" In *Meghillot: Studies in the Dead Sea Scrolls V-VI; A Festschrift for Devorah Dimant*, edited by M. Bar-Asher and Emmanuel Tov, 17–34. Haifa: University of Haifa, Bialik Institute, 2007.

Cowley, Roger. "The Beginnings of the Andǝmta Commentary Tradition." *Journal of Ethiopian Studies* 10/2 (1972) 1–16.

———. "The Biblical Canon of the Ethiopian Orthodox Church Today." *Ostkirchliche Studien* 23 (1974) 318–23.

———. *Ethiopian Biblical Interpretation: A Study in Exegetical Tradition and Hermeneutics*. University of Cambridge Oriental Publications 38. Cambridge: Cambridge University Press, 1988.

Bibliography

———. "Old Testament Introduction in the Andəmta Commentary Tradition." *Journal of Ethiopian Studies* 12/1 (1974) 133–75.

———. *The Traditional Interpretation of the Apocalypse of St. John in the Ethiopian Orthodox Church*. Cambridge: Cambridge University Press, 1983.

Cross, F. L., and E. A. Livingstone, eds. *The Oxford Dictionary of the Christian Church*. 3rd rev. ed. Oxford: Oxford University Press, 2005.

Crummey, Donald. "Church and Nation: The Ethiopian Orthodox Täwahedo Church (from the Thirteenth to the Twentieth Century)." In *Eastern Christianities*, part 3, *Church and Nation: The Ethiopian Orthodox Täwahedo Church from the Thirteenth to the Twentieth Century*, edited by Michael Angold, 457–87. Cambridge History of Christianity. Cambridge: Cambridge University Press,

Dalton, William Joseph. *Christ's Proclamation to the Saints: A Study of 1 Peter 3:18–4:1*. Analecta Biblica 23. Rome: Editrica Portificio Instituto Biblico, 1965.

de Bruyn, Theodore. "Papyri, Parchments, Ostraca, and Tablets Written with Biblical Texts in Greek and Used as Amulets: A Preliminary List." In *Early Christian Manuscripts: Examples of Applied Method and Approach*, edited by Thomas J. Kraus and Tobias Nicklas, 5:145–89. Texts and Editions for New Testament Study 5. Leiden: Brill, 2010.

de Jonge, Marinus. *Pseudepigrapha of the Old Testament as Part of Christian Literature: The Case of the "Testaments of the Twelve Patriarchs" and the Greek "Life of Adam."* Studia in Veteris Testamenti Pseudepigrapha 18. Leiden: Brill, 2012.

Dimant, Devorah. "The Biography of Enoch and the Books of Enoch." *VT* 33 (1983) 16–19.

"Discovery of Earliest Illuminated Manuscript." In *The Archaeology News Network*. https://archaeologynewsnetwork.blogspot.com/2010/07/discovery-of-earliest-illuminated.html.

Dunbar, David G. "The Biblical Canon." In *Hermeneutics, Authority and Canon*, edited by D. A. Carson and John D. Woodbridge, 293–360. Leicester, UK: InterVarsity, 1986.

Dunnett, Walter M. "The Hermeneutics of Jude and 2 Peter: The Use of Ancient Jewish Traditions." *JETS* 31 (1988) 287–92.

Ellis, E. Earle. "Biblical Interpretation in the New Testament Church." In *Mikra: Text, Translation, Reading and Interpretation of the Hebrew Bible in Ancient Judaism and Early Christianity*, edited by Martin Jan Mulder, 691–725. The Literature of the Jewish People in the Period of the Second Temple and the Talmud 1. Assen: VanGorcum, 1988.

———. *The Making of the New Testament Documents*. Biblical Interpretation Series 39. Leiden: Brill, 1999.

———. *Prophecy and Hermeneutics in Christianity*. Grand Rapids: Baker, 1993.

EOTC. *The Church of Ethiopia: Past and Present*. Addis Ababa: Commercial Printing Enterprise, 1997.

———. *Ethiopian Church Treasures and Faith*. [Paris]: Archange Minotaure, 2009.

———. *The Ethiopian Orthodox Tewahədo Church Faith, Order of Worship and Ecumenical Relations*. 2nd ed. Addis Ababa: Tinsae, 1996.

Erho, Ted M. and Loren T. Stuckenbruck. "A Manuscript History of *Ethiopic Enoch*." *JSP* 23.2 (2013) 87–133.

Eshel, Hanan. "An Allusion in the Parables of Enoch to the Act of Matthias Antigonus in 40 B.C.E." In *Enoch and the Messiah Son of Man: Revisiting the Book of Parables*, edited by Gabriele Boccaccini, 487–91. Grand Rapids: Eerdmans, 2007.

Bibliography

Eshete, Tibebe. *The Evangelical Movement in Ethiopia: Resistance and Resilience.* Waco, Tex: Baylor University Press, 2009.

Evans, Craig A. "The Scriptures of Jesus and His Earliest Followers." In *The Canon Debate: On the Origins and Formation of the Bible*, edited by Lee Martin McDonald and James A. Sanders, 185–89. Peabody, MA: Hendrickson, 2002.

Finneran, Niall. "Ethiopian Evil Eye Belief and the Magical Symbolism of Iron Working." *Folklore* 114 (2003) 427–33.

Fitzmyer, Joseph A. *The Dead Sea Scrolls and Christian Origins.* Grand Rapids: Eerdmans, 2000.

Flint, Peter. "'Apocrypha,' Other Previously Unknown Writings, 'Pseudepigrapha,' in the Dead Sea Scrolls." In *The Dead Sea Scrolls after Fifty Years: A Comprehensive Assessment*, edited by Peter Flint and James C. VanderKam, 2:62–66. Leiden: Brill, 1999.

Forslund, Eskil. *The Word of God in Ethiopian Tongues: Rhetorical Features in the Preaching of the Ethiopian Evangelical Church Mekane Yesus.* Studia Missionalia Upsaliensia 57. Uppsala: International Tryck AB, 1993.

Fossum, Jarl. "Kurios Jesus as the Angel of the Lord in Jude 5–7." *NTS* 33 (1987) 226–43.

Founderbruk, G. B. "Angel." In *The Zondervan Pictorial Encyclopedia of the Bible*, edited by Merrill C. Tenney. Grand Rapids: Zondervan, 1976.

France, R. T. *Jesus and the Old Testament: His Application of Old Testament Passages to Himself and His Mission.* London: Tyndale, 1971.

Fröhlich, Ida. "Enoch and Jubilees." In *Enoch and the Messiah Son of Man: Revisiting the Book of Parables*, edited by Gabriele Boccaccini, 141–147. Grand Rapids: Eerdmans, 2005.

Gadamer, Hans Georg. *Truth and Method.* Translated by Joel Weinsheimer and Donald G. Marshall. 2nd rev. ed.. London: Continuum, 2004.

Gaster, T. H. "Angel." In *The Interpreter's Dictionary of the Bible*, edited by George Arthur Buttrick 1:128–34. New York: Abingdon, 1962.

Gebre-Amanuel, Mikre Sellassie. "የቅዱሳት መጻሕፍት ታሪክ በኢትዮጵያ፡፡" በየኢትዮጵያ ኦርቶዶክስ ተዋህዶ ቤተክርስትያን ታሪክ ከልደተ ክርስቶስ እስከ 2000 ዓ/ም፡፡ 156–73፡፡ አዲስ አበባ: የኢትዮጵያ ኦርቶዶክስ ተዋሕዶ ቤት ክርስትያን፡, 2000.

Gilkes, Patrick. *The Dying Lion: Feudalism and Modernization in Ethiopia.* London: Friedmann, 1975.

Glenny, W. Edward. "Typology: A Summary of the Present Evangelical Discussion." *JETS* 40 (1997) 627–38.

Glessmer, Uwe. "Calendars in the Qumran Scrolls." In *The Dead Sea Scrolls after Fifty Years: A Comprehensive Assessment*, edited by Peter Flint and James C. VanderKam, 2:213–78. Leiden: Brill, 1999.

Gnisci, Jacopo. "Continuity and Tradition: The Prominent role of Cyrillian Christology in Fifteenth and Sixteenth Century Ethiopia." *Polyvocia SOAS Journal of Graduate Research* 4 (2012) 20–38. http://www.soas.ac.uk/research/rsa/journalofgraduateresearch/edition-4/file75708.pdf.

Gorgorios, Abba. (አባ ጎርጎርዮስ)። የኢትዮጵያ ኦርቶዶክስ ተዋሕዶ ቤተክርስትያን ታሪክ፡፡ አዲስ አበባ፡, 1974.

Greenfield, Jonas C., and Michael E. Stone. "The Enochic Pentateuch and the Date of the Similitudes." *HTR* 70 (1977) 51–65.

Bibliography

Green, Michael. *The Second Epistle General of Peter and the General Epistle of Jude: An Introduction and Commentary.* Tyndale New Testament Commentaries. Leicester, UK: InterVarsity, 1968.

Gunther, John J. "The Alexandrian Epistle of Jude." *NTS* 30 (1984) 550.

Günther, W. "Πλνάω, Lead Astray, Deceive." In *NIDNTT*, 2:457-61. Carlisle, UK: Paternoster, 1986.

Guthrie, Donald. *New Testament Theology.* Downers Grove, IL: InterVarsity, 1981.

Haile, Getachew. *The Mariology of Emperor Zär'a Yaqob of Ethiopia: Texts and Translations.* Orientalia Christiana Analecta 242. Rome: Pontificum Institutum Studiorum Orientalium, 1992.

Hannah, Darrell. "The Book of Noah, the Death of Herod the Great, and the Date of the Parables of Enoch." In *Enoch and the Messiah Son of Man: Revisiting the Book of Parables,* edited by Gabriele Boccaccini, 469-77. Grand Rapids: Eerdmans, 2007.

Harden, John Mason. *An Introduction to Ethiopic Christian Literature.* London: SPCK, 1926.

Hegermann, H. "Δόξα, Ης, 'H," In *Exegetical Dictionary of the New Testament,* edited by Horst Balz and Gerhard Schneider, 1:344-48. Grand Rapids: Eerdmans, 1990.

Henze, Paul B. *Layers of Time: A History of Ethiopia.* London: Hurst, 2000.

Hillyer, Norman. *1 and 2 Peter, Jude.* New International Bible Commentary. Peabody, MA: Hendrickson, 1992.

Holmes, Michael William, *The Apostolic Fathers: Greek Texts and English Translations.* Grand Rapids: Baker, 1999.

Institute of Ethiopian Studies. *Ethiopian Icons: Catalogue of the Collection of the Institute of the Ethiopian Studies.* Addis Ababa: Addis Ababa University; Milan: Skira, 2000.

Isaac, Ephraim. "1 (Ethiopic Apocalypse of) Enoch: A New Translation and Introduction." In *The Old Testament Pseudepigrapha.* Vol. 1, *Apocalyptic Literature and Testaments,* edited by James H. Charlesworth, 5-89. New York: Doubleday, 1983.

———. *The Ethiopian Orthodox Täwahïdo Church.* Lawrenceville, NJ: Red Sea Press, 2012.

———. "An Obscure Component in Ethiopian Church History: An Examination of Various Theories Pertaining to the Problem of the Origin and Nature of Ethiopian Christianity." *Le Muséon* 85/1-2 (1972) 225-58.

———. "A Study of Mashafa Berhan and the Question of the Hebraic-Jewish Molding of Ethiopian Culture." PhD diss., Harvard University, 1969.

Jackson, David R. "Jubilees and Enochic Judaism." In *Enoch and the Mosaic Torah: The Evidence of Jubilees,* edited by Gabriele Boccaccini and Giovanni Ibba, 411-425. Grand Rapids: Eerdmans, 2009.

Jauss, Hans Robert. *Toward an Aesthetic of Reception.* Translated by Timothy Bahti. Minneapolis: University of Minnesota Press, 1982.

Jembere, Admasu (አድማሱ ጀምበሬ). ዝክረ ሊቃውንት፡፡ አዲስ አበባ፤ ትንሣኤ ዘጉባኤ ማተሚያ ቤት፣ 1970.

Jones, A.H.M., and Elizabeth Monroe. *A History of Ethiopia.* Oxford: Clarendon, 1955.

Kaplan, Irving et al. *Area Handbook for Ethiopia.* Washington, DC: U.S. Government Printing Office, 1971.

Kaplan, Steven. *The Monastic Holy Man and the Christianization of Early Solomonic Ethiopia.* Studien zur Kulturkunde 73. Wiesbaden: Steiner, 1984.

Kelly, J. N. D. *A Commentary on the Epistles of Peter and of Jude.* Black's New Testament Commentary. London: Adam & Charles Black, 1969.

Bibliography

Kistemaker, Simon J. *Exposition of the Epistles of Peter and of the Epistle of Jude*. New Testament Commentary. Grand Rapids: Baker, 1987.

Knibb, Michael A. "Bible Vorlage: Syriac, Hebrew, Coptic, Arabic." In *Encyclopaedia Aethiopica*, edited by Siegbert Uhlig and Alessandro Bausi, 1:565. Wiesbaden: Harrassowitz, 2003.

———. "Christian Adoption and Transmission of Jewish Pseudepigrapha: The Case of 1 Enoch." *JSJ* 32 (2001) 396–415.

———. "The Date of the Parables of Enoch: A Critical Review." *NTS* 25 (1978–79) 345–59.

———. *Essays on the Book of Enoch and Other Early Jewish Texts and Traditions*. Studia in Veteris Testamenti Pseudepigrapha 22. Leiden: Brill, 2009.

———. *The Ethiopic Book of Enoch: A New Edition in the Light of the Aramaic Dead Sea Fragments, Introduction, Translation and Commentary*. Vol. 2. Oxford: Clarendon, 1978.

———. *Translating the Bible: the Ethiopic Version of the Old Testament*. The Schweich Lectures of the British Academy 1995. Oxford: Oxford University Press, 1999.

———. "The Translation of 1 Enoch 70.1: Some Methodological Issues." In *Biblical Hebrew, Biblical Texts: Essays in Memory of Michael P. Weitzmann*, edited by Ada Rapoport-Albert and Gillian Greenberg, 340–54. JSOTSup 333. Sheffield: Sheffield, 2001.

Kraftchick, Steven J. *Jude & 2 Peter*. Abingdon New Testament Commentaries. Nashville: Abingdon, 2002.

Ladd, George Eldon. *A Theology of the New Testament*. Grand Rapids: Eerdmans, 1993.

Landon, Charles. *A Text-Critical Study of the Epistle of Jude*. JSNTSup 135. Sheffield: Sheffield Academic, 1996.

Langmuir, Elizabeth Cross, et al. *Ethiopia: The Christian Art of an African Nation*. Salem: Peabody Museum of Salem, 1978.

Larson, Erik W. "The LXX and Enoch: Influence and Interpretation in Early Jewish Literature." In *Enoch and the Messiah Son of Man: Revisiting the Book of Parables*, edited by Gabriele Boccaccini, 84–89. Grand Rapids: Eerdmans, 2005.

Lawlor, George L. *Translation and Exposition of the Epistle of Jude*. International Library of Philosophy and Theology: Biblical and Theological Studies Series. Nutely, NJ: Presbyterian and Reformed, 1972.

Lee, Ralph. "The Ethiopic 'Andəmta' Commentary on Ethiopic Enoch 2 (1 Enoch 6–9)." *Journal for the Study of the Pseudepigrapha* 23/3 (2014) 179–200.

Levine, Donald. *Greater Ethiopia*. Chicago: Chicago University Press, 1974.

Lucas, Dick, and Christopher Green. *The Message of 2 Peter and Jude: The Promise of His Coming*. BST. Leicester, UK: InterVarsity, 1995.

Lucass, Shirley. *The Concept of the Messiah in the Scriptures of Judaism and Christianity*, 144–87. Library of Second Temple Studies 78. London: T. & T. Clark, 2011.

Manton, Thomas. *Jude*. Crossway Classic Commentaries. Wheaton, IL: Crossway, 1999.

Marsh, Richard. *Black Angels: The Art and Spirituality of Ethiopia*. Oxford: Lion, 1998.

Martínez, Florentino Gracía, and Eibert J. C. Tigchelaar. *The Dead Sea Scrolls Study Edition*. 2 vols. Leiden: Brill, 1997–1998.

McDonald, Lee Martin, and James A. Sanders, eds. *The Canon Debate*. Reprint ed. Grand Rapids: Baker Academic, 2001.

Mearns, Christopher L. "Dating the Similitudes of Enoch." *NTS* 25 (1978–79) 360–69.

BIBLIOGRAPHY

Melaku, Lule. (ሉሌ መላኩ)፤ የኢትዮጵያ ኦርቶዶክስ ተዋሕዶ ቤተክርስቲያን ታሪክ። አዲስ አበባ፤ ትንሣኤ ዘጉባኤ ማተሚያ ቤት፤, 1997.
Milik, Jozéf T. *The Books of Enoch: Aramaic Fragments of Qumran Cave 4*. Oxford: Clarendon, 1976.
Moffatt, James. *The General Epistles: James, Peter, and Judas*. Moffatt New Testament Commentary. London: Hodder & Stoughton, 1928.
Moo, Douglas J. *The Epistle to the Romans*. NICNT. Grand Rapids: Eerdmans, 1996.
Mountjoy, Alan B., and Clifford Embleton. *Africa: A New Geographical Survey*. New York: Praeger, 1967.
Munro-Hay, S. C. *Ethiopia, the Unknown Land: A Cultural and Historical Guide*. New York: Tauris, 2002.
Nicholl, Colin. "Michael, The Restrainer Removed (2 Thess. 2:6-7)." *JTS* 51 (2000) 27–53.
Nickelsburg, George W. E., and James C. VanderKam. *1 Enoch: A New Translation Based on the Hermeneia Commentary*. Minneapolis: Fortress, 2004.
———. *1 Enoch 2: A Commentary on the Book of 1 Enoch Chapters 37–81*. Hermeneia. Minneapolis: Fortress, 2012.
Nickelsburg, George W. E. "The Apocalyptic Message of 1 Enoch 92–105." *CBQ* 39 (1977) 309–28.
———. "The Book of Enoch in the Theology and Practice of the Ethiopian Church." In *Proceedings of the 15th International Conference of Ethiopian Studies, Hamburg July 20–25, 2003*, edited by Siegbert Uhlig, 611–19. Wiesbaden: Harrassowitz, 2006.
———. *1 Enoch 1: A Commentary on the Book of 1 Enoch Chapters 1–36; 81–108*. Hermeneia. Minneapolis: Fortress, 2001.
———. *Jewish Literature between the Bible and the Mishnah: A Historical and Literary Introduction*, 2nd ed. Minneapolis: Fortress, 2005.
———. Review of *The Books of Enoch*, by J. T. Milik. *CBQ* 40 (1978) 411–19.
———. "Scripture in 1 Enoch and 1 Enoch as Scripture." In *Texts and Contexts: Biblical Texts in Their Textual and Situational Contexts: Essays in Honor of Lars Hartman*, edited by Tord Fornberg and David Hellholm, 335–54. Oslo: Scandinavian University Press, 1995.
O'Leary, De Lacy. *The Ethiopian Church: Historical Notes on the Church of Abyssinia*. London: SPCK, 1936.
Oleson, John Peter. "An Echo of Hesiod's *Theogony* vv. 190–192 in Jude 13." *NTS* 25 (1979) 492–503.
Olson, Daniel C. "Enoch and the Son of Man in the Epilogue of the Parables." *Journal for the Study of the Pseudepigrapha* 18 (1998) 27–38.
———. "An Overlooked Patristic Allusion to the Parables of Enoch?" In *Enoch and the Messiah Son of Man: Revisiting the Book of Parables*, edited by Gabriele Boccaccini, 492–96. Grand Rapids: Eerdmans, 2007.
Osburn, Carroll D. "1 Enoch 80:2-8 (67:5-7) and Jude 12-13." *CBQ* 47 (1985) 296–303.
———. "The Christological Use of 1 Enoch 1:9 in Jude 14, 15." *NTS* 23 (1976) 334–41.
———. "Discourse Analysis and Jewish Apocalyptic in the Epistle of Jude." In *Linguistics and New Testament Interpretation: Essays on Discourse Analysis*, edited by David Alan Black, 287–319. Nashville: Broadman, 1992.
———. "The Text of Jude 5." *Biblica* 62 (1981) 107–15.
Pankhurst, Richard. *The Ethiopians*. The Peoples of Africa. Oxford: Blackwell, 1998.
Pankhurst, Richard, and Leila Ingram. *Ethiopia Engraved: An Illustrated Catalogue of Engraving by Foreign Travellers from 1681 to 1900*. London: Kegan Paul, 1988.

Bibliography

Parris, David. *Reading the Bible with Giants: How 2000 Years of Biblical Interpretation Can Shed New Light on Old Texts*. London: Paternoster, 2006.

———. "Reception Theory: Philosophical Hermeneutics, Literary Theory, and Biblical Interpretation." PhD diss., University of Nottingham, 1999.

Pedersen, Stoffregen, and Tedros Abraham, 'Andəmta' In *Encycleopaedia Aethiopica*, edited by Siegbert Uhlig and Alessandro Bausi, 2:258. Wiesbaden: Harrassowitz, 2003.

Perkins, Pheme. *First and Second Peter, James, and Jude*. Interpretation. Louisville: John Knox, 1995.

Piovanelli, Pierluigi. "The Apocryphal Legitimization of a 'Solomonic' Dynasty in the Kebra Nagast: A Reappraisal." *Aethiopica: International Journal of Ethiopian and Eritrean Studies* 16 (2013) 7–44.

———. "A Testimony for the Kings and the Mighty Who Possess the Earth: The Thirst for Justice and Peace in the Parables of Enoch." In *Enoch and the Messiah Son of Man: Revisiting the Book of Parables*, edited by Gabriele Boccaccini, 363–79. Grand Rapids: Eerdmans, 2007.

Porter, Stanley, and Jason Robinson. *Hermeneutics: An Introduction to Interpretive Theory*. Grand Rapids: Eerdmans, 2011.

Priest, John F. "Moses, Testament of." In *ABD*, edited by David Noel Freedman, 4:920–22. New York: Doubleday, 1992.

Rad, Gerhard von. "Typological Interpretation of the Old Testament." In *A Guide to Contemporary Hermeneutics: Major Trends in Biblical Interpretation*, edited by Donald K. McKim, 28–46. Grand Rapids: Eerdmans, 1986.

Reed, Annette Yoshiko. *Fallen Angels and the History of Judaism and Christianity: The Reception of Enochic Literature*. Cambridge: Cambridge University Press, 2005.

Reicke, Bo. *The Epistles of James, Peter and Jude: Introduction. Translation and Notes*. Anchor Bible 37. Garden City, NY: Doubleday, 1964.

Rietz, Henry W. Morisada. "Synchronizing Worship: Jubilees as a Tradition for the Qumran Community." In *Enoch and the Messiah Son of Man: Revisiting the Book of Parables*, edited by Gabriele Boccaccini, 111–18. Grand Rapids: Eerdmans, 2005.

Roberts, Alexander et al, eds. *Ante-Nicene Fathers*. Volume I, *Apostolic Fathers, Justin Martyr, Irenaeus*. Oak Harbor: Logos Research Systems, 1997.

———. *Ante-Nicene Fathers*. Volume II, *Translations of the Writings of the Fathers Down to A.D. 325*. Oak Harbor, WA: Logos Research Systems, 1997.

———. *Ante-Nicene Fathers*. Volume III, *Translations of the Writings of the Fathers Down to A.D. 325*. Oak Harbor, WA: Logos Research Systems, 1997.

———. *Ante-Nicene Fathers*. Volume IV, *Translations of the Writings of the Fathers Down to A.D. 325*. Oak Harbor, WA: Logos Research Systems, 1997.

Romm, James S. *The Edges of the Earth in Ancient Thought: Geography, Exploration, and Fiction*. Princeton: Princeton University Press, 2002.

Rowston, Douglas J. "The Most Neglected Book in the New Testament." *NTS* 21 (1975) 554–63.

Ruiten, Jacques van. "A Literary Dependency of Jubilees on 1 Enoch." In *Enoch and the Messiah Son of Man: Revisiting the Book of Parables*, edited by Gabriele Boccaccini 90–93. Grand Rapids: Eerdmans, 2005.

Sacchi, Paolo. "Qumran and the Dating of the Parables of Enoch." In *The Bible and the Dead Sea Scrolls: The Princeton Symposium on the Dead Sea Scrolls*, edited by James H. Charlesworth, 377–95. Waco, TX: Baylor University Press, 2006.

Bibliography

Schaff, Philip, ed. *The Nicene and Post-Nicene Fathers*. Vol. II. Oak Harbor, WA: Logos Research Systems, 1997.

———, ed. *The Nicene and Post-Nicene Fathers*. Vol. IV. Second Series. Oak Harbor, WA: Logos Research Systems, 1997.

Schuller, Eileen. "The Dead Sea Scrolls and Canon and Canonization." In *Kanon in Konstrüktion und Dekonstruktion: Kanonisierungsprozesse Religiöser Texte von der Antike bis zur Gegenwart: Ein Handbuch*, edited by Eve-Marie Becker and Stefan Scholz, 293–314. Berlin: de Gruyter, 2012.

Scott, James. Review of Kelley Coblentz Bautch, A Study of the Geography of 1 Enoch 17–19: "No One Has Seen What I Have Seen." *Journal of Biblical Literature* 123 (2004) 752–56.

Sergew, Hable Sellassie. *The Church of Ethiopia: A Panorama of History and Spiritual Life*. Addis Ababa: B.S.P.E, 1970.

Sidebottom, E. M. *James, Jude and 2 Peter*. New Century Bible Commentary. London: Nelson, 1967.

Smith, D. Moody, Jr. "The Use of the Old Testament in the New." In *The Use of the Old Testament in the New and Other Essays: Studies in Honor of William Franklin Stinespring*, edited by J. M. Efird, 3–65. Durham, NC: Duke University Press, 1972.

Smith, Larry Douglas. "Unlocking the Structure of Jude." *The Bible Translator* 55 (2004) 138–42.

Stegemann, Hartmut. *The Library of Qumran: On the Essenes, Qumran, John the Baptist, and Jesus*. Grand Rapids: Eerdmans, 1998.

Stone, Michael E. "Enoch's Date in Limbo; or, Some Considerations on David Suter's Analysis of the Book of Parables." In *Enoch and the Messiah Son of Man: Revisiting the Book of Parables*, edited by Gabriele Boccaccini, 444–49. Grand Rapids: Eerdmans, 2007.

Stone, Michael E., and Theodore A. Bergren. *Biblical Figures outside the Bible*. A. & C. Black, 2002.

Strauss, Stephen J. "Perspectives on the Nature of Christ in the Ethiopian Orthodox Church: A Case Study in Contextualized Theology." PhD diss., Trinity International University, 1997.

Stuckenbruck, Loren T. "The 'Angels' and 'Giants' of Genesis 6:1–4 in Second and Third Century BCE Jewish Interpretation: Reflections on the Posture of Early Apocalyptic Traditions in Relation to Emerging Demonology." *Dead Sea Discoveries* 7 (2000) 354–73.

———. "Apocrypha and Pseudepigrapha." In *The Eerdmans Dictionary of Early Judaism*, edited by John J. Collins and Daniel C. Harlow, 143–62. Grand Rapids: Eerdmans, 2010.

———. "The Book of Enoch: Its Reception in Second Temple Jewish and in Christian Tradition." *Early Christianity* 4 (2013) 7–40.

———. *The Book of Giants from Qumran: Text, Translation, and Commentary*. Texte und Studien zum Antiken Judentum, 63. Tübingen: Mohr/Siebeck, 1997.

———. "The Early Traditions Related to 1 Enoch from the Dead Sea Scrolls: An Overview and Assessment." In *The Early Enoch Literature*, edited by Gabriele Boccaccini and John J. Collins, 41–63. JSJSup 121. Leiden: Brill, 2007.

———. *The Myth of Rebellious Angels: Studies in Second Temple Judaism and New Testament Texts*. Wissenschaftliche Untersuchungen zum Neuen Testament 335. Tübingen: Mohr/ Siebeck, 2014.

BIBLIOGRAPHY

———. "Revision of the Aramaic-Greek and Greek-Aramaic Glossaries of the Books of Enoch: Aramaic Fragments of Qumran Cave 4 by J. T. Milik." *JSJ* 41 (1990) 13-49.

———. Review of *The Books of Enoch* by J. T. Milik. *CBQ* 40 (1978) 411-19.

Sundberg, Albert C. "Canon of the NT." In *The Interpreter's Dictionary of the Bible, Supplementary Volume*, edited by K. Crim, 136-40. Nashville: Abingdon, 1976.

———. *The Old Testament of the Early Church*. New York: Kraus Reprint, 1969.

———. "Re-Examining the Formation of the Old Testament Canon." *Interpretation* 42 (1988) 78-82.

Suter, David W. "Enoch in the Sheol: Updating the Dating of the Book of Parables." In *Enoch and the Messiah Son of Man: Revisiting the Book of Parables*, edited by Gabriele Boccaccini, 415-43. Grand Rapids: Eerdmans, 2007.

Tamene, Getnet. "Features of the Ethiopian Orthodox Church and the Clergy." *Asian and African Studies* 7 (1998) 87-104.

Tamrat, Tadesse. *Church and State in Ethiopia 1270-1527*. Oxford: Oxford University Press, 1972.

Thiselton, Anthony C. "Reception Theory, H. R. Jauss and the Formative Power of Scripture." *Scottish Journal of Theology* 65/3 (2012) 289-308.

Tromp, Johannes. *The Assumption of Moses: A Critical Edition with Commentary*. Studia in Veteris Testamenti Pseudepigrapha 10. Leiden: Brill, 1993.

Tzadua, Paulos. *The Fetha Nagast: The Law of the Kings*. Addis Ababa: Haile Sellassie I University Press, 1968.

Uhlig, Siegbert. "Chronography." In *Encyclopaedia Aethiopica*, edited by Siegbert Uhlig and Alessandro Bausi, 1:733-37. Wiesbaden: Harrassowitz, 2003.

Ullendorff, Edward. *Ethiopia and the Bible*. The Schweich Lectures of the British Academy 1967. London: Oxford University Press, 1968.

———. *The Ethiopians: an Introduction to Country and People*. 3rd ed. Oxford: Oxford University Press, 1973.

———. "Hebraic-Jewish Elements in Abyssinian (Monophysite) Christianity." *Journal of Semitic Studies* 1 (1956) 216-56.

Ullendorff, Edward, and Michael Knibb. "Book Review of J. T. Milik (ed.): The Books of Enoch: Aramaic Fragments of Qumran Cave 4." *Bulletin of the School of Oriental and African Studies* 40 (1977) 601-2.

Ulrich, Eugene. "The Jewish Scriptures: Texts, Versions, Canons." In *The Eerdmans Dictionary of Early Judaism*, edited by John J. Collins and Daniel C. Harlow, 116-17. Grand Rapids: Eerdmans, 2010.

VanBeek, Lawerence. "Enoch among Jews and Christians: A Fringe Connection?" In *Christian-Jewish Relations through the Centuries*, edited by Stanley E. Porter and Brock W. R. Pearson, 93-115. JSNTSup 192. Sheffield: Sheffield Academic, 2000.

VanderKam, James C. "1 Enoch, Enochic Motifs, and Enoch in Early Christian Literature." In *The Jewish Apocalyptic Heritage in Early Christianity*, edited by James C. VanderKam and William Adler, 33-101. Compendia rerum Iudaicarum ad Novum Testamentum. Section 3, Jewish Traditions in Early Christian Literature 4. Assen: VanGorcum, 1996.

———. *The Book of Jubilees*. Guides to Apocrypha and Pseudepigrapha. Sheffield: Sheffield Academic, 2001.

———. *The Dead Sea Scrolls Today*. Grand Rapids: Eerdmans, 1994.

———. *Enoch: A Man for All Generations*. Studies on Personalities of the Old Testament. Columbia: University of South Carolina Press, 1995.

BIBLIOGRAPHY

———. "Identity and History of the Community." In *The Dead Sea Scrolls after Fifty Years: A Comprehensive Assessment*, edited by Peter Flint and James C. VanderKam, 2:487–533. Leiden: Brill, 1999.

———. "Response: Jubilees and Enoch." In *Enoch and the Messiah Son of Man: Revisiting the Book of Parables*, edited by Gabriele Boccaccini, 162–70. Grand Rapids: Eerdmans, 2005.

———. "Some Major Issues in the Contemporary Study of 1 Enoch: Reflections on J. T. Milik's *The Books of Enoch: Aramaic Fragments of Qumrân Cave 4*." *Maarav* (1982) 385–97.

———. "The Theophany of Enoch I 3b-7, 9." *VT* 23 (1973) 129–50.

Veitch, Sophie F. F. *Views in Central Abyssinia*. London: Hotten, 1868.

Volmer, Mueller. *The Hermeneutics Reader: Texts of the German Tradition from the Enlightenment to the Present*. New York: Continuum, 2006.

Watson, Duane F. *The New Interpreters Bible*. Vol. 12, *The Letter of Jude*. Edited by Leander E. Keck. Nashville: Abingdon, 1998.

Westphal, Merold. *Whose Community? Which Interpretation? Philosophical Hermeneutics for the Church*. Grand Rapids: Baker, 2009.

Wiersbe, Warren W. *Be Alert: 2 Peter 2 and 3 John and Jude*. Amersham-on-the-Hill, UK: Scripture Press Foundation, 1984.

Wondmagegnehu, Aymro, and Joachim Motovu. *The Ethiopian Orthodox Church*. Addis Ababa: Ethiopian Orthodox Mission, 1970.

SUBJECT INDEX

1 Enoch, ix-x, 1–2, 5–24, 30–79, 82–120
1 Enoch as Scripture, 1, 13–17, 36n71, 37, 56, 73n57, 129
2 and 3 Enoch, 66, 77n69, 119
2 Baruch, 66, 119
2 Peter, 24, 69, 122–24, 126–27, 130, 132

Abba Frumentius. See Frumentius, Abba.
Abuna Selama Kesate Berhan (Father of Peace, Revealer of Light). See Frumentius, Abba.
Adam, 20–21, 30, 36–37, 41, 76, 102
Afnin the Archangel, 100
Africanus, Julius, 75–76, 98
Aksum, Aksumite, 78–81, 82n14, 84n21
Alexandrian, 57n1, 81, 85, 88, 126
Amharic Translation. See Translation of Amharic version.
Amulets, 12, 85, 106–8, 112, 124
Angelology, 41n97, 42–43, 49, 51n151, 52, 55, 85, 100, 103–4, 107, 116,
Angel(s), 24n4, 39–55, 64, 69–75, 92–94, 97, 100–104, 112. 108–16, 118, 125
Angel Story. See Story of the Watchers.
Animal Apocalypse, the Book of, 10, 66, 102, 109
Animal vision. See *Animal Apocalypse, the Book of.*
Anointed One, the, 70

Another Book by Enoch, 15
Anti-Christian, 77, 119,
Antinomian(s), 51
Apocalypse of Peter, 9n16, 10n18
Apocalypse of Weeks, 66
Apocalyptic literature/writer/thought, 8, 24nn4, 7, 31, 38–39, 40n94, 48–50, 55, 58, 59nn15–17, 60n18, 63n6, 101, 110n53, 123, 126, 128, 130–31
Apocrypha, Apocryphal, ixn1, 10, n18, 16n47, 57, 63n4, 64n8, 68, 75–76, 99, 120, 125, 129–31
Apocryphal Acts of the Apostles, 99
Apostolic Fathers, 56–58, 71n44, 126, 129
Appropriation of 1 Enoch, 1–2, 20, 24, 32, 62, 66, 68–70, 76, 78n69, 88–113, 116, 118–21
Arabic text, 79, 81, 83, 85, 119, 127
Aramaic Levi Document, The, 66, 119
Aramaic translation. See Translation of Aramaic version.
Aramaic fragments/text, 2n1, 6–8, 13–14, 33, 34nn59–61, 35, 122, 129, 132–33
Assumption of Moses, The, 52nn154–55, 121, 131
Astronomical Book, the, 2n1, 7–8, 10, 66
Athanasius, St., 75, 81, 119
Athenagoras, 71–72, 119, 121
Augustine, St., 12n30, 67–68, 76, 119

133

Subject Index

Authority, 3n6, 18, 24, 51, 56, 58n6, 65, 66n18, 69, 77, 86, 101, 120, 124
Canonical/Scriptural, 18n53, 56, 59, 73, 76–77, 86, 119–20
Of Angels, 45
Of (1) Enoch, 11, 16, 32, 37n78, 41, 45, 56n167, 58n6, 59, 65, 73, 101
Of God, 51n146, 54, 63n4
Azazel/Azaz'el/Asael, 44n109–110, 46, 72, 90, 108

Badima Yalew, Qes, 115n7
Balaam, 27–28, 29n29, 30, 47
Barnabas, Epistle of, 58, 70–72, 102, 119
Bauckham, Richard, 23, 24n6, 25–27, 28nn23–25, 30n34, 32, 34nn58–63, 35nn64–70, 36, 37n78, 38, 39nn85–88, 40nn91, 96, 43n104, 44nn106, 111, 45n117, 46, 47n130, 48, 50–51, 52nn153–55, 53, 54nn160–63, 56n168, 57, 61n25, 69n36, 122
Beta Israel, 79, 106n39
Bible Society of Ethiopia, 83n17, 114n5
Birth of Noah, The, 15
Book of Animal Apocalypse, the. See Animal Apocalypse, the Book of.
Book of Astronomical, the,
Book of Dream Vision, The. See *Dream Vision, The Book of.*
Book of Light, the. See *Matshafe Berhan.*
Book of Luminaries, the. See Astronomical Book, the.
Book of the Mysteries of Heaven and Earth, the. See *Metshafe Mistira Semay Womeder.*
Book of Nativity, the. See *Metshafe Mi'lad.*
Book of Parables, The. See *Parables, The Book of.*
Book of Watchers, the. See *Watchers, the book of.*
Bruce, James, ix, 122

Cain, 27–28, 29n29, 30, 47, 75, 89, 96–99, 101
Calendar, 67, 100, 114–15, 125

Canon, 1–2, 5, 17–18, 56n168, 57–61, 73, 77–78, 79n4, 81, 83–84, 86, 107n42, 114, 119, 121–23, 125, 127, 130–31
Canon of Scriptures. *See* Canon.
Canonical authority/works/writing/ text/collection, 2, 17–18, 30n35, 36, 56n168, 57–61, 64, 75–76, 83–84, 87
Canonicity, 17, 18n53, 64, 76n68
Celestial beings, 51n146, 75. *See also* Heavenly Beings.
Charles, R. H., ix, 9n10, 13
Children of Cain. *See* Cain.
Children of Seth, 89, 91, 96–98
Chosen One, the, 70
Christ, 21, 39n87, 102, 105n32, 109n48, 122, 130. *See also* Jesus Christ
Christian:
Art/iconography/painting, 108–9, 127
Belief/Faith, 108
Church, 21, 124
Communities, 10, 82, 102
Discourse, 2, 72
Education, 81
Festivals/holidays, 107n42, 114
Grave, 10n18
Interest, 8
Interpretations/Interpreters/translations, 32n47, 34n59, 77
Landscape, ix
Literature/Scripture/Texts/Writings, 10n18, 16, 18, 20, 23, 60n19, 61n23, 62, 67n26, 68–69, 71, 80–81, 118, 121, 124, 126, 131
Origins, ix, 62, 125
Polemics, 71–72, 77, 119
Rejection, 119
Teaching/Theology/Thought, 14, 20, 24, 55, 98
Tradition, x, 1–2, 5, 12, 16–17, 19, 21, 24, 52, 87, 99, 101, 114, 118, 120, 130
World, 10

Subject Index

Christianity in Ethiopia, *or* Ethiopian Christianity, 5, 12, 14–15, 19–21, 78–81, 107–8, 121, 126, 131
Christianity in Ethiopia, Evangelical, 113–19
Christology, 21, 105–6, 121
Christological:
　Controversies, Debate, 12n27, 105–6
　Hermeneutic, 56n167
　Themes, 11, 24n4, 34, 37, 70
　Understanding, 41, 70
Criticism, text/textual. *See* Text/textual criticism.
Chronographia of George Syncellus, 9
Chrysostom, John, 12n30
Church Fathers, 10n18, 12n30, 13, 50, 58, 61, 63, 68, 70–77, 85, 98, 119. *See also* Influence of 1 Enoch on Apostolic and Church Fathers.
Clement of Alexandria, 32n47, 70, 73, 119
Community(ies):
　Christian, 10, 82, 87, 102
　Eschatological, 59, 60n18
　Ethiopian Christian, 8, 15, 101
　Interpretive, 6
　Jewish, 6, 62
　Qumran, 56, 61–65, 66–67, 119, 129, 132
　Recipient, 12, 29n30
　Religious, 106, 116n10
Coptic:
　Church, 81, 82n14, 84–85
　Fragments/Texts, 13, 81, 83n15–16
　Synaxarium, 99
Cyprian, 71, 73n57

Daniel, the Book of, 8, 64n10, 105,
Daughters of Cain. *See* Cain.
Day of Judgment, 41, 44nn109–10, 46
Day of the Lord, 46
Dead Sea Scrolls, ix, xv, 6, 8, 13, 50, 56n169, 65, 68n28, 123, 125, 127, 129–32. *See also* Discovery of the Dead Sea Scrolls.
Debtera/däbtära, 21, 107n41
Delgue, the. *See* Flood, the story of the.
Demonology, 68, 101, 103–4, 116, 130

Dergue, the, 114n4
Deuterocanonical, xiv, 80n4
Devil, the, 26, 43, 51n149, 52–55, 104
Dream Vision, The Book of, ix, 7–8, 15, 66n19
Didache, 79
Discovery of the Dead Sea Scrolls, ix, 6–7, 13, 65, 123, 130. *See also* Dead Sea Scrolls.

Early Christianity, 16–17, 25, 34, 61, 62n1, 63, 77, 124, 130–31
Ecclesiastical, 12, 18, 107, 115
Egypt, 12n30, 53, 71, 83n19, 84, 109n48
Elijah, 101
Emperor Haile Sellassie I. *See* Haile Sellassie I, Emperor.
Emperor Menelik I. *See* Menelik I, Emperor.
Emperor Menelik II. *See* Menelik II, Emperor.
English Translation. *See* Translation of English version.
Enoch Seminar, 16–17, 62n1, 66n18, 122
Enochic Pentateuch. *See* Pentateuch, Enochic.
EOTC, x, 1–2, 5–6, 10–11, 17–18, 20–21, 60n21, 78–86, 87–112, 113–17, 118, 121, 124, 126, 130–32
EOTC Canon. *See* Canon.
Epistle of Barnabas. *See* Barnabas, Epistle of.
Epistle, The. *See Epistle of Enoch, The*.
Epistle of Enoch, The, 7–8, 10, 15
Epistle of Jude, The. *See* Jude, the Epistle of.
Epistle to the Romans, The. *See* Romans, The Epistle to the.
Eschatological:
　Community, 59, 60n18,
　Hermeneutic, 56n167
　Hero/witness, 55, 101, 103
　Judgment, 41, 44, 68
　Orientation/perspective, 42, 59, 118
　Redeemer, 34

Subject Index

Eschatological *(continued)*:
  Role, 55n165
  Understanding, 41, 51, 65n12
Ethiopian Christianity. *See* Christianity in Ethiopia.
Ethiopian Jews. *See* Beta Israel.
Ethiopian Orthodox *Tewahǝdo* Church. *See* EOTC.
Ethiopic. *See also* Geʻez.
Ethiopic Apocalypse of Enoch. *See* 1 Enoch *and/or* Ethiopic Enoch.
Ethiopic canon, 18, 83n20
Ethiopic Church, 84n22. *See also* EOTC.
Ethiopic Didascalia. *See* Didache.
Ethiopic Enoch, 88-99, 122, 124, 127. *See also* 1 Enoch.
Ethiopic manuscripts, 11, 14, 79
Ethiopic version, ixn1, 7-8, 10, 13-14, 18, 32-35, 79, 123, 127. *See also* Geʻez version
Extra-biblical. *See* "Extra-canonical."
"Extra-canonical," xv, 24, 61
Evangelical Christianity in Ethiopia. *See* Christianity in Ethiopia, Evangelical.
Evil Spirits, 20, 21n9, 98, 107, 109, 117. *See also* Satan.
Ezana, King, 80-81

Falasha. *See* Beta Israel.
Fallen Angels, the, 10n19, 13n34, 20, 27, 30, 42-43, 45n112, 46-49, 71-73, 76n67, 78nn70-71, 102, 117, 119, 130. *See also* Evil Spirits.
False Christ, 101
False Teacher(s), 25, 27, 32, 34-36, 38-39, 41, 43, 45, 47-48, 51, 54, 58
Festal Letter, 75
Fetḥa Nagast, 83
First Bishop of the EOTC, 10, 80-81. *See also* Frumentius, Abba
Flood, the story of the, 69, 72-73, 75, 102
Frumentius, Abba, *also known as* Abuna Selama Kesate Berhan (Father of Peace, Revealer of Light), 10, 80-81

Gabriel, 100n16, 101n16, 104, 109
Gadamer, Hans-Georg, 1-5, 126
Gadamer's hermeneutics. *See* Gadamar, Hans-Georg.
Gebre-Amanuel, Mikre Sellassie. *See* Mikre Sellassie Gebre-Amanuel.
Gebre-Ewostateos, Qes, 115n7
Geʻez, ix, 6, 10, 11n22, 14n38, 18n53, 21, 79-84, 86, 89, 115, 120
Geʻez version, ix, 2n1, 7, 10, 11n22, 14n38, 79-84, 86. *See also* Ethiopic version.
Genesis Apocryphon, 66, 119
German Translation. *See* Translation of German version.
Gnostic, 50, 77n69
God, v, xi, 29n30, 33n55, 36, 37n78, 38-39, 45, 51, 53, 55n166, 72, 75, 89-92, 95, 98, 103, 114n3,
Gospel of Peter, 9n16, 10n18
Gudina Tumsa, v

Haile Sellassie I, Emperor, 114
Hans-Georg Gadamer. *See* Gadamer, Hans-Georg.
Hans Robert Jauss. *See* Jauss, Hans Robert.
Heavenly:
  Army, 52
  Beings, 49n138, 50, 51n146
  Bodies, 47n128, 48
  Books, 30-31, 38
  Deeds, 89, 97
  Home, 48
  Honor, 89, 91
  Kingdom, 96
  Power, 45
  Prestige, 44
  Realm, 50
  Tablets, 38
  Tour, 38
  Watchers, 91
  Wisdom, 59
Hebrew Bible, 58, 60, 79, 124

Subject Index

Hermeneutic(s), 2–5, 15, 24n4, 25n12, 27nn20–22, 28n23, 29nn31–32, 30, 56n167, 58, 89, 123–24, 129, 132
Historical interpretations. *See* Interpretation(s), Historical.
Holy:
  Angels, 40, 49, 101, 104, 118
  Book, 103
  Church, 83
  Cross, 114
  Eternal place, 44n109–110
  Heaven, 46n120
  Men, 98, 111n57, 126
  Mount/Mountain, 91, 96–98
  Ones (as angels), 31, 33n52, 42, 52
  Spirit, 29n29, 72–73, 94, 96–97
  Trinity, 105
  Words, 95
Horizon(s), fusion of, 3–5
Hymnology/Music, Ethiopia cultural musical instrument 21, 107, 110–12

Iconography, 108–10, 112
Image(s)/Imagery, 32, 40, 42, 47–48, 64, 106–7, 109–10
Impact of 1 Enoch on Ethiopian Christianity, 1, 14, 87–112, 113–20
Influence. *See* Significance and/or influence.
Influence of 1 Enoch on Ethiopian Evangelical Christians, 113–17
Influence of 1 Enoch on Apostolic and Church Fathers, 70–77
Influence of 1 Enoch on early Jewish and Christian literature, 62–86
Influence of 1 Enoch on Jude, 22–23, 38–56, 118–20
Influence of 1 Enoch on Judaism, 63–68, 118–20
Influence of 1 Enoch on the New Testament, 1, 16, 51, 56, 62, 68–70, 85
Interpretation(s), 2–4, 25n13, 26–28, 29n31, 34n59, 35, 39, 47, 50, 51n146, 52n154, 53, 77, 85, 87–88, 122, 128, 131–32:
  Act of, 2, 59–60, 87

  Biblical, 25n8, 85n26, 88n4–7, 123–24, 129
  Ethiopian, 111–12
  Expository, 30
  Historical, 1–5, 14, 16–17
  Jewish 130
  Literal, 45n114
  Midrashic, 54
  Process of, 4
  Theological, 16
  Traditional, 85n26–25, 124
  Typological, 28, 49, 129
  Validity of, 2, 4
Interpreter(s), 2–3, 32n47, 58, 77n69, 118
Interpretive:
  Activity, 24
  Communities, 6
  History, 75
  Impacts, 1
  Method, 85
  Paradigm, 76
  Renderings, 25n8
  Theory 129
  Traditions, 5, 85, 98
  Strategies 24
Irenaeus, 71–73, 119, 129
Isaac, Ephraim, 7n5, 9, 10n17, 14, 15n41, 19–22, 68, 112n52, 123, 126
Isidore of Pelusium. *See* Pelusium, Isidore of.
Israel, 27–28, 29n29, 30, 43, 55n165, 79, 111

James Bruce. *See* Bruce, James.
James, the Epistle of, 36nn72, 74, 51n146
Jauss, Hans Robert, 2–5, 132
Jerome, 76n68
Jesus, Jesus Christ, xiii, 24n4, 28n24, 29n29, 34, 39, 41, 57n4, 70, 99, 105, 122, 125, 130
Jewish Enoch. *See* 2 and 3 Enoch.
Johannine Epistles. *See* John, Epistles of.
John, Epistles of, 37n80
John the Baptist, 130

Subject Index

Josephus, 66, 119, 121
Jubilees, Book of, 64, 65n13, 66–67, 79n4, 119, 122, 125–26, 129–32
Jude, the Epistle of, 24n7, 25n13, 26n15, 27nn19–20, 28n23, 30n34, 36n72, 51n148, 52nn154–55, 56n167, 57n1, 73, 76,
Judeo-Christian church/religion/scripture, 20–21, 79
Judgment, 24, 27–28, 30–31, 33n52, 36, 38, 40–41, 43–46, 48–49, 54, 59, 65, 68, 98, 102
Judith, Queen. *See* Queen Judith.
Julius Africanus. *See* Africanus, Julius.
Justin Martyr, 70–72, 119, 129

Kebre Negest/Kebra Nagast/Kebrä Nägäst, 20n6, 112n52, 129
King Ezana. *See* Ezana, King.
King Solomon. *See* Solomon, King.
King Wazeba. *See* Wazeba, King.
Kirubel, 100
Knibb, Michael A., 7–8, 9n10, 10nn19–21, 11, 12n27, 13n32, 14, 32n51, 33n53, 35, 44n110, 65nn13–14, 83nn15–16, 122, 127, 131
Knibb's translation of Enoch, 44n110
Korah, 27–28, 29n29, 30, 47

Latin version of 1 Enoch, 13, 32
Laurence, Richard, ix
Law, 51, 54, 83, 89, 96, 131
Literary:
 Appropriation, 20, 87–112
 Context, 52
 Dependency, 66n19, 129
 Device, 29–30, 35
 Evidence, 65n13
 Hermeneutics, 2
 History, 4, 15, 82, 108
 Production, 84
 Reception and influence of Enoch, 99, 112
 Renaissance, 82
 Structure, 1
 Style/strategy/structure of Jude, 23–25, 28, 30, 35, 57, 123
 Theory, 4–5, 129

Work, 4, 112n52, 115
Liturgy, Ethiopian, 21, 99, 107n41, 114
Lord, 29n29, 36, 39, 41, 46–48, 52–53, 54, 89, 94–95, 125. *See also* Jesus, Jesus Christ.
Lord of spirits. *See* Lord.
Lucius Aurelius Commodus, 72
Luminaries, the Book of. See Astronomical Book, the.
LXX. *See* Septuagint.

Magic, Magical, 12, 71–72, 75, 106–7, 108n45, 116, 125
Manicheans, 76n68
Manuscript(s), xi-x, 6–8, 9–15, 17, 63n14, 65, 79–80, 88n4, 124
Marcus Aurelius Anoninus, 72
Mariology, 12n27, 21, 104n29, 126
Mary, 21, 99, 108n45, 109. *See also* Mariology.
Masoretic text. *See* MT.
Master. *See* Jesus, Jesus Christ.
Meaning(s) of the text, 2, 4, 45, 47n127, 50, 74, 86, 89, 96–97, 119
Matshafe Berhan (the *Book of Light*), መጽሐፈ ብርሃን, 11, 21n10
Menelik I, Emperor, 79n2, 88n3
Menelik II, Emperor, 114
Messiah, 9n10, 16n46, 39, 68, 70, 121, 127
Metshafe Mi'lad (the *Book of Nativity*), መጽሐፈ ምዕላድ, 11, 105
Metshafe Mistira Semay Womeder (the *Book of the Mysteries of Heaven and Earth*), መጽሐፈ ምስጢር ሰማይ ወምድር, 11,
Miaphysite Christology/Theology, 82n13, 105n34, 106
Michael (the archangel), 26, 29n29, 30, 39, 40, 42–43, 46, 49, 52–55, 100n16, 101n16, 104, 109, 128
Midrash, Midrashic, Midrashim, 24–26, 27n17, 29, 32, 37, 43, 54, 85
Milik, J. T., ix, 7, 9n10, 11n23, 14, 35n69, 128, 131–32
Miracle of Mary, (Tea'mere Mariam), 108n45

138

Subject Index

MT, 83, 85, 119
Mikre Sellassie Gebre-Amanuel, 80n5, 83
Mosaic Law/Torah, Tradition, 54, 59n16, 66, 122, 126
Moses, 30-31, 51-55, 59, 66n18, 74
Moses, Assumption of. See *Assumption of Moses.*
Moses, Testament of. See *Testament of Moses.*
Mountain of righteousness, 89, 96-97
New Testament, ix, 1-2, 11, 14-17, 19-21, 23, 30, 37, 27nn21-22, 28, 31, 36-38, 41, 45n115, 51, 57, 60n19, 61-62, 68-71, 95, 99, 105, 109, 118-19

Nickelsburg, George W.E., 7nn1, 5, 9, 10n19, 13, 14n37, 15, 19, 39n89, 41, 58-59, 60n18, 63, 64n7, 65, 66n16, 67n22, 71n45, 72n49, 73nn54, 57, 74, 75nn63-64, 76n68, 104n30, 105, 106 n36, 110, 111nn54, 58, 128,
Nine Saints, the, 10, 78-79, 81
Non-canonical, 23, 30n35, 61
NT. See New Testament.

Old Testament/OT, 1, 12, 17, 26, 27n18, 28, 30-32, 36-37, 43-44, 49n138, 50, 61, 64n10, 76n67, 77-78, 88n3, 95, 109, 119, 122-31
Old Testament Canon. See Canon.
Old Testament Pseudepigrapha. See Pseudepigrapha.
Origen, 16, 70, 74, 119
Origin of, Original Sin, 20-21, 77n69, 116n9,
Origins, Christian. See Christian Origins.
OT. See Old Testament.

Parables of Enoch, The. See *Parables, The Book of.*
Parables, The. See *Parables, The Book of.*
Parables, The Book of, ix, 7-9, 15, 37n77, 70, 105, 121-32

Parousia/Christ's second coming, 34, 44, 52, 119
Patriarch, Patriarchate, 81, 82n14
Patriarch(s), the, 37n78, 55n166, 67n26, 73-74, 103, 124
Pelusium, Isidore of, 12n30
Pentateuch, Enochic, 9n10, 14n37, 125
Pentateuch, Pentateuchal, 8, 79
Philo, 66, 119
Pre-Christian tradition, 79,
Preservation of the text of 1 Enoch, ix-x, 2, 8-11, 13-14, 17, 37n77, 63, 73, 76, 77n69, 80, 112, 118
Primitive Christianity. See Early Christianity.
Principalities ... Powers, 45n115, 69
Prophecy(ies), 25n12, 26-28, 29n31-32, 32, 36-38, 43-44, 56, 58n6, 61n25, 63n4, 73, 101-2, 124
Prophets, Books of, 64, 72, 74, 119
Protestant, x, 17, 113-14
Protocanonical. See Biblical.
Pseudepigrapha/Pseudepigraphal/ Pseudepigraphical, 1, 12-14, 16n47, 56n167, 57, 70n41, 75, 82, 85-86, 115, 120-28, 130-31
Pseudo-Eupolemos, 66, 119

Queen Judith, 82 n14
Queen of Sheba, 79
Qumran:
(as place/venue), 7-8, 17n47, 30, 53n165, 63-65, 67, 128, 130
Community, 6-9, 36n74, 56, 61-65, 66-67, 119, 129, 132
Fragments/literature/manuscripts/ text, 6-9, 17n47, 27n21, 32n51, 54n160, 66n16, 123, 125, 129-30-31

Raguel, 100
Raphael. See Rufael.
Rebellious Angels, the, 28, 29n29, 130
Reception and appropriation of 1 Enoch. See Reception and Transmission of Scriptures in the EOTC.

Subject Index

Reception and Transmission of Scriptures in the EOTC, 1–2, 5, 24, 30, 66, 68, 69n38, 70, 77, 78–86, 87, 98–112, 118–20, 129–30
Reception History Approach, 2–5, 24, 126, 129, 131
Reception of Scriptures. *See* Reception and Transmission of Scriptures in the EOTC.
R. H. Charles, *See* Charles, R. H.
Richard Bauckham. *See* Bauckham, Richard.
Richard Laurence. *See* Laurence, Richard.
Romans, The Epistle to the, 37n79, 60n21
Rufael, Raphael, 100n16, 104

Satan, 20, 53, 55, nn165–66, 72. *See also* Evil Spirits.
Second Temple Period, ix, 16, 42, 49–51, 65, 70n41, 77n69, 119
Second Temple Period Judaism, 37n78
Second Temple period Literature, 16, 23, 24, 27n18, 45, 49–50, 53, 62, 65, 70, 119
Sénkéssar, 87, 99–103, 123
Septuagint, 8, 50n142, 61, 66n17, 82–83, 85, 119, 121, 127
Septuagint translation. *See* Translation of Ge'ez version.
Shemihaza, 108
Significance and/or influence:
 Christological, 34
 Of 1 Enoch, x, 2, 5, 7–8, 10–11, 16, 19, 38, 43, 55. 65, 67, 118,
 Of the EOTC, 2, 17
 Of tradition, 2, 103
 Theological, 1, 104
Similitudes of Enoch, The. See *Parables, The Book of*.
Sin, 20–21, 28, 39, 43, 72, 77, 90, 116. *See also* Origin of, Original Sin.
Sirach, Book of, 59
Slander/Slandering/Slanderous, 42n103, 51, 53–54, 122
Slavonic Enoch. *See* 2 and 3 Enoch.

Sodom and Gomorrah, 27–28, 29n29, 30
Sodomites, 43
Solomon, King, 79
Son of God, 70
"Sons of God, " 75–78, 98
Sons of heaven *as the Watchers*, 75
Son of Man, 11n22, 68, 70, 105, 121–32
St. Athanasius. *See* Athanasius, St.
St. Augustine. *See* Augustine, St.
St. Frumentius. *See* Frumentius, Abba.
St. Yared. *See* Yared, St.
STL. *See* Second Temple period Literature.
Story of the Flood, the. *See* Flood, the story of the.
Story of the Watchers, 16, 43, 64, 66n16, 67–69, 71–73, 75–76, 77n69, 111. *See also* Watchers, The.
Stuckenbruck, Loren T., ix–xi, 11n22, 16–17, 56n169, 124, 130
Surafel, 100
Synaxarium, Ethiopian. *See* Sénkéssar.
Syriac excerpt/text/fragment, 13, 79, 82, 83nn15–16, 85, 119

Tabot (the Ark of the Covenant), 21, 101n16, 104
Tanakh, 59, 65
Targum Pseudo-Jonathan, 66n16, 67
Tatian, 71
Tea'mere Mariam (the Miracle of Mary). *See* Miracle of Mary, the.
Tertullian of Carthage, 32n47, 58n9, 70, 73, 76, 119
Testament of Moses, 40n90, 52–53, 55, 129
Testament of Naphtali, 66n16, 67
Testament of Reuben, 66n16, 67
Testament of the Twelve Patriarchs, 55n166, 67n26, 124
Text/textual criticism, 7n5, 10, 15
The Book of Enoch. *See* 1 Enoch and/or Ethiopic Enoch.
The Book of Dream Vision. *See* Dream Vision, The Book of.

Subject Index

The Book of Parables. See *Parables, The Book of.*
The Book of Watchers. See *Watchers, the book of.*
Theophany/Theophanic expression, appearance, language, 30-31, 33nn53-54, 34, 41-42, 51, 118, 132
The Parables of Enoch. See *Parables, The Book of.*
The Parables. See *Parables, The Book of.*
Torah, 55, 59, 64, 119, 122, 129
Traditional beliefs. *See* Traditional religion.
Traditional religion, 12, 115, 117
Tradition(s):
Andəmta Commentary, 21, 85-86, 89
Apocalyptic, 131
Apocryphal, 100
Biblical, 24n6, 28n28, 30, 55, 58, 65n13, 86, 89n3, 132
Christian, x, 1-2, 4, 12, 16-17, 21, 24, 37n77, 88, 100, 102, 117, 119, 121, 131
Church, 100, 110, 126
Enochic, x, 1, 13, 46, 55, 65, 66n18, 67, 78n69, 109, 112, 116, 119, 128, 131
EOTC, x, 2, 18, 20-21, 80, 83-84, 86, 88, 105, 108, 110n48, 112-13, 115-16, 117n10
Ethiopian, 2, 19-21, 80, 84, 88, 107, 109n45, 110n48, 111, 113n52, 117n10
Evangelical, 114-16
Interpretive, 2-4, 86, 89n2-4, 59, 89, 99-100, 124-25
Jewish, ix-x, 27n18, 28, 30, 41-42, 45n112, 53, 65n13, 66n17, 70, 78n69, 125, 130, 132
Mosaic, 66
Nature and definition of, 2-3, 59
Oral, 27, 89
Religious, 12, 14, 19-21, 116
Translation of:
1 Enoch, 7n5, 8-11
Amharic version, 18n53, 83, 88

Arabic version, 83
Aramaic version, 6, 8n6, 33, 35
Dead Sea Scrolls, 8n6
English version, 14-15, 19n2, 32n51, 44n108, 88-98, 126
Geʽez version, ix, 10-12, 14, 19n2, 32n51, 33, 78-85, 119
German version, 14n38
Greek version, 8, 33, 35, 63n4, 119
Hebrew version, 79, 119
Latin version, 13,
Scriptures, 8, 10, 18, 78-85, 114
Scriptures into Ethiopic. *See* translation of Geʽez version.
Scriptures into modern languages, 14n38, 18, 79
The Bible *see* Translation of Scriptures
Transmission of 1 Enoch, x, 1-2, 5, 6-18, 78-86, 119
Transmission of Scriptures. See Reception and Transmission of Scriptures in the EOTC.
Throne of God, 50, 55, 94-95, 98, 100
Type(s)/Antitype/Typology, 26-31, 39, 43-45, 47, 54, 70, 125

Unfallen Angels, 42, 49-56, 118. *See also* Holy Angels.
Ungodly, 26, 28, 30n35, 31, 38, 40-41
Uriel, 100n16, 104

VanderKam, James C., 9, 14n37, 15-16, 33n53-54, 58nn6-8, 63nn2, 5, 66n19, 67n20, 68-69, 71nn43, 46, 72n53, 74n60, 105, 106n36, 125, 128, 131-32
Virgin Mary. *See* Mary.

Watchers, The, 17, 23, 39, 44-45, 47-48, 51, 66-67, 69, 72-73, 75-76, 92, 99, 103, 109, 112, 117, 119. *See also* Fallen Angels, the, *and* Rebellious Angels, the.
Watchers, the book of, 7-9, 13, 15, 37n77, 66n16, 69, 111
Wazeba, King, 80n9

Subject Index

Western church/culture/ideology/thought, x, 15, 20, 60, 77, 105, 108, 114
Wisdom of Jesus Ben Sira, 66, 119
Wisdom of Solomon, 66, 119
Wisdom Literature, 30n35, 31
Woman, women, daughter(s), 39, 67n24, 71–75, 89–90, 96–98, 116n11

Yared, St./Yaredic, 21, 111, 112n50

Zar'a Ya'qob/Zer'a Yacob, Emperor/King, 12n27, 105n34

AUTHOR INDEX

Aalen, S., 50n140–41
አባ ጎርጎርዮስ. See Gorgorios, Abba.
Abba Gorgorios. See Gorgorios, Abba.
Abraham, Tedros, 88n6
Achtemeier, Paul J., 121
Adler, William, 57n2, 69n33, 71n43, 121, 131
አድማሱ ጀምበሬ. See Jembere, Admasu.
Admasu Jembere. See Jembere, Admasu.
Albert, Ada Rapoport-, 127
Anderson, Cory D., 23, 56n167
Andersen, H. G., 52n154
Angold, Michael, 124
Appleyard, David, 107n41
Arcari, Luca, 9n10
Asale, Bruk A., x, 78n1, 83nn17&20, 115n6
Asres, Reda, 112n50
Athenagoras of Athens, 72
Ayenew, Hailemariam Melese, 105n32, 106n37
Aymro Wondmagegnehu. See Wondmagegnehu, Aymro.

Bakke, Johnny, 115n7
Bampfylde, Gillian, 9n10
Balz, Horst, 126
Bar-Asher, M., 123
Barclay, William, 51n148, 54n162
Barnet, Albert E., 54n162
Barr, James, 8

Bauckham, Richard, 23–28, 30, 32, 34–40, 43–48, 50–54, 56–57, 61, 69
Bausi, Alessandro, 99nn11–12, 127, 129, 131
Bautch, Kelley Coblentz, 110nn52–53, 111n56, 123, 130
Becker, Eve-Marie, 130
Beckwith, Roger, 17
Benton, John, 42n103
Berger, Klaus, 11n23
Bergren, Theodore A., 101n19
Bietenhard, H., 49n138
Bigg, Charles, 58n8
Black, David Alan, 128
Black, Matthew, 7n5, 8n9, 9n10, 10n18, 32n51, 33n53, 34n56
Blum, Edwin, 24n5, 36n73, 46n121, 51n146
Boccaccini, Gabriele, ixn2, 9n10, 16n46, 66n18, 121–32
Bratcher, Robert G., 51n146
Brooke, George J., 110n53
Brown, Colin, 122
Bruk Ayele A. See Asale, Bruk A.
Bruyn, Theodore de, 12nn28–30
Budge, E. A., 100nn13–15, 101nn17–18, 102nn20–23, 103n24
Buttrick, George Arthur, 122, 125

Carson, D. A., 37n80, 124
Cedar, Paul A., 51n146
Charles, J. Daryl., 24n4, 25n11, 28nn27–28, 30nn35–36, 31n43, 32n46, 41n99, 55nn164–65

Author Index

Charles, R. H., ixn3, 9n10, 13nn35–36, 68n30, 74n60
Charlesworth, James H., xn5, 9n10, 14n37, 62n1, 64n11, 126, 129
Clark, David J., 25n13
Colin, Gérard, 99nn11–12
Collins, John J., 63nn5–6, 130–31
Cowley, Roger, 18n53, 85nn26–27, 88nn2–5, 7
Crim, K., 11
Cross, F. L., 79n4
Crummey, Donald, 84n24

Dalton, William Joseph, 70n39
Dimant, Devorah, 14n37, 123
Dunbar, David G., 61n24
Dunnett, Walter M., 24n4, 58n7

Efird, J. M., 130
Embleton, Clifford, 111n54
Ellis, E. Earle, 24n8, 25nn9–13, 27nn20–22, 28n23, 29nn31–32
EOTC, 1–2, 5–6, 10–11, 17–18n53–54, 20–21n9, 60n21, 78, 79n4, 80n60, 81n11, 82n13, 83n17, 85, 87, 99, 100–101n16, 103nn25–26, 104n28, 105n32, 106nn37, 39, 107n42, 111, 113–17, 118–19
Erho, Ted M., ixn2
Eshel, Hanan, 9n10
Eshete, Tibebe, 113n1
Evans, Craig A., 57n4

Filho, Orlando Iannuzzi, 123
Finneran, Niall, 107n42, 108n44
Fitzmyer, Joseph A., 63n2
Flint, Peter, 63n4, 125, 132
Fornberg, Tord, 128
Forslund, Eskil, 114n3, 115n8, 116n9
Fossum, Jarl, 24n4
Founderbruk, G. B., 49n138
France, R. T., 28n24
Fransis, Charles, 122
Freedman, David Noel, 122, 129
Fröhlich, Ida, 66n17

Gadamer, Hans Georg, 2, 3n5–7, 10, 4n13, 5

Gaster, T. H., 49n138
Gebre-Amanuel, Mikre Sellassie, 80n5, 83n18
Getnet Tamene *see* Tamene, Getnet
Gilkes, Patrick, 84n23
Glenny, W. Edward, 31n45
Glessmer, Uwe, 67n21
Gnisci, Jacopo, 12n27
Gorgorios, Abba, 84n22, 107n42
Greenberg, Gillian, 127
Greenfield, Jonas C., 9n10, 14n37
Green, Michael, 28n26, 45n113, 46n122, 47n130, 48n131, 53nn158–60
Green, Christopher, 51n146, 152, 52n155
Gunther, John J., 57n1
Günther, W., 47n127
Guthrie, Donald, 36n71

Hable Sellassie, Sergew. *See* Sergew, Hable Sellassie.
Haile, Getachew, 104n29
Hailemariam Melese Ayenew (Abba). *See* Ayenew, Hailemariam Melese.
Hannah, Darrell, 9n10
Harden, John Mason, 112n51
Harlow, Daniel C., 130–31
Hartman, Lars, 128
Hegermann, H., 50nn139, 142
Hellholm, David, 128
Henze, Paul B, 80nn8–9
Hillyer, Norman, 50n140, 53nn158–59, 54n162
Holmes, Michael William, 71n44

Institute of Ethiopian Studies, 109n49
Ibba, Giovanni, 122, 126
Ingram, Leila, 111nn54, 57
Isaac, Ephraim, 7n5, 9n14, 14nn39–40, 15n41, 19nn1–2, 20nn4–8, 21n10, 68n31, 112n52, 123

Jackson, David R., 67n23
Jauss, Hans Robert, 2, 4n18, 5n19, 131
Jembere, Admasu, 105n32
Jones, A.H.M, 84n24
Jonge, Marinus de, 12, 13n31

Author Index

Kaplan, Irving, 111n54
Kaplan, Steven, 111n57
Kelly, J.nD., 35n68, 38n83, 39n87, 44n107, 45n115, 46n122, 48nn132, 134, 50n145, 54n162
Kistemaker, Simon J., 44n107, 45nn116, 119
Knibb, Michael A., 7nn3-5, 8n8, 9n10, 10nn19-21, 11nn22-26, 12n27, 13n32, 14, 32n51, 33n53, 35n65, 44n110, 65nn13-14, 83nn15-16, 122, 131
Kraftchick, Steven J., 29n30
Kraus, Thomas J., 124
Ladd, George Eldon, 36n71, 37n79
Landon, Charles, 29n33
Langmuir, Elizabeth Cross, 108n46, 109n46
Larson, Erik W., 66n17
Lawlor, George L., 36n72
Lee, Ralph, 88n1, 98n10
Levine, Donald, 106nn38-40
Lindars, B., 122
Livingstone, E.A., 79n4
Lucas, Dick, 51nn146, 152, 52n155
Lucass, Shirley, 70nn40-41,
ሉሌ መላኩ. *See* Melaku, Lule.
Lule Melaku. *See* Melaku, Lule.
Manton, Thomas, 45n114, 47n126
Marshall, Donald G., 125
Marsh, Richard, 110n50
Martínez, Florentino Gracía, 8n6
McDonald, Lee Martin, 17n52, 60-61n22, 121, 125
McKim, Donald K., 129
Mearns, Christopher L., 8n10
Melaku, Lule, 84n22, 105n32
Mikre Sellassie Gebre-Amanuel. *See* Gebre-Amanuel, Mikre Sellassie.
Milik, Józef T., ixn4, 7nn2-5, 9n10, 14n37, 35n69, 128, 131-32
Moffatt, James, 47n130
Monroe, Elizabeth, 84n24
Moo, Douglas J., 37n79, 47n130, 48n137, 54n162, 60n21
Motovu, Joachim, 18n54, 21n9, 103n26, 104n27, 31
Moule, Digby, 122

Mountjoy, Alan B., 111n54
Mulder, Martin Jan, 124
Munro-Hay, S. C., 84n21

Nicholl, Colin, 55n165
Nickelsburg, George W. E., 7nn1, 5, 9nn10-16, 10n19, 13n33, 14n37, 15nn42-44, 19nn2-3, 39n89, 41n99, 58nn8-11, 59nn12-17, 60n18, 63, 64n7, 65n12, 66n16, 67n22, 71n45, 72n49, 73nn54, 57, 74n61, 75nn63-64, 76n68, 104n30, 105-5nn33-36, 110, 111nn54, 58
Nicklas, Tobias, 124

O'Leary, De Lacy, 84n22
Oleson, John Peter, 40n94
Olson, Daniel C., 9n10, 11n22
Osburn, Carroll D., 24nn4, 7, 32n50, 33n54, 34nn56, 60-61, 40nn94-95, 41n98

Pankhurst, Richard, 81nn10, 12, 84n25, 111nn54, 57
Parris, David, 2n2, 3n4
Paulos Tzadua. *See* Tzadua, Paulos.
Pearson, Brock W. R., 131
Pedersen, Stoffregen, 88n6
Perkins, Pheme, 47n130
Piovanelli, Pierluigi, 9n10, 112n52
Porter, Stanley, 3nn6-12, 4nn14-15, 131
Priest, John F., 52n154

Rad, Gerhard von, 28n24, 49n138
ረዳ አስረስ, Reda Asres. *See* Asres, Reda.
Reed, Annette Yoshiko, 10n19, 13n34, 76n67, 77nn70-71,
Reicke, Bo, 36n74, 40n92, 51n146
Rietz, Henry W. Morisada, 65n13
Roberts, Alexander, 71n47, 72nn50-52, 73nn55-58, 74nn59, 62
Robinson, Jason, 3nn6-12, 4nn14-15, 131
Romm, James S., 110n53
Rowston, Douglas J., 23n3, 56n168, 61n25

Author Index

Ruiten, Jacques van, 66n19

Sacchi, Paolo, 9n10, 76n66–67
Sanders, James A., 17, 60–61n22, 121, 125
Schaff, Philip, 75n65, 76nn66–67
Schneider, Gerhard, 126
Schuller, Eileen, 68n28
Smalley, S.S., 122
Scholz, Stefan, 130
Scott, James, 110n53
Sergew, Hable Sellassie, 18n54
Sidebottom, E. M., 47n130, 53nn158–59
Smith, D. Moody, Jr, 61n23
Smith, Larry Douglas, 25n13
Stegemann, Hartmut, 64n11, 65n12
Stone, Michael E., 9nn10–11, 14n37, 101n19, 125
Strauss, Stephen J., 105n32
Stuckenbruck, Loren T., vii, ixn2, x–xi, 11n22, 16n47, 56n169
Sundberg, Albert C., 17n50
Suter, David, 9n11, 130

Tadesse Tamrat. *See* Tamrat, Tadesse.
Tamene, Getnet, 107n41
Tamrat, Tadesse, 84n23
Tenney, Merrill C., 125
Thiselton, Anthony C., 4nn16–17
Tibebe Eshete. *See* Eshete, Tibebe.
Tigchelaar, Eibert J. C., 8n6

Tov, Emmanuel, 123
Tromp, Johannes, 52n154
Tzadua, Paulos, 83n19

Uhlig, Siegbert, 14n38, 123, 127–29
Ullendorff, Edward, 7n3, 10n19, 11n24, 21n11, 34n61, 108n45, 111n55
Ulrich, Eugene, 64nn9–10

VanBeek, Lawerence, 58nn8–9, 63n3, 65n15, 66n16, 67nn25, 27, 68n29, 69nn34–37, 70n42, 71n43
VanderKam, James C., 9n12, 14n37, 15nn42–43, 16n45, 33nn53–54, 58n6, 8, 63nn2, 5, 66n19, 67 n, 20, 68n32, 69n36, 71nn43, 46, 72n53, 74n60, 105–6nn33–36, 125, 128, 132
Veitch, Sophie F. F., 111n54
Volmer, Mueller, 2n3

Watson, Duane F., 36n76, 44n107, 51n148, 54n163
Weinsheimer, Joel, 125
Weitzmann, Michael P. 127
Westphal, Merold, 3n9
Wiersbe, Warren W., 51n146
Williamson, W. G. M., 123
Wondmagegnehu, Aymro, 18n54, 21n9, 103n26, 104n27, 31
Woodbridge, John D., 124

SCRIPTURE INDEX

Old Testament/Hebrew Bible

Genesis
4:8	27
5:24	37n78
6:1–4	16n47, 76–7
19	27

Exodus
24:16–7	50
25:11	50
32:32–33	31n44
33:18–23	50

Numbers
14	27
16	27
22:1—31:16	27

Deuteronomy
10:18	31n40
17:6	28n28
19:15	28n28
33:1–29	31
33:2–4	51
33:2	31n38–9
34:5–6	52

Judges
5:4	31n38

Psalm(s)
18:9	31n38
19:1	50
40:4	31n44
46:8–9	31n41
56:8	31n44
68:17	31n39
69:29	31n43
76:3–6	31n41
76:9	31n40
96:13	31n40
139:16	31n44

Proverbs
25:14	54n160

Isaiah
4:3	31n44
19:1	31n38
19:3	31n41
26:21	31n38
27:1	31n41
31:4	31n38
31:27	31n38
33:5	31n40
40:10	31n38–9, 34n57
57:20	54n160
66:15–24	31n42

Scripture Index

Isaiah (continued)

66:15-6	31n41
66:15	31n39, 34n57

Jeremiah

22:30	31n44
25:31	31n40-42

Ezekiel

1:7	50
8:2	50
13	50
34:2	54n160

Daniel

5:25-6	39n88
7:10	31n39-40, 31n44
7:13	31n40
7:16	31n40
10:5-6	50
12:1	31n44

Joel

2:11	46
2:31	46
3:2	31n40

Amos

1:2	31n38

Micah

1:3	31n38

Habakkuk

1:12	31n40

Zephaniah

1:7	31n38

1:8	31n41
1:9	31n41
1:12	31n41
1:14	46
3:8-18	31n41
3:8	31n40

Haggai

2:22	31n41

Zechariah

1:10	39n88
1:19-20	39n88
3:1-5	53
4:10	39n88
4:14	39n88
9:14	31n38
14:1	31n38
14:2-3	31n41
14:3	31n38
14:5	34n57, 34n59, 52
14:12	31n41

Malachi

2:17	31n40
3:1-3	31n38
3:3-5	31n41
3:5	31n40
3:16	31n44
4:5	46

Apocrypha

Tobit

14:10	48n135

Wisdom of Solomon

3:1	95
12:12	95

Scripture Index

Pseudepigrapha

1 Enoch

Reference	Page
1—36	15
1	33n55
1:1—32:6a	9
1:4	33n55
1:9	27, 32-3, 35, 41, 58, 118
1:19	69n37
2:1—5:4	40
6—19	27, 44
6—9	98
6:1—9:4	9
6	111
6:1-6	13
7:1	39
8:4—10:14	9
9:8	39
10	46n125
10:4-5	48
10:4	44
10:5	46
10:6	44, 46n122
10:11	39
10:12	46, 46n125
10:20	38
12:4	39, 44, 46n120
13—15	88-98
13:1	46n123
14:1	46n122
14:5	46n123, 46n125
15:3	39, 46n120
15:4	39
15:7	46n120
15:8—16:1	9
16:3	74
17—19	110n53
18:13-16	47n129, 48
18:15	47-8
19:1	69
20:7	39
21	45n112
21:3-6	47n129, 48
21:16	48n132
22:4	46n122
22:10	46n122
22:11	46
37—82	15
37—71	ix
38:2	39
40	39
41:2	39
45:2	39
46:1—51:5	11
46	105
46:1-4	106n36
46:3	39
46:6	48n135
46:7	39
48	105
48:10	39
50—51	105
54:3-5	46n123
54:6	46
56:1-4	46n123
60—63	105
60:8	37
61:10	69
62:1-16	11
63:6	48n135
67:5-7	40
67:8	39, 41n102
67:10	39
69	105
70—71	105
70:1	11
71	110n50
77:7—78:1	9
78—82	2
78:8	9
80:2-8	40
80:6	54n160
81—108	15
81:1-2	31n44
82	47n128, 48
82:10-20	45n118
83—90	15, 47n129, 48
83—4	ix
84:6	46
85:10—86:2	10
86—88	45n112
86:1-3	47-8
87:1-3	10
88:1	46n123, 48
88:3	48
89:42-49	10

Scripture Index

1 Enoch (continued)

89:45–77	70
89:61–64	70
89:62–71	38
89:62	31n44
90:14	31n44
90:17	31n44, 70
90:20	31n44
90:22	31n44
90:24	48
91—105	15
91:7	34n57
92—105	40
93	13
93:3	37, 41n102
97:5	46n122
97:6—107:3	10
99:8	39
100:3	69
103:8	46n122, 48n135
104:7	31n44
106—7	15
106:13–15	45n112
106:17	45n112
108	ix, 15
108:3	31n44
108:7	31n44, 38
108:14	48n135

Jubilees

1:27–9	51n147
2:2	45n118
4:15	45n112
4:22	45n112
5:1	45n112
5:6	45n118, 46n123
5:10	46n125
7:39	37
17:15—18:16	53
48	53

2 Enoch

10:2	48n135
20:1	45n118
22:7	50n140
22:10	50n140

Sibylline Oracles

4:48	48n135

2 Baruch

24:1	31n44
56:10–14	45n112
56:13	46n123

Testament of Reuben

5	67
5:6–7	45n112

Testament of Levi

3:8	45n118
5:5–6	55n166
18:5	50n144

Testament of Judah

25:2	50n144

Testament of Dan

6:2	55n166

Testament of Naphtali

3:5—4:1	67
3:5	45n112

Testament of Asher

7:5	31n44

Ascension of Isaiah

3:16	40
9:32	50n140

Psalms of Solomon

14:9	48n135

Scripture Index

15:10	48n135

Epistle of Barnabas

4:3	70
16:5	70–71
16:6	71

New Testament

Matthew

1:22	37n81
2:15	37n81
2:17	37n81
3:3	37n81
4:14	37n81
8:12	48n135
8:17	37n81
12:17	37n81
13:14	37n81
13:35	37n81
15:7	37n81
16:27	52n153
18:16	28n28
21:4	37n81
22:13	48n135
22:43	37n81
25:30	48n135
25:31	52n153

Mark

8:38	52n153
12:26	27n22

Luke

9:26	52n153

John

5:31–3	28n28
6:36	95
8:17–8	28n28

Acts

2:16	32n49
2:20	46
4:11	32n49
7:38	51n147
7:53	51n147
8	79n3

Romans

8:38	45n115, 45n118, 69

1 Corinthians

10:1–5	27n17

2 Corinthians

10:17	27n22
13:1	28n28

Galatians

3:11	27n22
3:19	51n147, 55
4:24	27n21

Ephesians

1:10	73
1:21	45n118, 69
3:10	45n118
4:12	45n115
6:11	73
6:12	45n118

Philippians

2:10–11	73

Colossians

1:16	69
2:15	45n115, 45n118

2 Thessalonians

1:7	52n153

Scripture Index

1 Timothy

5:19	28n28

2 Timothy

3:8	27n21
3:16	60n19

Hebrews

2:2	51n147
2:6	37n81
2:12	37n81
7:1–3	27n17
9:5	50n144
10:28	28n28
12:26	37n81

1 Peter

1:19	69
1:20	69
1:21	69
2:4–10	30
3:2	69
3:19–20	69

2 Peter

2:4	69, 69n36

Jude

1–2	25,
1	28–9
2	29
3–4	25, 26
3	25, 29
4	25, 29, 31, 38–9
5–23	26
5–19	26, 43
5–16	40n94
5–10	47
5–7	25n13, 26, 54
5–6	43
5	27–9, 30n35
6	28–9, 38–9, 42–8, 69
7	28–9, 39, 46
8–10	25n13, 26
8	29, 30n35, 39, 42–3, 49, 51, 54
9	25n13, 26, 28–9, 39, 40n90, 42–3, 51n149, 52–4
10	29, 30n35, 51n149, 54
11	26–9, 30n35, 40, 47
11–3	47
12–3	26, 40, 47
12–4	54n160
12	29, 30n35
13	29n29, 42–3, 46n124, 47–8
14–5	26, 29n29, 31–3, 35, 38, 41, 43, 60n20, 118
14	27, 29, 30n35, 31, 42, 49, 51
15	29
16	26, 29, 30n35
17–8	26
17	27, 29, 30n35
18	29, 30n35, 38
19	26, 29, 30n35,
20–23	26
20–21	29n29
20	29
21	29
22–23	29n29
22	29
23	29, 31
24–5	26
24	29, 31
25	29

Revelation

3:5	31n44
5:1	31n44
5:7	31n44
5:8	31n44
7:14	39n88
10:8–11	31n44
11	69n38
11:3–13	101
11:4	39n88
14:4	39n88
14:20	69
16:18	46
20:12	31n44

Scripture Index

Dead Sea Scrolls

Damascus Document (CD)
1	63
2:17—19:1	45n112
5:17–18	53

Genesis Apocryphon (1QapGen)
2:1	45n112

Thanksgiving Hymns (1QH)
1:11	45n118
10:8	50n140

War Scroll (1QM)
10:12	45n118

Manual of Disciples (1QS)
2:8	48n135
4:13	48n135
8	63

Florilegium (4QFlor)
1:2	27n21
1:3	27n21
1:11	27n21
1:12	27n21
1:16	32n49
1:17	27n21

Pesher or Qumran Commentary on Isaiah (4QpIsa/b)
2:6–7	27n21
2:7	32n49
2:10	27n21
3:7	27n21
3:9	27n21
3:10	27n21
3:12	27n21

Early Christian Writings

Augustine of Hippo
De Civitate
XV	75

Athanasius
Festal Letter — 75

Athenagoras of Athens
Plea for Christians — 72

Clement of Alexandria
Comments on the Epistle of Jude — 73

Stromata
5	73–74
5.1.10, 2	70

Irenaeus
72–73

Julius Africanus
75

Justin Martyr
2 Apologia
5	70–71

Origen
de Principiis
3.3	74
4.35	74

Tertullian of Carthage
On the Apparel of Women — 73

www.ingramcontent.com/pod-product-compliance
Lightning Source LLC
Chambersburg PA
CBHW050820160426
43192CB00010B/1837